CROWDS
AND
SULTANS

CROWDS
AND
SULTANS

Urban Protest in
Late Medieval Egypt and Syria

Amina Elbendary

The American University in Cairo Press
Cairo New York

First published in 2015 by
The American University in Cairo Press
113 Sharia Kasr el Aini, Cairo, Egypt
420 Fifth Avenue, New York, NY 10018
www.aucpress.com

Exclusive distribution outside Egypt and North America by I.B.Tauris & Co Ltd., 6
Salem Road, London, W4 2BU

Dar el Kutub No. 25541/14
ISBN 978 977 416 717 1

Dar el Kutub Cataloging-in-Publication Data

Elbendary, Amina
        Crowds and Sultans: Urban Protest in Late Medieval Egypt and Syria / Amina Elbendary.—
Cairo: The American University in Cairo Press, 2015
        p. cm.
        ISBN 978 977 416 717 1
        1. Egypt—History—1250–1517
        2. Mamluks
        3. Syria—History—1260–1516
        962.024

1 2 3 4 5   19 18 17 16 15

Designed by Adam el-Sehemy
Printed in Egypt

To my parents,
Nawal Mehallawi and Attia El-Bendari,
In loving memory

CONTENTS

NOTE ON TRANSLITERATION

In transliterating Arabic words the American University in Cairo Press uses a modified version of the *International Journal of Middle East Studies* system. Accordingly, words that are part of the English lexicon are not italicized and diacritical marks are not used.

PREFACE

This book, as most projects do, has a prehistory. It began in a discussion in our kitchen with my mother's best friend, the late Lebanese novelist Layla Usayran. Having reunited with my mother in the mid-1990s after the Lebanese Civil War had kept them apart, Auntie Layla visited us in Cairo. As she tried—albeit with limited success—to explain to me just what the war had been about, we turned to protest and despotism. I made an offhand remark that maybe our populations, especially in Egypt, didn't resist and rebel against despotic rule historically because the stakes were too high and they knew better. Little did I know! When I started graduate studies at the American University in Cairo, I was struck to discover so many references to street riots and protests in the Mamluk period. Gradually a project came to develop, not on "Why did they not rebel?" but on "When and how did premodern people of Egypt and Syria protest?" And "What did protest look like before colonialism and modernity?" These questions were asked long before the Arab Spring was on the horizon, indeed in part in the hope that one would live to see such active protest in the political landscape of the region in the spirit of our medieval ancestors, or that one would come to better appreciate what appears as a calm surface. This project officially began in 2003, on the eve of the Second Iraq War and when the streets of the Arab world had begun grumbling, if in somewhat muted voices. It is laid to rest in 2015, well after a revolution and its aftermath.

I am grateful for all the support I received at the Faculty of Oriental Studies, University of Cambridge, from the Cambridge Overseas Trust, the Gibb Memorial Trust, and my college Clare Hall, without which I would not have been able to finish my research in a reasonable time frame.

I am indebted to many people in helping me write this book. I am thankful to my professor and mentor Professor Nelly Hanna for many reasons, too many to mention and do justice to. Since my graduate-student days Professor Hanna has made history seem so exciting, so crucial, and yet so easy. She continues to inspire me and to teach me lessons on why history matters. She is always generous with her time and thoughts and this book owes much to long, patient discussions with her. I am grateful to the steady advice of Professor Basim Musallam at Cambridge, who made the Mamluks seem less intimidating and the "project" an already existing whole whose parts one only had to assemble.

I am also deeply indebted to Professor Elizabeth Sartain at AUC. Her encyclopedic knowledge of medieval Islam and Egypt remains a beacon to aspire to.

I am also grateful for the supportive atmosphere and resources—and bottomless cups of hot coffee in the cold Cambridge winter—of the Skilliter Centre for Ottoman Studies and Professor Kate Fleet. I am also thankful to the students of ARIC 460/560 and ARIC 357 at AUC who endured the long reading lists on protest and dissent in premodern and early modern history, especially the group that persevered in Fall 2010, before protest was once more in academic fashion. Our discussions have greatly informed this project. I am also grateful for the insight and comments offered by colleagues at the Annemarie Schimmel Kolleg of Bonn University where I presented part of the arguments here. I also benefited greatly from the discussions at the Zukunftsphilologie Winter School on "Textual Practices beyond Europe 1500–1900" organized by Forum Transregionale Studien in Cairo in 2010. A pre-tenure leave from my university, the American University in Cairo, allowed me precious time to put the manuscript in order. The anonymous AUC Press readers made very thorough and insightful remarks and suggestions on the manuscript for which I am very grateful. I wish to thank the team at AUC Press, Nigel Fletcher-Jones, Neil Hewison, Nadia Naqib, and Nadine El-Hadi;

they have been particularly helpful and patient through all the stages of finalizing the manuscript.

I am immeasurably sad that neither of my parents lived to see this book in print or read its drafts, for it owes them much. I am indebted to my mother, Nawal Mehallawi, for her support and encouragement of my education, even from beyond; for giving me my first dictionary with continual instructions to "look it up"; and for instilling in me the idea that one can do almost anything "if you put your mind to it." To my father, Attia Elbendary, I am indebted to his down-to-earth backing. His support was an anchor far beneath the surface whose gravitation is fully appreciated only after it is gone. I am grateful to my brother Alaa Elbendary for his backing and matter-of-fact encouragement at all the crucial junctures. I am also deeply grateful to Hussein Basyouni, without whose help I would not have been able to leave my home and head to England, for being supportive in many subtle ways.

Last, but certainly not least, I am indebted to my friends and colleagues who endured years of talking about "the book" and about protest, and who made valuable suggestions and helped it materialize: Maggie Morgan, Amira Howeidy, Pascale Ghazaleh, Mona Anis, Sherine Hamdy, Adam Sabra, Camilo Gomez, Reham Barakat—thank you.

1

INTRODUCTION:
THE LONG FIFTEENTH CENTURY

Long-Term Transformations

Medieval as well as contemporary histories of the Mamluk period differ in their historiography and on many issues; they all agree, however, that the fifteenth century ushered in a new period for the regime. While many of these sources have understood these transformations in terms of a paradigm of decline—citing signs of the weakness and economic crisis the Mamluk regime was going through—this book will argue that things were more nuanced and complicated. Rather than straightforward and linear decline, I will argue that the fifteenth century witnessed crises that presented opportunities for various political and social groups, some of whom benefited and gained more power, while others suffered and were placed under increased stress. It will also show that the multiple crises were simultaneously the outward manifestations of deeper changes. These economic crises and political transformations led to changes and were themselves the outcome of changes in all of the domestic, regional, and international balances of power. Furthermore, while the changes led to distress in some areas, and for some groups at certain times, they also opened up opportunities for others, at other times. Rather than a linear regression, then, there was more dynamic change occurring, with ups and downs. This allowed some groups in society more access to power, and placed others under stress that led them to continually renegotiate their positions. On the whole, this social flux left non-elite urban populations in a position to negotiate power with rulers.

In order to better understand the deeper meanings of these crises, we need to look beyond dynastic history. Rather than narrate the history of this tumultuous fifteenth century solely from the point of view of the ruling dynasties, this book attempts to integrate into the total picture the point of view of the common people, especially the urban non-elites. And rather than presume that the non-elite took no part in those trans-formations and only stoically endured the oppression, it argues that the urban populations played various roles in those transformations. They were both the recipients of change and the agents of change in many cases. Their contributions are apparent and manifested in various ways, including the literary production of the time but also in references to urban protest.

Sources that refer to the fifteenth century include many references to incidents of protest, at rates that appear higher than those reported for other historical periods. These protests act as warning lights that point modern historians to areas of social and political tension. They also illu-minate some of the ways in which power was negotiated and shared in medieval Egyptian and Syrian cities.

The Mamluk sultanate went through various economic crises. While it is difficult to give precise dates for the start of the crisis (indeed, in some modern narratives it seems as if the regime had barely been established when it began to decline economically), it is clear that by the beginning of the fifteenth century the regime was under much stress, and ruling sultans attempted to come up with various solutions to a long-term crisis. There would be times in which the crises reached a nadir as well as times of noticeable recovery throughout the century.

By reconsidering some of the interpretations of the fifteenth-century crisis, one must confront another issue: that of periodization. The issue of periodization is one that challenges many historians; medieval Islami-cists are no exception. And while historians of the Arab-Muslim world have become reluctant to use the terminology of European historiography ('late antique,' 'medieval,' 'early modern,' etc.) to describe epochs of Arab-Mus-lim history, no standard alternative has been reached. Many scholars continue to date periods by referring to the contemporary ruling dynasties: thus Umayyad, Abbasid, Fatimid, Mamluk, Ottoman. I will use the terms 'medieval' and 'late medieval' with all the expected disclaimers. That is, it is important that the reader try to dissociate the European connotations of the Middle Ages when speaking of Islamic history. Instead I mean by 'medieval' the period and institutions that spread and characterized the Arab-Muslim region in the post-Abbasid, postclassical time, when the last semblance of a centralizing political entity gave way to multiple regional courts and military dynasties. By 'late medieval' I mean the tail end of this period, which is admittedly a blurred demarcation, but it includes early Ottoman rule of the Arab provinces. Similarly, I will concentrate on the fifteenth century, and I will argue that it was a long century for this part of the world. There is some merit in following the periodization of Mamluk historians, who saw the reign of Sultan Barquq (r. 1382–99 with a brief interruption) as the beginning of a new epoch. They based this largely on the racial shift in army recruits: Barquq's reign is seen as the beginning of the Circassian period, characterized by the predominance of Circassian recruits in the army. I will argue that that shift itself was reflective of the long-term changes referred to earlier.

The fifteenth century ended with the fall of the Mamluk sultanate that had ruled Egypt and Syria since 1250. As is well known, the Mamluks were originally slave soldiers who were recruited for the armies by the last Ayyubid sultan al-Salih Najm al-Din Ayyub, hence the title 'Mamluk,' since they were 'owned.' Brought in as young slave boys from the Kipcak steppes, the Mamluks were educated in special military barracks. They were converted to Islam and taught basic literacy and skills as well as martial arts. Upon their graduation, the soldiers were manumitted and assigned to positions in the army. However, they continued to be referred to as Mamluks, even after their manumission. In the final months and years of Ayyubid rule over Egypt and Syria, and as the regime faced increasing military threats by the Crusaders directing attacks on Egypt, the Mamluk officers came to play greater roles in governance and rule, until ultimately they named one of their number as sultan. It is in the context of a crusade targeting Egypt in AH 647/1249–50 CE that they seized power. Not long after that, another invasion of Islamic lands, this time from the east, arrived on the scene. The Mongols reached Baghdad, until then the capital of the Abbasid Caliphate, under which the Ayyubids had at least nominally ruled. The fall of Baghdad in 1258 was a dramatic watershed in the history of medieval Islam. The Mongol advance threatened to expand and include all areas under Islamic rule in the eastern Mediterranean. The Mamluks' victory against the Mongols at 'Ayn Jalut in 1260 sealed their reputation as defenders of Islamic Egypt and Syria. It created a border between Iraq and Syria that was to be upheld for centuries. The Mamluks went on under al-Zahir Baybars (r. 1260–77) and al-Mansur Qalawun (r. 1279–90) to found a strong and stable military-feudal regime that was in many ways the epitome of postclassical medieval military regimes in the region.[1]

The Mongol invasions of the thirteenth century had put paid to the Seljuk network of regimes and subsidiary principalities in Iraq, Mesopotamia, and parts of Asia Minor. This vacuum allowed for the rise of new Turkish military regimes, one of which, the Ottoman principality, was to continue to grow and expand into a world empire that rivaled the Mamluks and others. By 1453 the Ottomans had taken over Constantinople, the historic capital of the Byzantines, thereby ending the centuries-old rule of the Eastern Roman Empire. The fifteenth century saw further consolidation of power by the Ottomans and their expansion in the east. It also witnessed the rise of the Safavid state in Iran and the Mongol successor states in parts of Iraq and Mesopotamia. By the sixteenth century, the balance of power between the Mamluks and the Ottomans had tipped in favor of the latter, resulting in final confrontation. The defeat of the Mamluks at the battles of Marj Dabiq (1516) and al-Raydaniya (1517) sealed the end of the Mamluk ruling regime, although Mamluk officers would continue to be important in Egyptian politics until the nineteenth century.

The battles between the last Mamluk sultans and the Ottoman armies in 1516–17 and the fall of the regime were in many ways the culmination of a long period of transformation that took place over at least a century. The economic and political transformations that Egypt and Syria witnessed during the long fifteenth century had tremendous effects on the populations and societies under Mamluk rule.

'Decline and Fall' Paradigm

Much of the modern literature on the late medieval period and late Mamluk rule is written within the paradigm of 'decline and fall,' which implicitly moves backward from the Ottoman conquests and explains the fifteenth century retrospectively. The rise of the Ottomans is understood firmly as a defeat of the Mamluks, thereby ignoring many of the similarities between the two regimes and many of the elements of historical continuity. One of the main signs and causes of the decline is implicitly the economic crisis. The decline is also thought to have permeated all aspects of society, so that cultural production of the period is looked upon with condescension and populations are imagined to have toiled, silently and stoically, under rampant corruption and injustice. This book tries to look at things sideways and bottom-up to read the signs of decline as signs of transformation and to hear the echoes of the non-elite through the surviving narratives.

Who are the non-elite? In addition to the challenges of periodization, social categorization is also a perennial issue for the modern historian. While it is important for us, writers and readers about the past, to be aware of the historical contexts in which terms such as 'class' have developed, we must also acknowledge the challenges in trying to understand and imagine how historical societies conceived and imagined social order in a pre-class context. The main divisions among people in the pre-modern Islamic world are usually imagined along the lines of rule and military power (rulers and ruled; sultans and subjects), religion (Muslims and non-Muslims), and gender (men and women). Economic privilege is of course understood to have played a role in people's social position, although the rich as such do not seem to have constituted a visible social group on their own; rich people belonged to other apparently more dominant identities. They could be rich officers, rich ulama, rich merchants, and so on. The poor, on the other hand, sometimes appear in the sources as one undifferentiated block, usually in the contexts of certain crises, such as famine, for example. Such discursive references do not necessarily reflect social reality.

Then there are the elusive 'amma. I tend to translate this term as 'commoners,' since the two words carry very similar connotations, or else as 'non-elites.' The *'amma* of the medieval Arabic sources are easier to define in negative terms: they are *not* Mamluks, for example; they are not even poor Mamluk soldiers. They are not necessarily uneducated, although some of the poorer members of the ulama class cannot have enjoyed much greater material benefits than the *'amma*, aside from education. They are not necessarily poor either; they could provide for themselves.

The difficulty of understanding medieval social distinctions in the spirit of their times is best understood by the terminology the contemporary sources themselves used. The Mamluk historian al-Maqrizi divided contemporary society into seven groups. The first were the rulers,

> those who hold the reins of power. The second [is formed of] the rich merchants and the wealthy who lead a life of affluence. The third [encompasses] the retailers, who are merchants of average means, as are the cloth merchants. This also includes the small shopkeepers. The fourth category embraces the peasants, those who cultivate and plow the land. These are the inhabitants of the villages and of the countryside. The fifth category is made up of those who receive a stipend *[al-fuqara']* and includes most legists, students of theology, and most of the *ajnad al-halqah* and the like. The sixth category [corresponds to] the artisans and the salaried persons who possess a skill. The seventh category [consists of] the needy and the paupers; and these are the beggars who live off the [charities of] others.[2]

Thus wealth alone was not the main marker of difference among groups of people in society, though al-Maqrizi does offer a quasi-hierarchical structure that begins with the rulers at the top and ends with beggars at the bottom. In the middle are various categories of people who are distinguished by their roles in society and the functions they performed.

Therefore, in discussing the roles of the non-ruling/non-Mamluk classes, including common people, I refer to them as the 'non-elites.' It is not an ideal term but it is meant to convey to the reader the sort of individuals who were not formally part of the ruling structure, who were not part of power, and who were not particularly wealthy or well connected, but who increasingly came to play roles in matters of power and politics, often through protest and negotiating power. They might have included craftsmen, artisans, and tradesmen of the Egyptian and Syrian cities, small-scale and local merchants. They might have included minor clerks and employees of ruling institutions, minor employees of educational institutions, *katibs* (scribes), janitors, muezzins, copyists. These members of society were traditionally marginalized in contemporary historiography, yet—as this book will argue—they made increasing appearances in the narratives of the late Mamluk period, which arguably reflects their changing social and political roles.

Economic crises

Contemporary and modern scholars agree that the Mamluk regime faced an economic crisis by the fifteenth century. Various reasons have been suggested for this, especially the long-term and cumulative effect of the waves of the plague, including the Black Death of 1348, that swept through the eastern Mediterranean. Contemporary historians recognized that something was amiss, prompting the famous Mamluk historian al-Maqrizi (d. 1442) to pen his treatise *Ighathat al-umma bi kashf al-ghumma* (Helping the community by revealing the causes of its distress). He and others placed the blame squarely on the shoulders of the rulers; the crises were a function of corrupt government. A similar argument is reflected in another treatise by Muhammad ibn Muhammad ibn Khalil al-Asadi (fl. 1450) titled *al-Taysir wa-l-i'tibar* (The book of relieving hardship and learning lessons), in which the author called for administrative and fiscal reforms. The book analyzes the corruptions of the time and then describes the basic principles of sound administration and political practice that should be followed by Muslim rulers. According to al-Asadi there were four main reasons behind the disorder that Egypt suffered, all relating to matters of governance: the administration's neglect of the land and irrigation; the state's failure to quell rebellious Bedouin; the tyranny of government officials, especially inspectors, governors, and tax collectors; and the extortions levied by armed men and men close to the sultan.[3]

With the benefit of hindsight, we now recognize a number of economic challenges and difficulties that befell the Mamluk state simultaneously or else in close enough succession to be at times inseparable. A predominant factor must have been the successive waves of plague that decimated the population. That in turn had effects on both the workforce (i.e., the peasants) and the armies. Whole villages were reported to lie fallow as their dwindling populations fled to other areas, ultimately affecting agrarian production, especially in Egypt. When we keep in mind that Egypt was largely an agrarian society and that the land taxes did constitute a significant percentage of the state's income, we can appreciate the compounded effects of decreased agrarian production on tax revenues. New military recruits were also severely affected by the epidemic; young and unaccustomed to the disease as they were, many perished during the plague epidemics. This meant that money, dearly obtained to buy young slaves for the army, was lost. Another economic challenge was that the Mamluk regime suffered from a cash crisis. Gold was difficult to obtain during the late Mamluk period, a situation clearly reported in surviving sources and reflected in the decreasing percentages of gold and silver in currencies. At the same time, the Mamluk state was increasingly facing new rival powers that threatened or cut off its control over certain trade routes and its supply of various materials including slaves, wood, and bullion. The rise of the Ottomans and the Safavids in Asia affected trade patterns. So did the increasing encroachment of the Portuguese into Red Sea trade.

In explaining the fifteenth-century crisis, modern historians fall roughly within two main schools. One school tends to explain it by stressing internal factors of decline. By looking within the Mamluk system, some historians have questioned not only its economic productivity, but also its politics. E. Ashtor, for example, considered government monopolies, taxes, corruption, and technological stagnation largely responsible for the collapse of Egyptian and Syrian industries such as the sugar and textile industries, and the ultimate triumph of European trade and commerce in the second half of the fifteenth century.[4] Within this paradigm, the cruelty and greed of sultans such as Barsbay (r. 1422–38) led them to monopolize commodities and enterprises such as the spice trade and sugar production through various measures. The excessive taxes they levied from private, non-Mamluk producers and the system of *tarh*, or forced purchases, they imposed on traders in effect strangled competition and is the main reason, Ashtor argued, for the closing of many sugar factories. This led to both corruption in the management of surviving sugar factories and an aversion to technological innovation.[5] Meanwhile, Europeans were developing more innovative techniques using horses instead of oxen, and a new sugar press was introduced by the mid-fifteenth century.[6] Ultimately the Levantine products could not compete in price or quality with European sugar, especially after the introduction of New World plantations. While Ashtor did make allowance for demographic realities, mainly the depopulation of Egypt and Syria following the series of epidemics of the fourteenth and fifteenth centuries and the detrimental effects on the Syrian economy of Tamerlane's invasion at the dawn of the fifteenth century, his analysis stresses the effect of the structure and organization of medieval Mamluk government itself, in addition to the decrees of particular rulers.[7] Similarly, though he disagrees with some of the arguments of Ashtor, Sato Tsugitaka sees political corruption and natural disasters—rather than technological stagnation—as the main causes for the decline of sugar production in late Mamluk Egypt.[8]

Carl Petry has focused on studying the politics of Egypt's last two important and long-reigning sultans, Qaytbay (r. 1468–96) and Qansuh al-Ghawri (r. 1501–16). In his studies of the late Mamluk period in Egypt, published in two volumes as *Protectors or Praetorians? The Last Mamluk Sultans and Egypt's Waning as a Great Power* and *Twilight of Majesty: The Reigns of the Mamluk Sultans al-Ashraf Qaytbay and Qansuh al-Ghawri in Egypt*, Petry focused on the history of the two sultans and the policies of the senior men of state who surrounded their regimes.[9] Petry was able to bring to life the economic and political crises these two sultans faced and the ways in which the ruling men dealt with and unintentionally aggravated the challenges before them. While medieval historians like Ibn Iyas idolized Qaytbay—and demonized Qansuh al-Ghawri—Petry takes issue with their judgment. According to his reading, Qaytbay championed the old Mamluk order and did not attempt to reform it. He was more a custodian of a tradition, who did not introduce any significant innovations in foreign policy, administrative style, or economic production.[10] Qaytbay bequeathed his eventual successor, Qansuh al-Ghawri, a legacy of bankruptcy, confiscation, and oppression.[11] And although Qansuh al-Ghawri's foreign policy also aimed at maintaining a regional environment in which Mamluk institutions could continue to function as they had for centuries instead of adopting proactive initiatives, Petry credits the sultan with innovations in armament and financial administration.[12] Al-Ghawri's military and fiscal experiments had the potential of altering the power structure itself in the face of crisis. However, Petry remarks that historians' pessimistic assessments of both reigns show that members of the lettered classes saw that the conduct of the soldiers and military, their exploitation of society at large, had gotten out of hand[13]—a situation confirmed by analyses of urban protests during that period. Indeed, the frequent rioting of the *julban* (new army recruits) for more pay is a recurring motif in all the historical sources and is assumed to be one of the main reasons behind the state's imposing more and more taxes. It was also a frequent cause of unrest and disorder in Cairo. Petry offers a rather daring hypothesis to account for Qansuh al-Ghawri's appropriation of *awqaf* (pious endowments), funds, and the hoarding of resources. Rather than see al-Ghawri's decisions as either erratic acts or else the behavior of a tyrant (as the ulama and contemporary Mamluks who stood to lose from all this seemed to believe), Petry connects this policy with that of establishing the fifth corps who were experimenting with firearms and were paid direct salaries and not through *iqta'*s (tax farms). By placing more and more of the state's resources directly under royal control, Petry argues, al-Ghawri might have been trying to gradually phase out the traditional Mamluk regiments and their system, which was based on *iqta'*, and replace it with a different kind of army.[14] It is a daring hypothesis, but surviving sources do not offer enough details to either confirm or refute it, and time was unkind to Qansuh al-Ghawri; the Ottomans arrived at the doorstep before such a master plan—if it really existed—could reach fruition.

Petry's analysis of the late Mamluk period stresses the stasis and lack of innovation in the system rather than any decline in agricultural production. It is such stasis that encouraged mismanagement of resources, the exploitation of subjects, and the hoarding of assets over innovative investment. What ingenuity existed lay chiefly in devising ways to hoard assets and keep them out of other people's hands; the same attitude informed the strategies of both the state and its subject population.

The second school of modern interpretation attributes the fifteenth-century crisis to the changes in the world economy at large. Rather than a decline in Egyptian and Syrian economic productivity due to despotism and oppression, it was changes in European patterns of investment, capital production and accumulation, and manipulation of markets that changed the international world order to a degree with which a traditional economy, such as Egypt and Syria, could not immediately compete.[15] This argument, which focuses on external world explanations for the crisis, is best exemplified by the works of Immanuel Wallerstein and Janet Abu-Lughod. Wallerstein refers the decline in eastern Mediterranean trade and the ensuing crisis that evolved to structural changes in world trade.[16] Sugar production did not decline only in Egypt and Syria, for example; the decline reached the whole eastern Mediterranean by the end of the fifteenth century largely due to failure to compete with sugar imports from American plantations with their abundance of new land, favorable climate, and slave labor.[17]

Abu-Lughod identifies two main external factors as precipitating the decline and turning Egypt and Syria from a hegemonic diversified economy to a dependent one: firstly the aggressive trade policies of Venice, by which the Italian city-state dumped large amounts of fabrics on the Egyptian and Syrian markets and turned Egypt and Syria into exporters of raw cotton, rather than textiles, and secondly the double impact of the Black Death and Tamerlane's invasion at the beginning of the fifteenth century.[18]

My own interpretation considers the way that these various crises were interrelated. It stresses the dynamic relationship between economic problems and challenges and the administrative decisions taken in response to them, showing that the acts of the Mamluk sultans were often in answer to pressures from below. This crisis led various Mamluk rulers to resort to a number of policies in order to raise income and save cash. Historians of medieval Egypt and Syria are familiar with the policies of monopolization, forced sales, and extra-legal taxes that different sultans and *amirs* enforced. Most famous of course are the monopolies imposed by Sultan Barsbay (1422–38). Igarashi Daisuke's study of the *diwan al-mufrad* shows that the establishment of this *diwan* by Sultan Barquq in 1383 in order to pay monthly salaries to the sultan's Mamluks was part of a wider restructuring of Mamluk finances and the collapse of the *iqta'* system, which meant a deep restructuring of the Mamluk state.[19] Indeed, even as late as the period of Sultan Qaytbay (r. 1468–96), when the *diwan al-mufrad* was abolished, the ruler was trying to find ways of restructuring the administration to better control resources. While some of these policies were viewed as corrupt and evil by contemporary scholars, we can in retrospect see them as ways in which rulers tried to circumvent strenuous conditions. Indeed, some scholars, such as Toru Miura, have argued that some of these policies, such as bribery and the sale of offices, were not deviations from the norm but rather were so institutionalized they were part of the financial policy followed to compensate for the state's loss of income, allowing it to function in a somewhat decentralized mode.[20] Even if the state did not formally recognize these latter practices, or if rulers did not officially condone these as state policies, their prevalence confirms that they had overarching long-term cumulative effects on the ability of the state to penetrate society and to impose its will—even at times over its own employees. Thus, hand in hand with the image of autocratic military rulers that we have of the Mamluk sultans, we must also recognize the limitations they faced in exercising their powers and their repeated attempts to restructure their institutions. Much of the coercive power of the state was gradually usurped over the span of the century even by the officials appointed by the state itself.[21] This does not deny that the sultan remained powerful—indeed, the almost endemic confiscations of the same century are testament to the sultanate's ultimate supremacy over the *amir*s (senior Mamluk officers)—but it is a power that was shared, and exercised brutally when the hegemony of the state itself and of the sultan was seriously threatened and imperiled. It's also a situation that allowed room for other members of society to participate in politics.

It is important to question and study how these policies were implemented, and how they were received by the populations. An analysis of the surviving sources shows that despite the autocratic nature of the Mamluk regime, many of these policies were adjusted or modified in order to accommodate popular dissatisfaction, expressed through protest. The urban non-elite managed on many occasions to negotiate these policies to their advantage or at least to ameliorate some of the burdens that befell them.

The straitened financial and economic situation meant that the Mamluk state and its functionaries were forced to share power with other groups in society, albeit in indirect and subtle ways. Continuous negotiation was one avenue through which power was shared and redistributed. This did not always work smoothly or to the satisfaction of all parties involved. Yet it was a premodern, non-institutionalized form of power sharing and political participation. Perhaps because these developments were not rarefied in institutional formats, they were perceived as signs of decline, as signs of the breakdown of an imagined order. That is in any case how they were often perceived by the ruling classes, including some of our chroniclers—as signs of breakdown rather than restructuring and transformation.

Social mobility, the "bourgeois trend," popularization

My analysis also considers the various social groups that were affected by the transformation taking place. The diffusion of power and the state of social and political flux that characterized late Mamluk rule allowed some groups and individuals in society to rise and flourish. Thus we see increasing references to members of the non-elite, commoners and people from craftsman backgrounds, who were able to rise through the administration, reaching high levels of authority. Some also left their mark on surviving literature and historiography. Contemporary medieval sources—and not a few modern sources—interpret this as one more sign of the corruption and decline of the Mamluk system. However, one can read these developments differently. In place of the rigid hierarchical system that was roughly based on merit, whether among the ranks of the ulama for the intellectuals or Mamluks for the military administrative apparatus, and through which only the tough first-generation slave soldiers were able to occupy senior positions in the army and top administration, commoner upstarts were recorded as occupying official positions from *muhtasib* (market inspector) to *nazir al-khass* (supervisor of the Royal Fisc). These include Abul-Khayr al-Nahhas, who started out as a coppersmith and went on to occupy senior positions in the bureaucracy,[22] as well as Sharaf al-Din Muhammad ibn 'Ali al-Hibri, a one-time sugar trader and convicted felon of bad repute who was appointed to the *hisba*.[23] However, rather than the simple value judgment of "decline" with which many fifteenth-century changes are stamped, the modern historian can see this as part of a bigger trend throughout the century, one that allowed for more participation in some quarters, and for a relaxation of some of the rigid dichotomies in others—even perhaps for a "popularizing" trend. Some historians see this as a reflection of social mobility, or of a "bourgeois trend." By referring to these developments as indicating a "bourgeois trend" I mean to argue for the genesis of a new type of culture, new forms of cultural expression, and new genres, that reflect the burgeoning of a potential new class. It is important, however, not to over-stretch these indications. That is, these indications, these hints, that survive to us in the sources, are not enough to argue for the rise of a bourgeois class as such (in the Marxist sense) in Egypt and Syria in the fifteenth century. They do, however, suggest that the germs of such developments are perceptible.[24]

This book argues that deep economic and social transformations were taking place in the late Mamluk period, especially during the fifteenth century, and that these changes allowed for a greater space for the non-elite. It also argues that it is these transformations that were behind the many popular protests that are reported for the century. Rather than reading the changes through the lens of decline, and the protests as a sign of breakdown, it will argue that the changes were more dynamic, with benefits to some and losses to others, and that the protests—while they were naturally against perceived injustices—were themselves a mechanism through which some of the urban non-elites participated in the politics of their communities. It will argue that this was all part of the transformations occurring at the time.

The gradual rise of the non-elite and the 'bourgeois trend' are quite palpable in literature, including historical literature. Medieval Egyptian and Syrian historiography is remarkable for the concern and attention it shows to daily life and the affairs, not only of the ruling elite and their caste, but of the cities and their people. In doing that, medieval chroniclers and scholars brought common people into history. Biographical dictionaries came to include people of craft and petty-bourgeois background. Some historians were themselves of modest background, such as Ibn al-Sayrafi, whose father was a money-changer. The very language that was used by some of the chroniclers, such as Ibn Iyas, reflects echoes of the vernacular. This is a complex development. In part it is due to the fact that some of the people who were putting their pens to paper during this period came from various non-scholarly backgrounds. That is, there was a widening of the scope and social base of the literati. Many of those people were writing history books. Furthermore, it would seem that what contemporary writers thought of as history broadened to include affairs of their own societies. Historians were no longer solely interested in the history of early Islam or the golden years of the caliphate, but they came to see their own lives, and their own contemporaries, as worthy of historicization and documentation. And this they did in a language that sometimes bore echoes of their everyday lives. This suggests that they had an awareness of their role in history as being important and their times as being worthy of note. It includes new references to the writers' sense of individuality as well, and to changing attitudes toward public space.

This is a question that will be discussed further in the book. I will argue that this shift in the historiography is related to a general shift in society, a flexibility and a broadening of the power base that also allowed non-elite urbanites and social groups outside the scholarly and military establishments or on their margins to express their political opinions and wills, often enough, through negotiation and protest.

A world upside down

Much of the literature on the fifteenth century has portrayed the period as being one of disruption of the social order. The reactions to this disruption varied. On the one hand, contemporary scholars perceived changes as signs of the decline of the regime and the horrors of the times. Thus, for instance, the social mobility that allowed for the rise of a coppersmith like Abul-Khayr al-Nahhas to levels of senior administration were interpreted by contemporary scholars such as the historian Ibn Taghribirdi as a sign of the weakness of the regime and the corruption of the social order. Social upstarts were viewed with suspicion, and indeed much of the information that contemporary historians provide about these historical figures relates to the administrative "corruption" and sale of offices that prevailed during the late Mamluk period—itself a consequence of the economic crisis that strained the state and the attempts to alleviate it. Rarely is this presented as a successful "rags to riches" narrative to be emulated. Instead, the dire consequences of such social trespass are often the moral of the tale. The upstarts invariably ended up in prison, or executed, usually having been deprived of the properties and wealth they had (illegally) amassed.

Similarly, this social mobility was reacted to on the streets by riots and protests that aimed at restoring an imagined traditional social order that was perceived to be under threat, or to advance claims or protest injustices. Thus repeated attacks on non-Muslim administrators and on non-Muslim places of worship often invoked the legendary "Ordinances of 'Umar." These were once more revived as part of the social and political discourse, and Mamluk sultans and elite, former non-Muslim born slaves, were eager to demonstrate their loyalty to the Muslim faith and social order by upholding such traditional regulations. The sense of crisis that permeated the Egyptian, and to some extent Syrian, societies resulted in violence against non-Muslims. At times, non-Muslim administrators were targeted by angry crowds. So were Muslim administrators, especially those charged with collecting taxes and levies. When levies were deemed unfairly high, crowds negotiated.

These changes and transformations also took their toll on people. In addition to their cumulative economic effects, the recurrent waves of plague had a psychological impact on society. The rate of change might also have left many uneasy; references to cases of suicide and violent crime suggest some form of social malaise. Some of the protests that are reported are also indications of the unease and difficulties people faced. After all, a limited number of people benefited directly from the transformations, and some stood to suffer.

By stressing transformation over decline I do not intend to deny the hardships that many contemporaries suffered or the corruption that existed. Rather, I mean to dig beneath these impressions and problematize them, to stare at the cracks that such pressures exposed in order to better understand how these societies functioned, and to better understand the role of a larger segment of the population in their histories. This is not intended to evoke a romanticized narrative of "the people" nor to make grand claims over the power of the urban non-elites in premodern times. Instead it is meant to aid the student of history to imagine a more complicated social and political landscape for premodern Egypt and Syria; rather than focusing on a hegemonic, autocratic power structure, it allows us to see various groups acting to further their interests. In short, it aims to look at society from the bottom up, or sideways, and to write a greater percentage of the population into its history.

After the Fifteenth Century

The economic, social, and political transformations that occurred over the fifteenth century left indelible marks on the Egyptian and Syrian societies, and influenced their history long after the fall of the Mamluks. Many of those transformations continued in effect under Ottoman rule. While Ottoman rule brought a measure of stability to Arab cities, and introduced some administrative changes, many of the aspects of the reorganization of the social order that had occurred during the fifteenth century remained in place. Thus, the sense of civic engagement that can be felt in medieval/Mamluk chronicles is very much apparent in seventeenth- and eighteenth-century sources. The series of chronicles by non-scholarly authors, including the Barber of Damascus, have already been subjects of historical inquiry. This literature, and the popular politics it narrates, indicates that many of the trends that were burgeoning in the fifteenth century bore fruit in the late-seventeenth and eighteenth.

Book outline

After this introduction, chapter two focuses on the transformations in the state structure and organization of power that occurred in Egypt and Syria in the late Mamluk period. It will study the various economic and political challenges that the Mamluk order faced and the attempts of the rulers to deal with them.

Chapter three deals with the social transformations that were occurring at the same time. Issues such as social mobility were heavily influenced and affected by the changes occurring in state and regime structure, especially during the fifteenth century.

Chapter four discusses the popularization of literature and historiography and the development of the bourgeois trend. As society was changing, more people were expressing themselves in literary and historical texts. They were doing this using new linguistic styles and genres. Their surviving writings reflect a changing awareness of themselves and their roles in history. They therefore suggest a new social trend, a kernel of a potential bourgeois class.

Chapters five and six are concerned with the various instances and reports of popular protest during the late Mamluk period. The discussion considers the ways in which different groups in society negotiated their interests with the powers that be. It shows that the deep transformations that were occurring to the state structure and to society were also reflected on the streets of the major cities and on the ways in which the urban non-elites dealt with their rulers. It brings the commoners into the viewfinder of history and argues that the behavior of common people, especially the urban non-elites, their decisions, and their protests, were part of the transformations occurring at the time. They reflect a way in which larger groups in society were participating in the politics of their time. Rather than assume that they were silent or ineffectual, these chapters bring out many examples from the historical literature to highlight the dynamic relationship between rulers and ruled.

Finally, chapter seven offers general conclusions on the transformations that Egypt and Syria were undergoing during the fifteenth century and the importance of studying urban protest in the premodern period.

2

THE MAMLUK STATE TRANSFORMED

As discussed in chapter one, the fifteenth century was one of many changes in Egypt and Syria. This chapter discusses the transformations that were occurring during the century and their effects on the state and its structures, and chapter three will discuss their effects on society. Deep transformations of the kind discussed here are ones that are accompanied by significant social and political flux and rearrangement of established social categories—a situation that I argue prompted the increasing protests of the period. The Mamluk rulers were pressed for financial and economic resources, and sultans devised various means to make ends meet. These challenges reached a peak of sorts by the fifteenth century, prompting the ruling Mamluk authorities to undergo a number of policy changes and employ different tools—with varying degrees of success—to deal with these situations. The challenges and the policies devised to meet them created a prolonged process of transformation that changed many aspects of state and society. Some of the very policies adopted to relieve the economic pressure unwittingly eroded the power of the state, compounding the difficulties the regime faced. Steadily, and as a result of different developments and policies adopted by the regime, power was diffused and de-concentrated and the Mamluk army on which the regime was based was itself transformed. There were many signs of reform and recovery during the late and long reign of

Sultan Qaytbay (1468–96). However, by the early sixteenth century the culmination was a state that ultimately struggled in dealing with the challenges before it, and a society that was under increasing pressure, some of whose members managed to do well out of tough times, while others did not. The policies that the Mamluk rulers followed were not only a reaction to these changes, but also factors that shaped them, and they resulted in many people's suffering and/or social displacement. This in turn prompted more acts of protest, as cries against injustice sometimes, but also as mechanisms against the injustice and attempts to relieve some of the burdens at other times. By the end of the century, both state and society had been transformed and were different from what they had been during the Early/Bahri Mamluk period. Many of the acts of Mamluk rulers which have been attributed to greed, corruption, or misrule can be analyzed in a different light if we place them in a wider context. This chapter discusses how some of the policies of late Mamluk rulers can be better understood as part of much deeper economic, and social, transformation.

The Mamluk regime, which ruled Egypt and Syria from the mid-thirteenth to the early sixteenth century, rested on the institution of military slavery. Military slavery was ancient in the Middle East but it gained importance, probably for various demographic and political reasons, roughly from the tenth century onward as more regimes relied on military slaves as the backbones of their armies. The Kipcak Turks who were recruited by the Ayyubid sultan al-Salih Najm al-Din Ayyub as troops for his army in the thirteenth century eventually took over power after his death. They gradually came to replace the Ayyubid network of rulers and kings, descendants of the famous Salah al-Din, who had among themselves controlled Egypt and much of Syria. Mamluk officers came to choose one of their own as leader, granting him the title "Sultan." With the collapse of the Abbasid Caliphate in Baghdad after the Mongol invasions of 1258, the Mamluks welcomed a descendant of the Abbasids to Cairo and proclaimed a continued caliphate from there. Henceforth they could legitimize their rule by claiming to be invested in the sultanate by the caliphs. These Cairo-based caliphs played minimal roles in Mamluk and Cairene society; they occupied a symbolic position in official ceremonials and were regarded with some religious respect. However, their movements and influence were severely curtailed. As army officers, the Mamluks were faced with several military challenges throughout the history of their regime. Coming to power in the midst of a Crusader attack on Egypt in Mansura, they continued to fight the Franks until the last principality succumbed in 1291. In 1260 they faced the Mongol invasions. Having conquered Baghdad and most of Iraq and Mesopotamia in 1258, the Mongol forces were advancing westward toward the Mediterranean. The Mamluk victory over the Mongols at 'Ayn Jalut in southern Palestine in 1260 sealed their reputations as defenders of Islam. The Mongol forces had committed numerous atrocities in the areas they conquered. Their reputation had preceded them, bringing panic and anxiety to Syrian and Egyptian cities. This made the Mamluk victory, for which there were probably several fortuitous causes, an important one.

Having achieved military victories over two formidable allies, the Mamluks went on to consolidate power under the sultans al-Zahir Baybars (r.1260–77) and al-Mansur Qalawun (r.1279–90) and his descendants. One of the main features of the regime was the continuation of militarization. Mamluk officers came to occupy major positions of state and administration. The regime also came to rely on the tax-farming system of *iqta'* in order to both pay its officers and manage a considerable part of the administration. In practice this meant that Mamluk officers were granted, according to their rank, certain enterprises from which to collect taxes on behalf of the state, and that was the way in which they—and their own Mamluk soldiers—were paid and maintained. *Iqta'*s were typically of land, granting officers the right to collect land taxes from particular villages, or else of particular ports or customs duties. Ideally, the *iqta'*s were rotated frequently as a check against corruption.

Mamluk historians devised the tradition of dividing Mamluk rule into two distinct periods, the Early (Bahri) period (1250–1380) and the Later (Burji/Circassian) period (1380–1517). While this distinction rested mainly on the racial background of the majority of Mamluk officers and soldiers recruited at each period, since with the Burjis more Mamluk recruits were of Circassian origins, it also carries within it other, similarly objective, reasons for the periodization.

One of these is that the fifteenth century witnessed a real transformation in the shape of the Mamluk state, in the ways in which the Mamluks exercised and wielded power over the populations, and in the ways in which they controlled and managed state resources. Indeed, some scholars, notably 'Imad Abu Ghazi, have suggested that the transformations occurring in the late fifteenth century were so deep as to have placed Egypt in particular on the threshold of a real social and cultural development of a magnitude akin to modernization, a development—Abu Ghazi argues—that was thwarted by the Ottoman conquest and the incorporation of Egypt and most of the Arabic-speaking lands into the Ottoman Empire.[1] While such a possibility remains a stretched hypothesis, it serves to highlight the depth of the transformations that were occurring during the late Middle Ages.

The Challenges before Them

The economic challenges and crises that the Mamluks faced were manifold and interconnected. They were also compounded over time by the effects of some of the policies the regime resorted to. Several of these were long-term developments and had long-term consequences. The responses of the Mamluk sultans resulted in long-term transformations that changed the nature of the state and of the Mamluk institutions. Many of these responses have been viewed as deviations from the proper norm of rule and governance, as signs of the corruption and greed of the *amir*s and administrators, and as causes for the "decline" of the Mamluk state, a motif quite recurrent in Mamluk literature. These policies had deep effects on various groups in society, pushing for the social, cultural, and political transformations that the fifteenth century witnessed.

Plague and its discontents

The economic challenges, as mentioned earlier, were manifold and interconnected. Scholars agree that the recurrent waves of plague had tremendous effects on the economy. While historians have long speculated that the Black Death of the mid-fourteenth century had long-term positive effects on Europe, leading the way from the Medieval to the Early Modern, the effects on the Middle East have largely been perceived as negative. Not only the famous epidemic of 1348 but also successive waves in the early fifteenth century heavily decimated the population in the Egyptian countryside, an effect which did not promote the rise of capitalism and ultimate economic growth in this part of the world.

As Michael Dols pointed out in his seminal study of the Black Death in the Middle East, many of the epidemics that hit the Arab central lands were most probably of pneumonic plague, either as the primary epidemic or a secondary epidemic as a complication of bubonic plague. Pneumonic plague is characterized by rapid death, and because of its infectious nature it has much higher mortality rates than bubonic plague.[2] This explains the rapid decimation of the population.

Young people and children were most heavily affected by the spread of the plague. The armies were also negatively affected as large numbers of soldiers perished. For example, commenting on Qaytbay's expenditures, especially on the purchase of new soldiers, Ibn Iyas reports: "He was also a prodigious purchaser of Mamluks, so that had the plagues not ravaged his reign, he would have accumulated eight thousand troopers."[3] One thousand Mamluks died during the epidemic of 1437–38. During the 1460 epidemic, 1,400 Mamluks—roughly a third of them—perished.[4] Indeed the total number of Royal Mamluks in service are thought to have dropped by half from 12,000 under al-Nasir Muhammad during the first half of the fourteenth century.[5] Historians also point out that Royal Mamluks, especially the *mushtarawat* (newly purchased slave soldiers) and *julban* (new recruits) of a reigning sultan, were more vulnerable and suffered higher losses than other groups; because they were among the younger members of the army and had probably been serving in Egypt and Syria for a shorter period, they would not have developed sufficient immunity against the disease.[6] The death of Mamluks by the plague was a loss of important resources to the state, requiring as it did their replacement and further expenditure. It was probably also one reason behind the recruitment of increasing older *julban* in the fifteenth century.

In general, modern historians differ in estimating the total medieval population of Egypt before the French Expedition of 1798, when the earliest modern census was conducted, and the populations of Syria before sixteenth-century Ottoman censuses. Similarly, they differ in estimating the percentage of the population that fell to the plagues. Some modern historians estimate the total population of Cairo around the mid-fourteenth century, by the reign of al-Nasir Muhammad ibn Qalawun, to have been somewhere between 450,000 and 600,000.[7] André Raymond offers more conservative figures, arguing for a population of 200,000 to 250,000 at the demographic height during al-Nasir Muhammad's reign in the mid-fourteenth century, 150,000 to 200,000 at its nadir during al-Maqrizi's time in the mid-fifteenth century, and no more than 200,000 in 1517.[8] Similarly, estimates for total population figures for Egypt as a whole vary between four and eight million, before the Black Death.[9] Figures for Syrian cities and provinces are even harder to estimate. However, historians have suggested a population of 900,000 to 1,200,000 for Syria, Palestine, Lebanon, and Transjordan prior to the Black Death.[10] The population of Damascus alone is estimated to have been around 80,180.[11] The degree of depopulation in Damascus during the Black Death alone is estimated at about 38 percent, while the total population of the Syrian provinces might have been reduced to around 400,000.[12]

Despite this wide margin of difference in estimating the total population figures, at least for Cairo, all modern historians agree that the plagues decimated the populations of Egypt and Syria. Raymond and Dols, agreeing with medieval historians, estimate that between a third and two-fifths of the population perished,[13] while Abu-Lughod estimates that around 40 percent of the population of Cairo was wiped out after the 1347 plague and that the decline in population continued as plagues recurred during the following half-century.[14] And while some historians suggest that the population recovered somewhat later during the fifteenth century, they argue it did not reach its earlier zenith. The decimation also affected the countryside since, unlike their European counterparts, Egyptian and Syrian peasants did not have many areas to flee to. Raymond suggests that out of the 2,200 villages in Egypt, forty were completely abandoned and 462 saw their tax burden reduced, indicating that the loss of lives was huge because otherwise the authorities would not have decreased the taxes they expected to collect. Tax revenues are estimated to have declined by 12 percent overall between 1348 and 1420.[15] Overall, between 1215 and 1517, the land tax of Egypt is said to have fallen from nine million dinars to less than two million, while Syria was even further impoverished.[16]

Such drastic decline in population figures, due to the effects of the successive waves of plague, must have affected the economy detrimentally, in particular the agrarian part of it. Both farming and the maintenance of irrigation works and industry were extremely labor-intensive and would have been negatively affected by the loss of manpower. There are indications that as the rural population shrank, a great deal of land was left to lie fallow and in fact many people, unable to survive in the countryside because of the added pressures of high and extortive taxation and decreased manpower, fled to the cities.[17] All this must have led to a drop in resources that agrarian lands yielded.[18]

Yet other indicators lead some historians, such as Petry, to argue that "no significant disruption in agrarian output plagued Egypt during these otherwise turbulent decades."[19] This is based mainly on reports of Nile floods and the prices of staple goods. The main source on agricultural taxation that survives from the period is Ibn al-Ji'an's (d. 1480) fifteenth-century cadastre, but unfortunately it only lists *iqta*'s and *iqta*'-holders' names.[20] An analysis of the information he provides can suggest the number of *iqta*'s parcelled up in a given province or, as Garcin has used it, the division of *iqta*'s among various social groups such as the Bedouin.[21] However, in the absence of cadastral surveys for the fifteenth century as well as the absence of surviving tax registers predating the Ottoman conquest, it remains impossible to gauge the area and productivity of cultivated land. Given the decimation in population it is highly likely that the area of arable land had decreased, with many lands lying fallow, and production sustaining the shrinking population without much left for investment or export. Similarly, the relative stability of the prices of crops is not necessarily an indicator of stable production, given the manipulation of the market by excessive taxation and hoarding.

While exact estimates are elusive, various sources allude to villages that lay fallow, and to agrarian productivity that presumably dropped. This led to a decline in both available foodstuffs and resources available to the central government, the land tax having traditionally been a main source of revenue. Indeed, throughout the century prices of food increased repeatedly, and famine, while seldom a reality, was a real fear.

This shrinkage of the economy intensified the struggle over resources and affected demographics. The depopulation of many villages in the countryside was also connected to a change in the demographics and population distribution. The ratio of peasants to Bedouin seems to have been sharply affected as a consequence. This in some part explains the rise of the Bedouin during the fifteenth century and repeated attacks on villages.[22]

In his comparative study of the effects of the Black Death on Egypt and England, Stuart Borsch stresses several important developments. While the plagues themselves were an environmental and natural disaster, their outcome was not predetermined, nor was it uniform in different parts of the world. One main reason the plague was so detrimental in Egypt, he argues, is related to the landholding system in place under the Mamluk regime. This system, and its slowness and inability to reform, led to further complications in the agrarian economy that compounded the negative effects of the plague over time and led to a near collapse of the agrarian economy by the sixteenth century. As the state system continued to privilege the Mamluk officers as a caste, and continued to pay them mainly through the *iqta‘* system, the depopulation caused by the plague did not lead to lower land rents but instead to a higher burden placed on the surviving and following generations of peasants. This led to major neglect of the irrigation system and waterworks. Lacking a clear incentive to finance the maintenance, repairs were generally delayed until some disaster occurred, by which time the expenses required were so huge that they were more often abandoned.[23] When they were carried out, the locals more often bore the brunt of the expenses.[24] The gradual collapse of the system of canals, dams, and dikes that connected various villages to the main waterways of the Nile led to a number of opposing outcomes in various areas and villages. Some ended up being overly flooded by the annual rise of the Nile while others remained unirrigated; both situations meant the loss of some arable land.

As Mamluk *amir*s based in the main urban centers (mainly Cairo where Egypt was concerned) were fighting over dwindling resources among each other, the system came to be further decentralized and additional burdens were placed on peasants. Furthermore, the system of *iqta‘* did not create enough incentives for the *amir*s to invest in maintenance, which furthered the collapse. And instead of paying peasants to work seasonally on the sultan's irrigation works, they turned to corvée labor in order to retain a higher percentage of the earnings.

What is most important for us to keep in mind here is that these developments were interrelated and that they placed a heavier burden on peasants, drove down agrarian revenues, and sharpened competition among the elite over dwindling resources.[25] They also ultimately changed the relationship of central authorities in Cairo to their peasant populations in the countryside. With the collapse of irrigation works and fighting and competition among rival factions of the army, the Mamluk landholding system came to be increasingly decentralized. The *iqta‘* system, on which the Mamluk institution was based, was breaking down.

Gold shortage and devaluation

Another long-term economic challenge to the Mamluk state was ensuring its supply of bullion, especially gold. As the state was dealing with the aftermath of the plague epidemics, drastic changes in currency rates occurred in late Mamluk times. The Mamluk regime used a three-tiered currency system: gold, silver, and copper coins were minted. The supply of bullion was threatened and affected over several stages during the fifteenth century. Italian merchants and then the Portuguese cut off the supply of gold reaching the Mamluks from Sudan and Mali. Similarly, the supply of silver was affected by the political changes in Asia Minor, especially the rise of the Ottoman state. As the supply of gold and silver was curtailed, coins included less of the heavy metals. While gold dinars continued to be minted, the silver currency was debased and largely disappeared, to be replaced by the copper currency. This created a severe cash crisis in the Mamluk sultanate and had various deep-seated consequences. The corruption of the currencies was recognized as a problem by contemporaries, and the regime repeatedly issued various exchange rates to deal with the devaluation problem. This in turn destabilized the markets, including rural markets, leading to demonetization and decommercialization in rural areas and a return to a barter system and paying rents in kind.[26] It is not coincidental that many of the protests that are reported for the fifteenth century relate to the currency exchange rate. Shortage of money made paying soldiers and officials more difficult, thereby urging the state to increasingly resort to indirect forms of payment. And it meant that the Mamluk sultans were constantly in need of cash, and devised ingenious ways of obtaining it.

The effects of the devaluation of the currencies were reflected on the streets and markets of Egypt and Syria, which were cash economies, especially in their cities (as well as the rural areas before the crisis). One of the recurring motifs in the literary sources is the minting of new coins and the protests and revolts that issued from repeated devaluation. In other cases merchants refused to trade and closed down their markets to protest changing currency rates, which they deemed unfair to their interests.[27] Often the negotiation process that followed allowed for a compromise.

The Mamluk authorities were trying various policies to manage this crisis, mainly by devaluation. But the success of this policy was uncertain. The population, and especially traders and merchants, were clearly aware of the crisis and therefore authorities could not just enforce an arbitrary policy. Sometimes they had to adjust currency rates in the face of social concerns and reactions. Unlike other policies—to be discussed later in the chapter—devaluation was one that was harder to implement. It was public and required the participation of the market.

The degree of popular involvement and awareness of the importance of the exchange rate is best revealed by a report from 1481 during the reign of Qaytbay. While riding back to the city from visiting the mausoleum of his recently deceased *dawadar*, the sultan was met by rioters complaining about new copper coins that had been minted and circulated at a higher rate and caused an increase in prices. So when he reached the citadel he ordered that a meeting of senior men of state be convened in the Salihiya Madrasa to resolve the issue. The four chief qadis, the *katib al-sirr*, the *nazir al-khass* al-'Alay ibn al-Sabuni, and the *muhtasib* (market inspector) met at his orders to discuss the coins. In the account of Ibn Iyas, the *nazir al-khass* is portrayed as having had the plan of setting different exchange rates for the old and the new coins. When the "common people" heard this they rose up against him in the center of the Salihiya Madrasa and pelted him with stones. Had it not been for the intervention of the *katib al-sirr*—Ibn Iyas assures his readers—they would have killed him. After a long meeting, it was agreed that the same rate would be set for all the copper coins, the old and the new—in effect canceling this particular devaluation.[28]

Among the interesting aspects of this report is that the sultan ordered that the meeting be held, not at the Citadel where rulers resided and ruled, but rather in the Salihiya Madrasa, which served as the main courthouse of the city. Conveniently located in the heart of the capital on one of its main streets, the courthouse was at the center of urban life. These decisions and negotiations were not occurring behind closed doors. Furthermore, some members of the population, other than the qadis and senior administrators, were either in attendance or had access to the deliberations. It is very possible that the discussions were public. Indeed, it is possible that by calling for the meeting to be held there, the sultan was trying to manipulate and channel popular reactions. The public or semi-public nature of the discussion is also something to note, for it suggests a communal aspect to the decision and the negotiation, and shows a politicized awareness from the population of the intricacies of exchange rates. It also shows that the policies the rulers resorted to in order to deal with the economic crunches were not simply arbitrary decisions taken from above within the confines of the Citadel; there were limitations on what they could decree, and members of the subject population had their input in the decisions. It was difficult for authorities to follow through with some policies, even if they were expected to have positive consequences, because they did not have the necessary power to implement and enforce them. Power was becoming de-concentrated, diffused, and inconsistent.

In 907/1502, when new coins were introduced, the markets of Cairo stopped trading until a favorable exchange rate was worked out.[29] When new coins were issued in 922/1516 in the last days of the Mamluk regime, Cairene markets were naturally destabilized; products had dual prices depending on the currency used. Markets shut down and bread was scarce.[30] Thus, rather than suffer and accept royal decrees, merchant communities and the urban population at large resorted to various tactics in order to resist and negotiate state policies, including refusing to trade and shutting down markets.

Through these acts of devaluation, protest, and negotiation, both state authorities and urban populations were devising ways to deal with acute financial crises. It is important to note here that very often the rates settled were not exclusively the result of decrees from above, but various groups among the population had a say in reaching them. The hesitancy and constant reworking of the value of the currency also betrays an insecure policy and a rather haphazard one.

Mamluk Administrative Policies in Crisis

In addition to currency devaluation, Mamluk sultans and the Mamluk administration in general resorted to a number of different policies at various junctures to deal with the enormous economic challenges that faced them. These policies were for the most part not well received, by contemporaries and modern historians alike. Some of these were general, macro-level policies that affected a wider sector of the population.

Monopolies and Red Sea trade

Among the most important fifteenth-century Mamluk policies were the trade monopolies that the sultans, especially Barsbay (r.1422–1438), imposed. These came to be applied to sugar production as well as to the spice trade.

Although contemporary historians reproached Barsbay for his greed, it is possible to read the situation differently. The various factors that combined to challenge the Mamluk administration meant that agrarian revenue from Egypt dropped. At the same time, in the early fifteenth century, the wars of both Tamerlane (Timur-Lenk) and the Turcomans in Mesopotamia and Iraq were a challenge in themselves, but they opened up an opportunity that Barsbay seized. These wars made trade routes through Iraq unsafe, and so the Red Sea became the safest route for the shipment of spices from India to Europe and the Mediterranean world. Barsbay sought to maximize this benefit by ensuring exclusive rights on this transit route to Egypt. Furthermore, he wanted the sultanate to have exclusive benefits of trading with the Europeans. So merchants were encouraged to discharge their goods at the port of Jeddah, rather than Aden, to make sure it was the Egyptian authorities who collected the taxes, since the Mamluks enjoyed hegemony over the Hijaz. The sultan then established a monopoly over the sale of spices.[31]

Different historians have studied the importance of the Red Sea trade to the Mamluk economy, some even arguing that, at least during the reign of Barsbay, Egypt subsisted solely on the income from its spice imports to Europe.[32] Meloy, however, sees Barsbay's "interference" in the trade not simply as a policy necessitated by the economic constraints but rather as one part of an imperial strategy to expand the Mamluk state.[33] Indeed, rather than a fixed policy, Meloy argues that Barsbay employed a dynamic approach to control trade, and building on Jean-Claude Garcin's analysis, he sees coherence in Barsbay's policies. Faced with a stagnant economy, his commercial policy was based on imperial expansion, argues Meloy.[34] Be that as it may, the monopolies were one policy the Mamluk state devised to maximize the profit it could make through the spice trade passing through its Red Sea ports on its way to the Mediterranean and European markets. However, it was a policy with multiple long-term consequences. With time, and as part of the same policy, the sultan's agents came to replace and take over from the Karimi spice merchants, striking a blow to free trade.[35] It was probably one of the more successful policies by the Mamluks, one that was maintained until the fall of the dynasty. It ensured enormous funds to the treasury. However, the exorbitant custom duties also prompted European merchants to search for alternative routes.

Taxation

Unsurprisingly, one of the first policies rulers short of cash resort to is additional taxation. The Mamluk period was notorious for these additional levies, referred to as *mukus* in the sources. These included weekly *(muja-ma'a)* and monthly *(mushahara)* taxes that were levied on merchants and tradesmen, resulting in increases in prices that everyone suffered from.[36] Rulers were ingenious in trying to figure out excuses for taxation. Occasionally they instituted seasonal taxes as well, levying duties on products such as watermelon, grapes, particular vegetables, leather, and fisheries.[37] These resulted in various reactions among the population. It is very difficult—if not impossible—to gauge how effective these levies were and how successful the population was in evading them. But they must have brought in some revenues, or else individuals working for the state would not have clamored to win the right to collect them. There was fierce competition among officers and bureaucrats over the right to collect different levies. Some even paid to get these positions. Consequently, they must have been a burden on the population. The sources do occasionally report on more obvious forms of resisting taxation. Abolishing the *mukus* was considered a pious deed. Therefore, in times of calamities such as natural disasters or illnesses befalling a sultan, the state would abolish the *mukus* as a form of charity.[38]

Occasionally the state imposed additional levies in order to finance the armies. Since the Mamluk regime repeatedly went to war in the fifteenth century, and since it was suffering from a cash crisis, the rulers continued to turn to the urban populations to help finance their military campaigns. These attempts were often met with resistance by the merchants and the ulama, the two urban groups most often affected. Whenever sultans tried to tax the lucrative funds of the *awqaf* (pious endowments) that were controlled by the ulama, the latter mounted scholarly battles. The merchants had various other means to protest levies.

Merchants occasionally succeeded in negotiating the levies down, if not in canceling them completely. Thus when Sultan Qaytbay imposed a levy of 40,000 dinars on the notable merchants of Cairo in Rajab 892/ June 1487 to finance the army going into battle, they refused and negotiated the sum down to 12,000 dinars.[39] (Chapter five discusses more detailed examples of how groups within the population protested various taxes and levies.)

One example in particular serves to highlight the ingenuity of rulers in finding ways to collect money and coming up with unusual taxes. In 876/1471, Qaytbay issued a decree specifying a certain long head cover for women to wear in public, one which included a royal stamp from the sultan's textile workshops on both sides. That was an indirect form of taxation: by making those head covers the only acceptable ones to wear in public, the sultan was in essence monopolizing women's headwear. Women who did not obey were publicly punished and humiliated. The decree was effective for a while before women began ignoring it.[40]

If Not Taxes, Then What?

Taxes, whether the *shar'i* (legal taxes sanctioned by Muslim jurists) ones—
zakat (alms tax) and *kharaj* (land tax)—or the *mukus*, were, it would seem,
not enough. In times of crisis, which were prolonged during the fifteenth
century, rulers resorted to other means to raise funds, including bribery,
sale of offices, extortion, confiscation, and land sales. Medieval chronicles include ample reference to bribery and extortion by senior state
officials, both military and civilian. That it was widespread is a matter
fairly evident in the sources, but historians disagree on how to interpret it.
Contemporaries saw it as a sign of decline and corruption; some modern
scholars, however, see it as "a routine feature that allowed the state to
function."[41] Indeed, even a contemporary observer such as al-Asadi (fl.
1450), in discussing the levying of protection money *(himaya)* by powerful state functionaries, accedes that they were compelled to follow such
practices partly because of the financial circumstances:

> If the sultan were to grant for each of them what was sufficient in
> [terms of] land allotment and fiscal register *(diwan)*, and did not autho-
> rize his command to whomever he wishes complete mastery over the
> people of the villages and the countryside, then he would never dare
> to contravene the law *(al-hudud)* and he would avoid tyranny, being
> afraid of what would come from it.[42]

Such comments give us an inkling of the various factors behind these
policies in the fifteenth century. The *himaya* that al-Asadi refers to
was a sum of money paid to a Mamluk *amir* in return for enjoying his
protection. Whereas in times past this protection was sought out by
various groups in the population, by the fifteenth century it had come
to be more often imposed by Mamluks on others, in effect being a form
of extortion.

The *amir*s resorted to imposing protection money on others, at least
in part because they were not paid sufficiently. And while land rents
did not fall and in fact increased in real terms, as already discussed, the
total agrarian production fell. Thus there was increased competition
among the Mamluk officers over those resources and they needed to

supplement their income by other means, extracting more revenue from the population under various guises.

Another mechanism of levying funds that the state used frequently in the fifteenth century was that of forced sales or *tarh*. According to this levy, merchants were forced to buy certain quantities of commodities at prices fixed by the state. We can consider it a form of extortion since, like the *himaya* levies, merchants had little choice in conforming; they could not choose not to buy the commodity (especially when it was one that was monopolized by the sultan). The sources contain various references to the ways in which merchants and tradesmen resisted and maneuvered around the *tarh*.

The reasoning and impact of the imposition of *tarh* is clear in a report about a protest that followed such a decree in 1471 in Cairo. At a time when Mamluk authorities were preparing to go to war against the Dhu'l Qadrids, they dumped leather on the market and forced its sale at double the market price. This was part of the process of preparing for and financing the war. It was also a mechanism to levy funds. It is highly likely that the leather itself had come from slaughtering animals confiscated after an attack on Bedouin tribes. When forced to buy leather at a price double the market value, some shoemakers accepted, while others started a riot and managed to negotiate the sum down.[43]

Even though taxes and extortion techniques such as the *tarh* probably had more immediate and pressing effects on members of the population, they were part of a longer chain of policies and mechanisms to raise funds. In fact, they were probably practiced toward the end of this chain of money levying. As crises and the shortage of funds intensified, problems accumulated and rulers needed to resort to more intense money-raising policies. Among the most prominent, and most alluded to in the sources, are sales of offices and land.

Sales of office

The practice of selling appointments in the official bureaucracy of the state is reported to have become established Mamluk practice by the fifteenth century.[44] In some cases the turnover rate of particular positions in government was so high that an occupant, having paid the sultan a hefty sum for the appointment, would be replaced within a few months or even weeks—naturally to a higher bidder. That bids continued and that the sultans remained able to collect cash by this mechanism is testament to the cash crisis that plagued the rulers, but also to the ways in which officials who did buy themselves offices were able to make up the amounts they paid, *with* profit. For example, the increasing role of the *muhtasib*s in collecting revenues for the state provided lucrative opportunities for amassing wealth, a situation state authorities were quite aware of as they ensured that appointees paid the state a considerable sum on their appointment[45] and periodically confiscated their properties, as they did with other middle-ranking and senior employees. The first mention of the sale of the office of the *muhtasib* of Cairo is thought to have been that of Najm al-Din al-Tanbadi in 789/1387, for 50,000 dirhams.[46] The types of positions open to this practice were numerous and various, from qadis to fiscal officers.[47]

The pressure the state imposed on its servants was translated into pressure on the markets. In Rajab 823/July 1420, when Sarim al-Din Ibrahim ibn al-Wazir Nasir al-Din Muhammad ibn al-Husam al-Saqri was appointed to the *hisba* of Cairo, he was asked to pay the treasury a thousand dinars, which, al-Maqrizi commented, he would duly collect from the tradesmen.[48]

Confiscations

The increasing involvement of senior military officers in the affairs of the administration allowed opportunities to amass wealth. Officers were assigned various *iqta*'s as part of their payment, and many managed to circumvent the system, overburden the subject populations with taxes, and create huge fortunes. Many also corrupted the system in order to pass on some of this wealth to their children—against the rules of *iqta*' and Mamluk regulations. However, sultans regularly confiscated the properties of senior military officers; the career of a successful officer often included prison time and confiscation of property at one point or another. The confiscations came to be so common that a *diwan* was established to specialize in those transactions.[49]

Manipulating the awqaf

Not only the holdings and property of members of the Mamluk class, but also the *awqaf*, or pious endowments, came to be included in the Mamluk machinations over resources.[50] Members of the elite—especially Mamluk officers, who should not, according to the rules and regulations, pass on wealth to their children—had placed substantial properties under *waqf*. This was one way in which Mamluks sought to save some of the resources they controlled from the frequent confiscations. However, *awqaf* funds were not always immune from state hands; toward the end of the century sultans repeatedly tried—with varying degrees of success—to either take over *awqaf* properties, tax their income, or channel *awqaf* incomes and rents to the state and especially to war efforts. Naturally the ulama were the group most vocal in its opposition to these policies, and they resisted strongly the attempts by sultans to siphon the funds allocated to the religious establishment, the main sources of income for the scholars themselves. These state policies were met with condemnation in the literary sources and stand out as further evidence to the corruption of the times. However, it is not difficult to see how removing substantial properties off the market and relieving them from taxation, as the *waqf* regulations allow, was denying the economy possible sources of income. In times of financial and economic crisis, they would be resources to resort to. Carl Petry, for one, reads Qansuh al-Ghawri's appropriation of *awqaf* funds as an attempt to bring back more of the state's resources directly under royal control in order to gradually phase out traditional Mamluk systems, dependent on *iqta'*, and replace them with a different kind of army.[51]

Land sales

As if appropriating *awqaf* funds were not enough, Mamluk sultans also managed to sell state lands in order to raise funds. 'Imad Abu Ghazi has studied surviving documents from the fifteenth and sixteenth centuries, covering the late Mamluk and early Ottoman periods, and has argued that the state repeatedly resorted to sales of lands from the *bayt al-mal* (treasury), especially during the late fifteenth century. Abu Ghazi argues that, contrary to what the documents claim, land sales were not correlated to periods of military expansion or increased spending on defense. Instead, he connects them to what he labels "political corruption." While Abu Ghazi cannot provide solid proof of why certain Mamluk sultans were more active in land sales than others, his survey shows that Mamluk officers were among the groups in society that most benefited from these sales. In fact, many of the estates that were turned into private property through land sales had previously been part of the holdings of their new Mamluk owners, frequently through *iqta'*. So, in essence, Mamluks were turning *iqta'* into private property. Furthermore, Abu Ghazi also shows that many of these sales were nominal: no actual money exchanged hands (hence he justifiably deems it "politically corrupt"). This suggests that it was not done to raise cash per se. Maintaining the Mamluk caste system and its privileges was costly, but in doing so the Mamluks ended up transforming the system and the state that was based on it. And they might have been in the process of creating a landowning class.

Iqta' and militarization

Increasing taxes, extortion, bribery, and the sale of offices were all mechanisms that brought in money in the short term, but they were also necessarily limited financial tools. More long-lasting and deep-seated were the changes that occurred to the *iqta'* system, the backbone of the Mamluk institution. Indeed, the *iqta'* system, at the heart of the Mamluk structure of power, was undergoing significant change, and was collapsing by the fifteenth century.

One means to which the state resorted in order to find funds to cover its main expenses, especially to pay its officers and soldiers, was through the expansion of the *iqta'* system and allotting administrative positions to military officers. Increasingly, larger areas of land were turned into *iqta'* land (instead of *kharaj* land), and the *iqta'*s of many officers were divided into several allotments that were dispersed across various provinces and often for short terms.[52] It is arguable that the multiplication of *iqta'*s and their dispersal over different provinces of Egypt negatively affected the ability of military officers to oversee the administration of any of those estates and encouraged them to focus on collecting funds and taxes, without much attention to maintenance and infrastructure.[53] In the long run, along with other factors mentioned earlier, this had negative effects on the productivity of the lands.

Similarly, as military officers came to depend almost completely on *iqta'*s for their payment, the *iqta'*s turned into business ventures and were up for sale. Thus some military officers would lease their *iqta'*s to others—including persons of non-Mamluk origins—to run them.[54] Al-Maqrizi comments on how common people of lowly backgrounds, including tradesmen and craftsmen, bought *iqta*'s, thereby infiltrating the *halqa* regiment.[55] All of these machinations affected the *iqta'* system and the army, as well as Egypt's income-generating projects.

Furthermore, just as civilians of undistinguished backgrounds were allowed into the administration in return for payment, military officers also came to be involved in the administration, "encroaching" on positions previously the exclusive domain of the ulama and bureaucrats, positions that did not normally require a military background. Increasingly, Mamluk officers were appointed to administrative positions such as the *hisba*. The *muhtasib*—often referred to as a 'market inspector'—had usually been a qadi or scholar. In the fifteenth century a series of military officers came to occupy the positions of *muhtasib* of Cairo and Fustat.

Why did sultans increasingly appoint *amir*s to manage the markets rather than qadis and religious scholars? On the one hand, these posts could have been means to pay back useful Mamluk allies. One of the ongoing challenges for rulers facing a shortage of cash, as explained earlier, was paying their military officers. Over the course of the late Mamluk period, many administrative posts were paid through the *iqta'* system. Another means of payment was by appointing the officers to lucrative administrative positions, such as the *hisba*. This was one indirect way of paying soldiers and providing an income for allies of one faction or another. The involvement of the military in this aspect of administration can be understood in this light—an attempt to find a new source of income for soldiers.

Berkey has argued that the function of the post of *muhtasib* underwent a gradual transformation during the late Mamluk period, one that brought to the fore the administrative and financial duties of the *muhtasib* at the expense of that of regulating public morality. The interference of *muhtasib*s in the economy became deeper and more arbitrary, he argues. This transformation he interprets in relation to the state's attempt to extract more revenues from a shrinking economy.[56] A *muhtasib*'s duties included supplying the main urban centers with food and controlling the prices of the main commodities as much as possible, a function that complemented the state's expanding monopolies. Perhaps as the markets witnessed more resistance and opposition, the post of the *muhtasib* came to require a more police-minded attitude rather than a legal one, hence the move to appointing more military men to the post. Stilt, for example, connects Barquq's appointment of the officer Dawlat Khuja (d. 841/1438) to the position of *muhtasib* with the period of plague and the need for an energetic man to carry out the sultan's orders.[57]

The skills that military officers brought to such jobs could have been an end in themselves. As the Mamluk sultans struggled to come up with adequate resources, controlling the markets was one of their goals. *Muhtasib*s played an important role in this overseeing of markets and in collecting market dues, and so it might have been a tactic to raise more funds to appoint individuals with particular skills to these posts, and with the ability to do so coercively. While traditionally and up to the early fifteenth century the post was more often assigned to an *'alim*, by the mid- to late fifteenth century Mamluk *amir*s were interfering more directly in the appointment of *muhtasib*s, preferring to choose men who belonged to one or another political faction, and more Mamluk officers were assigned to the post.[58]

This aspect of militarization and of the increased involvement of the Mamluk *amir*s in various aspects of administration is a major transformation in the structure of the state and how it carried out its functions. Regardless of the impetus or reasoning behind those policies, the result was a different state structure. It is therefore not surprising that in discussing the category of *amir*s or ruling officials, in his book of guidance to the naive and gullible, the scholar 'Abd al-Wahhab al-Sha'rani includes not only Mamluk military officers but also market inspectors, judges, treasurers, and Bedouin tribal shaykhs; the categories become interconnected. As Sabra explains, "the clear distinction between military and administrative officials of the early Mamluk sultanate had long since been blurred by the sixteenth century."[59] The blurring of differences between military and administrative functions and posts meant that military men came to occupy positions of civil administration and that men of non-military and non-Mamluk background also came to occupy positions formerly reserved for Mamluks. In practice this was part of the diffusion of power in the late Mamluk regime.

Similarly, Robert Irwin has written on the increasing involvement of Mamluk officers in the administration of justice. Whereas previously, and according to the norms historians believe were established in the late Abbasid and especially the post-Seljuk period, the religious establishment—that is, the ulama—were responsible for education, administering the *awqaf*, and the administration of justice, the fifteenth century, in contrast, witnessed increasing involvement of Mamluks in the judiciary, even though *amir*s were not appointed as qadis. Indeed, Irwin shows that, increasingly, military officers replaced qadis as administrators of justice and many, including *hajib*s (chamberlains), came to "usurp judicial powers that were formerly exercised by the qadis."[60] Irwin has termed this "the privatization of justice." It could also be viewed as one more manifestation of the militarization of the administration. Senior Mamluk *amir*s and the sultans also held *mazalim* court sessions in their households, to which common people would resort to settle disputes with their opponents.[61] While on some level this was a deviation from the norms, a corruption of the system, on other levels it reflects the changing ways in which Mamluk officers were exercising power over society, even though in a less centralized manner. The justice of the Mamluks would now be available to a wider segment of society—always at a price. And even though this meant more involvement of Mamluks in the administration, it also—ironically perhaps—worked to diffuse the power of the system they were supposed to uphold.

The transformations that were occurring in the Mamluk state during this century not only affected the Mamluk class itself, but had their ramifications on other sectors and levels of society as well. The appointment of military men to positions in the administration and the judiciary brought them into direct contact with the urban populations in new ways and meant, in practice, a transformation in the ways in which the Mamluks ruled. Transformations in the administration affected wider segments of society. The administration of justice was not a matter of concern only to the ulama; it also affected merchants, tradesmen, craftsmen—a wide array of city dwellers. These are transformations in state structure that affected not only the people on top, but also those below.

It is important to keep in mind that the *mazalim* courts in and of themselves were traditional. However, while in previous times the *mazalim* courts dealt mainly with issues relating to the Mamluks and to administrative justice, as Irwin argues, chroniclers of the second half of the century report that increasingly other members of the population resorted to the justice of the Mamluks rather than the qadis, because it seemed more expedient. Historians such as Ibn Taghribirdi were critical of this development, but for our purposes the new behavior shows the more direct ways in which Mamluks soldiers were interacting with the day-to-day affairs of the populations, at least in the cities. In his chronicle (under the events of 863/1458–59), Ibn Taghribirdi explained that at this time,

> the power of the purchased mamluks exceeded all limits, while the authority of the judges of Egypt was absolutely null. Anyone who had a just claim, or the semblance of such a claim, brought his charge against his opponent only before the purchased mamluks, and immediately he would secure what he claimed from his opponent, justly or otherwise. So everyone, especially merchants and sellers of any kind of wares, feared the mamluks and most men gave up their businesses, fearing the loss of their capital.[62]

As with the spread of *himaya*, the expansion of the Mamluks into the arena of administering justice could also have been another manner in which they found alternative sources of income. In this case, it further decentralized the administration of justice—one of the most important functions of governing. Some of the solutions that the Mamluks resorted to had unintended consequences: they led to a diffusion and de-concentration of power.

Structure of the Army

The composition and structure of the Mamluk army underwent significant change in the fifteenth century. Various factors contributed to this change. As previously mentioned, the late Mamluk period was generally designated the "state of the Circassians" by contemporary historians because of the racial element and the dominance of Circassian Mamluks throughout the period. Mamluks from other backgrounds, including Turks and Greeks, continued to be recruited and to rise up the military ladder, but the Circassians for the most part gained dominance.

Sultans, starting with Barquq, managed to accumulate a large percentage of state funds under their own direct control. Policies such as the trade monopolies and confiscation facilitated this. Furthermore, as the revenue coming from agrarian land decreased, so too did the yield of the *iqta*'s on which the *amirs* lived, creating a growing imbalance between the resources of the sultans and those of the *amirs*.[63] The *diwan al-mufrad* was created in 1383 in response to this and to manage the maintenance of new troops. These funds allowed the sultans to recruit new Mamluks swiftly.[64] The swift recruitment of large numbers of new troops meant that assimilation was not perfect, as integration needed time, and training and discipline were therefore compromised. For example, training time for new recruits seems to have been reduced to twelve or eighteen months.[65] Furthermore, recruits reportedly arrived in the Middle East at an older age, making the process of their training and discipline more challenging.

However, while the sultans were recruiting more royal Mamluks, the Mamluk structure became more factionalized, with groups of soldiers more loyal to their own *amirs* than to the sultan. At the same time the *amirs* themselves had fewer Mamluks. This is one factor behind the increasing rivalries and competition between the various factions. Sultans were to various degrees incapable of imposing discipline on all factions at once. The Mamluk aristocracy, as Garcin put it, was "dividing into clans."[66] This disintegration led to repeated rioting, especially by the new recruits, the *julban*.

Conclusion

The various changes that sultans from Barquq onward brought to Mamluk administration all point to the overall process of transformation that both Egypt and Syria were undergoing at the time. Greed and corruption, while surely part of the narrative since medieval times, do not alone account for the new policies. Al-Asadi's comments on the causes behind some of the "corrupt" practices of the state functionaries remind us of the connections that bound the economic and political challenges and policies together. The spread of the *iqta*' and its metamorphoses during that century, as well as many of the hateful policies such as bribery, sale of offices, and extortion, were all connected to the economic crisis and shortage of cash. While they might have been pursued as measures to compensate for the loss of income and allow the regime to function in some measure, they also—unwittingly—eroded the control of the rulers and diffused the power of the state. Many of them negatively affected different sectors and groups within the population, and thereby prompted various forms of protest. However, these policies aimed at solving economic crises, even if only in the short term. Some of the long-term consequences would have been unforeseeable and unpredictable for contemporaries. For example, the trade monopolies, especially on Red Sea trade, brought in considerable sums to the treasury, at times exceeding the revenue from land taxes, especially given the fall in agrarian production. It is only in retrospect that scholars have come to surmise that the excessively high taxes and regulations limiting the maneuverability of European merchants were among the factors that prompted the search for an alternative route to India, ultimately leading to the discovery of the route around Africa and the Cape of Good Hope. Similarly, policies that were meant to find resources to pay soldiers might not have been intended to erode the power of the state—yet they did. Thus it was no doubt unintentional that many of the policies to which the Mamluk administrators resorted exacerbated their problems in the end.

The policies themselves also had long-term effects that transformed the shape of the state and its relation to society. Indeed, as many historians have pointed out, the very policies of militarization and safeguarding the privileges of the Mamluk elite left the administration encumbered and largely dysfunctional. This dysfunction took its toll on society, which underwent various transformations during that century. Yet it also allowed room for political participation. The sultan—and the Mamluk establishment—could not monopolize on politics. The numerous reports of protest attest to the ways in which larger groups of society were sharing and negotiating power. By the beginning of the sixteenth century, the Mamluk state had become much less centralized, power was diffused among numerous actors, and it was a less wealthy state than before. The Mamluk institution itself on which the regime was based had become a costly burden. These transformations left a mark on society, exacting a heavy toll on some people and affording opportunities to others.

3

A SOCIETY IN FLUX

As explained in chapter two, the late Mamluk period, and the fifteenth century in particular, was one of deep transformations in Egypt. The economic challenges that faced the sultans' regimes and the ways in which rulers and administrators responded to those changes had profound effects on the economy and the state. However, as might be expected, this was a period of deep transformations for society and culture as well. A form of social flux prevailed over the fifteenth century, in part as a result of some of the state policies implemented to deal with various challenges, and in part as a reaction to some of those policies. It is not surprising that people—common people and the non-elite, and society at large—came to behave differently, and express themselves differently.

Studying the fifteenth century by looking beyond rulers and dynasties allows us to see a different picture. In fact the fifteenth century witnessed considerable social mobility in Egypt. People of different social classes were moving in new circles or rising to positions of authority, while simultaneously members of the Mamluk military class came to be more involved in matters of administration and hence more integrated with society at large, no longer isolated in the *tibaq*s (barracks) of Rawda or the Citadel. Others of that class lost previous privileges. Simultaneously, changes resulting from the plague epidemics and their aftermath affected the demographic structures in society, creating a new balance in the countryside between Bedouin and peasants, which in turn changed social realities.

This chapter will demonstrate that these social and economic changes touched many sectors of society, urban and rural, rich and poor. It is one more piece of the puzzle in arguing that all these changes were connected and went deep in society, and that we are thus seeing not simply a crisis and decline but a process of transformation. Those transformations were reflected in the way people expressed themselves culturally as well. Indeed, scholars have spoken of a "vernacularization" and a "bourgeois trend" during this period. (This will be the subject of the next chapter.)

A sense of social malaise permeates many of the writings of the late Mamluk period, probably caused by the deep transformations occurring in society at the time. In particular, the historiography of the period is replete with nostalgic references to the past, even as writers criticized their own times. This social tension, anxiety, and discomfort were also reflected on the streets in various acts of social violence and protest. We see it reflected in attacks on government officials, but also in attacks on non-Muslims. The acts of protest that historians of the period reported occurred against this backdrop of long-term social change and flux.

Population and Demographic Changes

The late Mamluk period witnessed many kinds of social changes that affected different groups. Those included major changes both in population levels and in the distribution of these populations across the landscape of Egypt in particular, and to some extent Syria. These in turn had an impact on various groups in society. Of course discussions of population composition and levels in the premodern period are notoriously difficult. However, two in particular are quite apparent in the sources: the demographic superiority of Muslims, and the prominence of the Bedouin. It is fairly well established in the literature that by this period the majority of the Egyptian population had become Muslim. We are not as well informed about the rate of conversion in other provinces. For example, conversion seems to have occurred much earlier and faster in Syria and was aided by the presence and subsequent movement of Arab tribesmen to the region after the initial Arab conquests, who were faster in adopting Islam. However, by the fifteenth century it would seem that the Coptic community was becoming a numerical minority in Egypt—a major social transformation.

Thus this period witnessed major transformations in society with groups and individuals moving both laterally—that is, from the peripheries of social power closer to its core (such as the experience of the Bedouin), and from the core to the periphery (as in the experience of the Coptic community becoming a minority)—but also moving up and down the social scale, as will be discussed in this chapter. These phenomena took place in addition to the overall drop in population levels. As discussed in the previous chapter, one of the main ramifications of the successive waves of plague that hit the region in the second half of the fourteenth and the fifteenth centuries was a decimation of the population. By some estimates, around a third of the population perished. This had numerous consequences, on demographics and distribution of population, and on what we can tentatively call the collective psyche of contemporary societies.

Indeed, it would seem that the recurrent plagues and their drastic effects on the population resulted in a shortage of urban labor, which in turn resulted in an increase in the wages of skilled and unskilled urban workers. Despite the horrors and drastic effects of the plagues, laborers seem to have been better off in the late Mamluk period compared to the Bahri period. Sabra, who has studied standards of living and surveyed wages of the poorer classes depending on salaries listed in *waqf* documents, posits an increase in wages in the period following the major plague epidemics in the second half of the fourteenth century.[1] Similarly, Ashtor has argued that workers and members of the lower classes in the late Mamluk period could afford a diet of sufficient nutritional value and that an increase in the bread and meat that they could afford followed the plagues and the Black Death of the fourteenth century.[2] The increase in average wages of urban laborers might in part explain how some of them came to accumulate wealth that granted them more visibility in the sources and more access to official positions. This accumulated wealth might also explain the increasing representation and reflection of artisans and craftsmen in the cultural life of the period. With some wealth at their disposal, some artisans and craftsmen could afford to enjoy various types of entertainment and perhaps even to patronize some cultural production.

Rise of the Bedouin and Bedouinization

The transformations of the fifteenth century can be observed not only in the main urban centers, such as Cairo or Damascus, but beyond in regions which for many other historical periods we know little about, and which are mentioned rarely in historical literature. Moreover, they are also apparent among sectors of the population that medieval chronicles are usually silent about, such as the Bedouin. That Bedouin should be so present in the late Mamluk sources is in itself an indication of change.

During the late Mamluk period, the Bedouin come to be more visible in the history and historiography, reflecting their increased political prominence and authority, especially in parts of the countryside and in Upper Egypt. Bedouin chiefs appear more prominently in the sources; their names are mentioned in texts such as the chronicle of Ibn Iyas. It is important to keep in mind that Bedouin tribes, though existing almost in parallel to Mamluk society, fulfilled various functions within the system. Despite their tribal organization, not all the tribes were nomadic, and some were agriculturalists. They were also a main source of riding animals and cattle—and hence meat and leather—for medieval Egypt and Syria. Furthermore, the patterns of their geographic settlement mean that the Bedouin of Upper Egypt controlled the supply of grain from the south to Cairo and other cities in the north as well as the trade routes with Sudan. The Bedouin of Syria controlled the grain harvest as well as pilgrimage and trade routes. Therefore, tense relations between medieval governments and the Bedouin of Egypt and Syria affected the urban populations. The Bedouin could and did threaten both peasants and urban dwellers, especially when their relations with the ruling authorities soured. The periodic campaigns that the state organized against the Bedouin were in part meant to provide cattle and foodstuffs for the army and urban communities. They were also a means by which the state extorted cash from the population: looted cattle were sold by force at fixed rates to merchants in the capital, for example.[3] The rise of the Bedouin is part of the general transformations occurring during this period. It was, in part, one of the demographic consequences of the plague epidemics. It was also partly due to the decentralization and relative weakness of the central ruling authorities and government—a recurring pattern in Egyptian and Syrian history.[4]

One reason for the rise and expansion of the Bedouin is the plague. The plague is thought to have negatively affected the Mamluk caste, the urban population, and the rural population of Egypt. In contrast, the Bedouin population seems to have been spared its detrimental effects. Similarly, the composition of the Mamluk army had changed considerably by the late fourteenth and fifteenth centuries. The troops were sent out to various distant battlefields and many soldiers fell in battle or to the plague, prompting continuous and rapid recruitment, which in turn affected the integration of the new troops and led to a change in the balance and composition of the armies in terms of different racial and age groups. Sources speak of the decline of the Mamluk army, but this is probably also due to changes in its composition and training, as discussed in the previous chapter. Also, the economic and state transformations meant that more officers came to be involved in the administration. The decentralization of government, diffusion of power, and factionalization of the Mamluk troops opened up political and martial space for the other armed group in society: the Bedouin. The balance of power seems to have shifted somewhat in favor of the Bedouin in the fifteenth century, leading to more attempts at rebellion and gaining leverage. This might explain not only the repeated, almost seasonal, campaigns against various Bedouin groups but also the elevation of some Bedouin chiefs to the position of *amir*s, and hence their very partial incorporation into the Mamluk state system. As we saw, Bedouin insurrection was a particular problem during parts of Qaytbay's reign, prompting repeated expeditions by his *dawadar* Yashbak min Mahdi to subdue rebellious Bedouin tribes. The emergence of the Bedouin tribes as a force to be reckoned with is one of the main transformations during this period.

Some Bedouin were also recruited in the heterogeneous *halqa* regiment that was open to numerous groups of hereditary and honorary semi-Mamluk statuses, such as the sons of Mamluks (*awlad al-nas*), eunuchs, the *wafidiya* (Kurdish and Mongol free warriors), Turcomans, Ayyubid princes, and even civilians with special affinities to the Mamluk Turkish caste.[5] Indeed, by the late fifteenth century, the Bedouin had taken over major parts of Sharqiya province, as the feudal registers show.[6] More than 20 percent of the *iqta*'s of Buheira and 46 percent of the *iqta*'s in

Sharqiya had gone to the Bedouin. While this is not easily convertible to corresponding areas of land, it does indicate that Bedouin shaykhs played an important role in levying taxes. That is, these Bedouin shaykhs had become in fact official authorities in the countryside, in a way replacing the *kashif*s of prior times; they had become part of the Mamluk system.[7] In those provinces of the delta, rural labor abandoned lands to the Bedouin and agriculture retreated.[8]

Bedouinization and Bedouin encroachment and takeover of rural areas was an added pressure on peasant communities. It was in part allowed by the depopulation and by the growing weakness of the state system.[9] It contributed to further rural depopulation and peasant flight in turn as Bedouin raids pushed peasants off the land. As Borsch points out, the collapse of the irrigation system left a broad spectrum of weedy plants, known as *khirs*, as the only species suited to the transformed ecology, replacing more traditional crops. Silted canals, collapsed dikes, and weed-clogged basins were ruins that were unfarmable and could not sustain an agricultural community, even when peasants resorted to alternative crops such as dhurra and sorghum. Instead, *khirs* grew in such conditions. They provided excellent pasture for the Bedouins' sheep and goats, further promoting their expansion out of the desert margins of Egypt and into the rural areas. The Bedouin thus benefited from the collapse of the irrigation system and the depopulation of the countryside of Egypt; at times they actively promoted it by cutting dikes and ruining basins to further their expansion.[10] In some cases, however, peasants in heavily disadvantaged areas joined forces with the Bedouin tribes.[11] It was in Upper Egypt in particular that the effects of Bedouinization were most acute; it was completely overrun by Bedouin tribes.[12]

Two issues were of prime importance in the relationship between Bedouin tribes and central government authorities: the harvest season and the transfer of grain to the storehouses in the capital, and the pilgrimage season and guaranteeing the safety of pilgrimage caravans. In times when the Bedouin tribes were on the rise, they threatened the movement of grain and of people; they could withhold the grain and plunder the goods on pilgrimage caravans; they could threaten the safety of pilgrims. In times when the central government was strong, its authorities managed to assure the safety of the transfers, and usually to confiscate some of the livestock of the tribes as well.

The harvest season was an annual period of tension between the Bedouin and the Mamluk authorities. This was particularly true in Upper Egypt, where the Bedouin controlled a large percentage of the grain harvest and its transportation routes. In Rabi' II 819/May 1416, Mamluk officers were sent north and south to ensure that supplies reached the capital. Al-Maqrizi writes that troops were sent to fight rebels in Upper Egypt, "these being the times of the grain harvest and their loss was feared."[13] Similarly in Rabi' II 821/May 1418, again the harvest season, al-Maqrizi reports more campaigns against the Bedouin in Upper Egypt.[14] The extent of booty was enormous: the *amir* Fakhr al-Din ibn Abi al-Faraj is said to have returned to the capital from this campaign with 20,000 sheep, 3,000 cows, 9,000 water buffaloes, 2,000 camels, 1,300 male and female slaves, and sugar cane, honey, and grain worth 100,000 dinars.[15] The following year in Jumada I 822/May–June 1419, again the *ustadar* returned to the capital with the booty from the Hawwara tribe: 200 horses, 1,000 camels, 600 water buffaloes, 1,500 cows, 15,000 sheep. The plunder was so great, al-Maqrizi writes, that Upper Egypt was deprived of cattle.[16] Such wars appear to be almost a part of the system, a way for the state to obtain whatever income it can from Upper Egypt and a way for the Bedouin to hold onto whatever resources they could. The outcomes of those skirmishes and battles are an indication of how far central authorities controlled the countryside.

A similar dynamic occurred in Syria. In Jumada I 894/April 1489, the viceroy of Damascus went out in a large expedition to quell the Bedouin of Hawran in order to save the harvest of that area.[17]

The Bedouin who patrolled the areas on the main pilgrimage routes were intimately connected with the routes' security—a situation they manipulated to their own advantage. Thus the fear of Bedouin attacks was a feature of the annual pilgrimage, one which necessitated special provisions on the part of the rulers of Damascus, including the payment of dues to Bedouin tribes as well as ensuring adequate security for pilgrimage caravans. Medieval chronicles not only scrupulously recorded the preparations for the annual pilgrimage caravan—an important event in the social and economic life of their cities—but they also reported on the letters the pilgrims periodically sent home to reassure their families and business partners of their safety. The pilgrimage journey was often a dangerous one; pilgrims could be attacked by the Bedouin. For example, in 905/1405, Bedouin attacked the pilgrimage caravan on its way back from Gaza, but the *amir* of the Hajj that year came to their rescue.[18] Again, the ability of the Mamluk authorities to ensure the safety of the pilgrims was a testament to their sovereignty and to their power as Muslim rulers.

In Muharram 900/October 1494, the pilgrimage caravan was intercepted by Bedouin on its way back to Damascus. The pilgrims reported that the *amir al-hajj* had abandoned the caravans and sped ahead with his own group and harem, which left the caravan unprotected and prey to the Bedouin. Even though the pilgrims had to buy their own safety from the Bedouin, later on the road they were once more attacked, losing their money and harem. Many women and children died of cold and hunger.[19] This happened during the interregnum that followed the death of Qaytbay and shows the breakdown in central state authority and the failure of the state to fulfill one of its most traditional and symbolic responsibilities: guaranteeing the safety of the *hajj*. Ibn Tulun's report makes it clear that the pilgrims were attacked primarily because the *amir al-hajj* did not carry out his duty properly. Finally a few years later, in 903/1498, the *na'ib* of Damascus attacked Bedouin of Banu Lam because they had repeatedly attacked pilgrims.[20] The following year, in Shawwal 904/June 1499, when news arrived that pilgrims on their way to Mecca were in fear of the Bedouin, the viceroy rode out with his troops to defend them.[21] Similarly, in Ramadan 906/March 1501, the viceroy himself went out in pursuit of Bedouin who had pillaged camels on the pilgrimage road.[22] Later, when some of the Egyptian pilgrimage caravan had ridden ahead of the others on the way back in Muharram 913/May 1507, they were attacked by Bedouin, their properties and money pillaged, and their women kidnapped. Ibn Tulun explained that this was because highway robbers and criminals knew that the *na'ib* was only interested in bribes and money and would not really go out to fight them.[23]

This annual dynamic would continue into the Ottoman period. As the incidents Ibn Tulun reports in his chronicle explain, when the state refused to pay the customary fees of highway protection to the Bedouin

tribes of Syria who guarded the pilgrimage routes, they attacked the caravans. This happened to the caravan returning to Damascus from the Hijaz
in Muharram 931/November 1524.[24] This is one of the few instances in
the sources where we can glimpse, vaguely, the triggers behind Bedouin
insubordination. That the Bedouin might have an excuse for rebelling
against the state is not an idea that is readily entertained by the sources.
Such attacks, though a serious affront to the ruling authorities, were
not unusual and would happen centuries later under the Ottomans in
1171/1757, when again the pilgrimage caravan was attacked and robbed.[25]

In these cases, state authorities had failed to uphold what the Bedouin might have considered their customary rights. Paying protection
money to Bedouin tribes for passing through their areas of influence helps
explain some of the tensions between various competing legitimacies, and
also elucidates the limits of the power of premodern rulers. Other similar examples occasionally appear in the sources. In Jumada II 895/May
1490, the Khalidiya Bedouin attacked caravans traveling from Aleppo to
Damascus carrying tribute and merchandise. They killed several people
and kidnapped women and concubines. Ibn Tulun explains that their attack
came as revenge for the arrest of their chief, Qarqamas al-Badawi.[26] We are
not told why the authorities had arrested Qarqamas, but apparently for his
tribe this constituted a breach of customary conduct that allowed them in
turn to breach their obedience to the state, hence the attack on the caravan.

The high number of Bedouin attacks on traders and caravans is an
indication of their increasing authority in many areas of the countryside. In Muharram 825/December 1421 the Upper Egyptian Bedouin of
Lahana and Hawwara rebelled and attacked the highways. They set fire
to several villages. Alas, al-Maqrizi, who reports this rebellion, does not
explain the reasons. He does mention, however, that there was a grain
shortage in Upper Egypt at the time, so severe that supplies were sent
from storehouses in Cairo to the south, rather than the other way around.
Many lands lay in ruin.[27] The rebellion continued throughout that spring;
in Rabi' II 825/April 1422 the *wali* of Qus was assassinated and the state
could not collect *kharaj* taxes from the Sa'id.[28] In Shawwal 912/Febru-
ary 1507, Bedouin in Sharqiya attacked a caravan leaving al-Mahalla and
including tax money destined to the sultan.[29] As we can see, the economic

crisis and the dearth resulting from decreased agriculture affected the countryside as well as the balance of power in the provinces, leaving the Bedouin in a more powerful position.

It was not just the countryside that was affected. War with the Bedouin affected urban life. It had the potential of disrupting the grain trade, as for example in 902/1497, when Mamluk factional wars led to the breakdown of law and order everywhere and encouraged the Bedouin to rebel. The Bedouin burned stores of wheat and barley in various provinces which, naturally, led to an increase in grain prices.[30] Bedouin wars also occasionally spread into the cities. In 876/1472, the Bedouin of Haram and Wayil of Sharqiya were rebellious; they attacked travelers so that the highways were unsafe. The fighting reached the capital; they attacked Cairo and pillaged markets in al-Husayniya.[31] Similarly, in Jumada II 890/June 1485, rebelling Bedouin attacked Damascus and its environs.[32] Another Bedouin attack on Damascus occurred on 12 Rabiʻ II 893/26 March 1488. The attackers were immediately put down by force; some were strangled to death, others beheaded.[33] But they had reached the city.

The overall effects of the Bedouinization on the rural societies, especially of Egypt, is difficult to document, if easier to imagine. It added to the pressures that peasant communities increasingly felt, in addition to increased rents and malnutrition, and prompted peasant flight into the cities in response. It also prompted peasant uprisings.[34]

Racial Groups

Studies of the fifteenth century have often focused on the shift from the Bahri/Turkish Mamluks to the Burji/Circassian Mamluks, indicating the origins of the ruling caste. In reality, however, the racial changes went much deeper. Just as the late Mamluk period witnessed the rise of the Circassians as the elite ruling group among the Mamluk establishment, other racial groups also moved from the peripheries of society closer to the core. These included the *habashi*s.

The *habashis*

Among the social groups that enjoyed some opportunities of advancement were Sudanese former slaves and clients of military officers, referred to as *habashi*s in the sources. Many of them were eunuchs and manumitted slaves, and found opportunities for advancement in the service of military officers, but also as merchants in Red Sea trade and even as scholars.[35] Scholastic achievement, learning, and piety opened doors for popular esteem. Thus there were various paths to upward mobility for such individuals of former lowly status. Several *habashi* eunuchs who reached notable status within the bureaucracy and accumulated large fortunes went on to endow religious institutions by setting up *awqaf*, in common with elite members of this society and emulating their own patrons.[36] This is an ethnic group that had been occasionally looked down upon, but in this period more and more individuals from this group came closer to the elite circles of the Mamluks. Being black and often eunuchs, the *habashis* were not on the same social or political level as the ruling Mamluk caste. However, their positions and fortunes allowed some of them to come closer to this elite and to behave in ways similar to it—to emulate its patronage patterns, for instance, by endowing *awqaf*. This could similarly be related to changes in the slave trade routes and the recruitment patterns of Mamluks. That is, the changes in the composition of the Mamluk caste during the fifteenth century opened up opportunities for advancement for other ethnic groups, such as the *habashis*.

Emerging Landowning Class

Just as significant were the shifts in the composition of certain social groups. In the domain of the economy, for example, 'Imad Abu Ghazi has argued for the emergence in the late fifteenth century of a new landowning class that was more indigenous in its makeup and that included the sons and grandsons of Mamluks, members of the *awlad al-nas* who were Egyptianized in their social placement. Abu Ghazi's claim is that the rise of this potential new social class was thwarted by the Ottoman conquest of Egypt. While the full ramifications of this transformation were not yet apparent in the fifteenth century, it was a change in the making, and a change that had echoes in society, as the Mamluks, who were traditionally an exclusive caste distinct from the rest of society, came to be further incorporated into local Egyptian and to some extent Syrian milieus. The land sales that increased toward the end of the period are one mechanism through which this was happening and which, had they continued, would have changed the land-holding system altogether. Otherwise, the involvement of Mamluk officers in more aspects of the administration also meant more assimilation with their local populations, making them less isolated than in earlier times.

Islamization

The spread of Islam more broadly among the Egyptian population is another domain where significant social transformations were taking place. Scholars of the history of Copts during the Mamluk period point both to the transformation of the community into a numerical minority and to increasing pressures placed on them. These pressures varied from decrees issued by various sultans prohibiting the employment of Copts in the service of Mamluk *amir*s, to restrictions on dress codes and riding animals. They also include popular attacks on non-Muslim individuals and groups. Tamer El-Leithy has shown how Coptic conversion to Islam accelerated during this period and how it became increasingly difficult for Copts to circumvent some of the restrictions placed on them by rulers. Many went so far as to choose martyrdom in defiance of those restrictions.[37]

While scholars agree that by the fifteenth century the Islamization of Egypt had reached an advanced stage, explanations for the reasons behind this major transformation are few. Huda Lutfi, for example, in her study of Coptic Nile festivals, has traced how the attitude of various Muslim rulers and regimes toward the indigenous Coptic population differed sharply over the centuries. Whereas some earlier rulers, including the Fatimids, were famously tolerant of their (majority) non-Muslim subjects to the extent of participating in Coptic festivals, the situation had changed considerably by the late Mamluk period. For Lutfi, this is a sign of the Muslim culture becoming hegemonic. Indeed, when comparing Egypt to other provinces of the Muslim caliphate and post-Abbasid regimes, it seems to have been much slower in its conversion. The question might be why it took so long for Egypt to convert compared to other areas. In addition to established hegemony, one could also point out to the non-Muslim background of the Mamluks for possible explanation. As is well known, the Mamluk *amir*s and sultans were all—in theory—born non-Muslim and enslaved. They were converted to Islam as part of their training for the army and manumitted upon graduation. This non-Muslim slave background of the elite who came to be the rulers of Egypt and Syria placed them at some moral and religious disadvantage, making their credentials as Muslim rulers somewhat suspect. They tried to boost those credentials by various means: mainly by defending the realm of Islamic lands from non-Muslim invaders such as the Mongols and the Franks, but also by patronizing the religious establishment and all its institutions. They even revived the Abbasid Caliphate in Cairo, by recognizing a Abbasid claimant to the caliphate, thereby re-establishing the Caliphate if only in name. Finally, they also tried to appear as good Muslim rulers versus the non-Muslim other within, namely the Copts. By claiming to uphold the ancient "Ordinances of 'Umar" or "Pact of 'Umar," the Mamluk rulers were trying to appeal to their (now majori-ty-Muslim) subjects. It is perhaps significant that this aspect gains more momentum during the late Mamluk period and not the early formative period, that is, *after* the major threat of both Mongols and Franks had been subdued. Possibly one might imagine this came as a result of state and army feeling a bit weaker and trying to consolidate themselves by enhancing their image as Islamic rulers.

In several surviving narratives, Mamluk sultans are urged by visiting Muslim dignitaries or ulama to revive the Ordinances of 'Umar and tighten restrictions on their non-Muslim subjects. This happened, for example, during a visit of the *wazir* of the ruler of the Maghrib in 700/1301, who was astonished to see the behavior of some Christian senior officials in Egypt, who rode on horseback among the Muslims, wore white turbans, and humil-iated Muslims.[38] Under the pressure of fellow Muslim authorities, Mamluks were shamed into living up to the requirements of upholding Muslim hege-mony, here mainly through subjugating their non-Muslim subjects. It is also worth noting that the impetus for reviving restrictions on non-Muslims in several narratives comes from Spanish and Morroccan émigrés to Egypt, scholars who were probably well aware of the Catholic advances in Spain and whose sense of Muslim identity was sharpened as a result.

Furthermore, some of the restrictions on non-Muslims might be understood as part of the state transformations discussed in the previous chapters. For example, one of the first decisions that Barsbay took as sultan was to renew the ban on Christians and Jews entering government service. However, this may have been an indirect form of taxing, or another example of the extortions rulers resorted to, like the sale of offices, "since when non-Muslims were the object of such a decree, they usually circumvented it by payment of a sum of money."[39] However, even though many senior Coptic officials found ways to circumvent the decrees, others were forced to convert to keep their positions, which would partly explain the demographic shift.

This changing social placement of the Coptic community—notwithstanding the difference in experience between Copts of various social classes, and the different experiences of the cities and countryside, about which we know much less—is probably partly behind the rise of popular attacks and acts of violence against non-Muslims during this period. Popular riots and mob attacks on non-Muslim officials could have been ways of restoring an imagined traditional social order. This in turn might have been a factor which accelerated the conversions.

Social Mobility

As we have seen, some groups in society were moving from the periphery to the core while others were moving in the opposite direction; groups that had been outsiders to the system, such as the Bedouin, came to be partially incorporated into the Mamluk system, while senior Coptic officials and bureaucrats were squeezed out and struggling to maintain their positions. It was a society in flux. There was in addition to this another dimension of mobility, of individuals moving from one social category to another, both up and down.

The late Mamluk period saw the rise of unexpected personalities to fame and infamy, or at least to lucrative administration positions. The flux that the changing administration was going through meant that, increasingly, cracks were opening up into the neatly-divided social categories and classes. The divide between the *khassa* and the *'amma*, the elite and commoners, ever-so-idealized if never fully realized, was giving way to let some people from the commoner classes rise up in administration and society, and to let some Mamluks down to integrate with the non-Mamluk population.

Increasingly during the late Mamluk period, especially the fifteenth century, men from lower social backgrounds, upstarts, started making their way into the literary historical narratives. They appeared in the documented history because they increasingly played roles in the administration and in politics. They also appeared in the cultural life of the time. This could be a consequence of the vacuum left by the changing conditions we have been discussing; social barriers were becoming a bit looser as the century progressed. Through the surviving sources it is possible to follow specific individuals who rose from modest beginnings and within a relatively short time were able to rise to unprecedented levels of wealth and power. This was often met with disdain by contemporary scholars, which suggests that such upward mobility was not easy or smooth. In a study of some ninety commoners who are listed in Ibn Hajar's biographical dictionary, Irmeli Perho shows that lineage, family relations, and social networks were very important for social advancement.[40] Even though the religious establishment was ostensibly open to all on grounds of merit, there were limits to how far individuals from a commoner background (artisan or trade) could rise within the field. However, despite serious challenges, many individuals managed to rise through the social ranks and attain powerful administrative positions. Others moved into different circles from those of their fathers and grandfathers, or even those of their own early careers—for example, from being a *shahid* (clerk) in court to being a copyist,[41] or from butcher's son to linen worker to *faqih* and assistant judge.[42] Most of the commoners who gained prestige in scholarly circles, as reflected in Ibn Hajar's biographical dictionary, were *muhaddith*s (scholars and transmitters of prophetic hadith).[43] Even if these individuals did not come to occupy the highest possible positions among the civilian elite, such as that of chief judge for example, they were still able to move from one social category to another, often slightly upward from where they started. These changes also allowed for more participation of women in the scholarly life of the time.

Mamluk patronage was another path for social mobility. We have seen in the previous chapter how bribes and the sale of offices were criticized as methods through which the rulers sought to increase their income, and in the process occasionally allowed unqualified persons to assume office.

In trying to find necessary resources, sultans such as Qaytbay also turned to men from civilian society and trade backgrounds, probably for their know-how and "lack of scruples," as Garcin puts it.[44] Money-changers, retailers, suppliers of meat must have had inner knowledge of the working of the markets and the ways in which various merchants and tradesmen conducted their business and hid their wealth—knowledge that would have been of value to the tax collectors. This knowledge was especially beneficial to the *hisba*; indeed, several *muhtasib*s come from a commoner background, such as Muhammad ibn Subayh (d. 1325) who began his career as chief muezzin in Damascus,[45] or Muhammad ibn 'Ali al-Sharrabi (d. 1420), who was a seller of beverages before getting a legal education and later buying himself the post of *muhtasib*.[46] Others must have attracted the attention of Mamluk *amir*s and officers because of their talents. It is also possible, though difficult to substantiate, that the decimation that was caused by the plagues also affected the civilian bureaucracy and the training and production of new generations of bureaucrats, leading to a loss of certain expertise and qualified men.[47] Be that as it may, this very mechanism allowed for social mobility.

Whereas we often think of medieval government as static, and administrative procedures before the nineteenth century as lacking in innovation, the changes that were happening, though they were not revolutionary, had long-lasting effects on society. The sale of offices meant that positions in the administration were increasingly occupied by people from backgrounds different from those who had occupied them earlier. Positions that were often exclusive to scholars with a jurisprudential background came to be open to individuals with less education, and also to military officers. In some cases, positions that had been the domain of officers came to be occupied by civilians. This turn of events was looked upon unfavorably by contemporaries. It was an overturning of the traditional order of things, and a sign of corruption. What it does show the modern historian, however, is the degree of change this society was undergoing.

The career of Abul-Khayr al-Nahhas (d. 1459), followed and analyzed by Richard Mortel, serves as an excellent example of the opportunities and limitations facing commoners rising in society during the late Mamluk period.[48] His climb up the bureaucratic ladder was quick, and involved all the characteristics of the time: buying office, intrigues, plotting against rivals, confiscation, and imprisonment. It is a dramatic Mamluk story of rags to riches to rags again. Abul-Khayr, as his epithet indicates, started out his career in the footsteps of his father, apprenticing as a copper-smith *(nahhas)*. He also received a religious education, studying *fiqh* in Cairo and Aleppo, an opportunity presumably afforded by the spread of *awqaf*-funded education during the period. Although al-Nahhas did not distinguish himself as a scholar, he continued to recite the Qur'an in several mosques while working in his father's workshop. In 1446 he gained the attention of Sultan Jaqmaq after presenting a case against one of the leading qadis of the day. From then on, he began a career in the adminis-tration, covered by Ibn Taghribirdi in his chronicle and in notices about him in biographical dictionaries. Having won the favor—and it would seem, more importantly, the ear—of Sultan Jaqmaq, al-Nahhas plotted to replace several senior men of state and came to occupy positions as varied as supervisor of the treasury, supervisor of the *jizya* collection, supervisor of the *kiswa* of the Ka'ba (the embroidered silk covering of the Ka'ba at the Mosque of Mecca sent annually by the Mamluk rulers from Cairo), supervisor of the Sufi khanqah of Sa'id al-Su'ada' and of the mosque of 'Amr in Fustat.[49] Equally important, al-Nahhas's closeness to Jaqmaq gave him an opportunity to interfere in the appointment of other men to posi-tions within the administration, so he filled many bureaucratic posts with his clients. This was information known to urban crowds and to Jaqmaq's recruits and earned him many enemies.

True to form, al-Nahhas himself was subjected to the intrigue of his rivals. He was also the target of popular protest as well as attacks by the sul-tan's *julban*. In 1449 he was attacked and in 1450 his house and properties pillaged.[50] He was subsequently imprisoned, exiled to Syria, and his prop-erties confiscated, and even though he managed to make a comeback under the reign of Sultan Inal in 1458, it was short-lived and doomed; he died a few months later penniless.[51] His fall from grace was as dramatic as his rise. And while many historians, contemporary ones such as Ibn Taghribirdi or even modern ones such as Mortel, interpret the rise and fall of al-Nahhas in the context of the decline of Mamluk bureaucracy, we can also read fur-ther into this example. It shows us that there were opportunities for men from artisan and commoner backgrounds to enter the civil bureaucracy, especially if they had entered the ranks of the educated by studying *fiqh*, but that this also required much maneuvering, ruthlessness, and social survival skills. His story involves much intrigue and sales of offices. It was also a risky business. Men such as al-Nahhas obviously brought much-needed skills to Mamluks such as Jaqmaq, but it was dangerous getting so close to power. And it was resented by various groups in society: the learned elite, such as Ibn Taghribirdi, and commoners alike.

As we saw, al-Nahhas was able to enter the civil bureaucracy after studying *fiqh*. Indeed, the spread of literacy through the establishment of *sabil-kuttab*s (public water fountains attached to primary schools for religious education) and their generous endowments, as well as the popularization of culture to be discussed further in this chapter, also allowed opportunities for social mobility. One prominent example is the famous scholar and Sufi 'Abd al-Wahhab al-Sha'rani (d. 1565). Though he himself came from a peasant background, he immigrated to Cairo and rose to become a highly respected scholar of his time.[52] Indeed, the late Mamluk period also witnessed the emergence and rise of Sufi artisans who continued to practice their crafts and professions and yet came to occupy leading positions within the Sufi community.[53] Even though some of them were illiterate and despite their lowly backgrounds, their mystical knowledge awarded them a place of pride within Sufi circles and even promoted them to positions of leadership. In a sense the popularization of Sufism during this time period also created a new avenue for social mobility and advancement. It further created a new group of "everyday saints," as Sabra labels them, organic intellectuals and leaders whom common people could and did resort to in their day-to-day affairs. Sufism and learning were paths to advancement in society. In this period Sufism itself ceased to be exclusive to an intellectual and spiritual elite but rather became open to people from humble backgrounds, even those who were illiterate.

Downward mobility

The social changes of the fifteenth century clearly cannot be understood as simply a set of people who succeeded in attaining a higher status. The challenges and transformations of the fifteenth century did not provide occasions and opportunities only for upward mobility and advancement in society; some people, naturally, stood to lose some ground. There are references in the sources to members of the Mamluk caste/elite who lost their *iqta*'s. The Mamluk state was under financial pressures during this period, and much of its liquidity went to financing, shoring up, and maintaining this military caste with all its privileges, which from a later, early-modern point of view was not economically efficient. It would seem that under pressure, the rulers tried to cut off the *iqta*'s and stipends of members who were not really working for the state or providing services. The individuals we hear of losing their *iqta*'s are mostly people who inherited those rights from forefathers. They perceived these *iqta*'s as their established privileges and complained when they were jeopardized. Similarly, the sources also adopt their point of view by presenting such loss of privilege as a sign of the corruption of the rulers and the times, and as an injustice to which some individuals were subjected. For example, the historian Ibn Iyas himself narrates how his own *iqta*' was canceled at one point and how he petitioned the sultan to regain it. As he explains, in Jumada II 914/ September 1508, the sultan canceled some of the *iqta*' of *awlad al-nas* who were members of the *halaqa* and others, including women, who received stipends and *iqta*'s, re-assigning them to Mamluks. Ibn Iyas writes of this in indignation, presenting it as an injustice, although we can appreciate the logic behind al-Ghawri's policy. Mamluks attacked many of the *awlad al-nas* in their houses to take possession of their *iqta*' deeds. Ibn Iyas himself was affected and his *iqta*' was re-assigned to four Mamluks, however he explains that with God's help, he was able to retrieve it. In discussing events of a year and a half later in Dhu'l Hijja 915/March 1510, he mentions that he read out a complaint to the sultan in the *maydan* and in response the sultan returned his *iqta*'.[54] Despite the good fortune of Ibn Iyas, we can imagine how many members of the Mamluk caste stood to lose some or all of their privileges due to changing economic circumstances and the Sultan's attempts at fiscal reform. Similarly, the battles that the Mamluks were fighting in the fifteenth century led to pressures on recruitment, as previously discussed, which in turn created tension and struggle between the veteran Mamluk officers and the recruits, with some of the old-timers and former sultans' Mamluks losing benefits.

Integration

The social flux that allowed for upward mobility for some commoners, and led more members of the Mamluk classes to come to be involved in trade and civil administration, created a new type of social integration as well. As previously discussed, some scholars, like Abu Ghazi, surmise that this development would have led to the rise of a new landowning class. The immediate effects, however, meant that the Mamluk officers were no longer confined to their barracks and their military careers, but instead came to be more involved in matters of civil administration, even judicial administration. This brought some of them at least into more direct contact with the urban populations, and could have provided more causes for the social friction and violence that permeates the late medieval narratives. The policies to which the rulers and administrators resorted in order to make ends meet changed the relationship between rulers and ruled. Thus, for example, the *himaya* levies that powerful *amir*s collected created a web of alliances and clientship networks that brought together officers and civilians. Hence, in discussing the extortions levied under the rubric of *himaya*, Meloy has argued for a symbiotic relationship tying the military and civilian elite. Just as military officers increasingly dispensed justice, thereby usurping some of the powers of the judiciary, so too judges connived with military men to seek profit from the system. Similarly, "the benefits gained from corruption in the justice system trickled down the social pyramid as well: . . . members of the judiciary at all levels, from judges down to scribes, 'had some kind of connection to the powerful *amir*s, with whom they cooperated for profits instead of for the upholding of the law and for governance by law.'"[55] Meloy concludes: "just as lower functionaries within the courts came to depend on the system of corruption so did the tradesmen mentioned earlier rely on the protection they received."[56] That is, the *himaya* was not *only* a form of extortion. Individuals, clerks and tradesmen and others, who agreed to pay the protection money might have often done that under duress, but others might have also sought this protection as a way of indirectly resisting the pressures that they were suffering, of circumventing the levying powers of the state. The process was just like evading taxes. When the *himaya* payers acted in this way, and when the *amir*s provided the expected services, the two groups came to be joined to each other in new ways and formed new alliances.

Anxiety and Social Malaise

All of this social change and turmoil left its mark on the populations. There were both collective and individual manifestations of social anxiety and tension during the late Mamluk period.

As previously discussed, the Middle East, including Egypt and Syria, was hit by successive waves of plague during the fourteenth and fifteenth centuries. This repeated occurrence left its mark not only on the state and economy of the Mamluk sultanate, but also on society. The main challenges that the plague posed to these societies were that it appeared suddenly, people were for the most part defenseless before it, and those infected died rapidly, sometimes within hours of falling sick. It also affected different classes of the populations and people of various nationalities. It is quite difficult for us in the modern period to try to imagine the anxiety and insecurity that such a threat posed to medieval societies. However, it is palpable in the sources of the period. That society was struggling to come to grips with such instances of death is reflected in the plague treatises that survive from this period. Several jurists penned treatises relating to the plague, trying to explain its causes and aiming to console bereaved parents over the loss of their children.

One particular narrative, recounted by both al-Maqrizi and Ibn Taghribirdi, gives a sense of the fear that at least urban dwellers lived through.[57] Rumor had spread that a particular day, in 841/1438, a Friday, would be the end of time and that all people would perish. People crowded at the public baths so that when death overcame them they would be in ritual purity. When the preacher apparently fainted while leading the Friday prayers, hysteria broke out, as people imagined he had died and that it was in fact the end of time. The anxiety that the narratives reflect, concerning death and the obsession with ritual purity, give us an inkling of how present these concerns were in people's lives.

The anxiety caused by the plague is evident even in sources that do not purport to be writing directly about the epidemic. We see, for example, how an ordinary low-level clerk like Ahmad ibn Tawq, who lived in

Damascus in the fifteenth century, faithfully noted down when one of his ulama acquaintances was down with a fever. For just as he notes down in his chronicle-cum-diary the important events of the city, his own comings and goings and judicial dealings, protests, and food he has consumed, he also mentions when someone he knows falls sick, often but not exclusively with fever, in very short, curt references.[58] He also notes when they are cured or when their health improves.[59]

It is this constant fear of succumbing to the plague that is palpable between the lines when Ibn Tawq notes down which night his little baby girl started a fever. His references are curt and concise but in the entries of several days we learn that his daughter, Umm Hani, was sick and had stopped eating.[60] At first he guesses that it was due to teething.[61] Yet finally, around two weeks later, he writes, "Umm Hani, my daughter, died on this day. . . . She was one year old and one month and fourteen days. She died between the two prayers. She was buried during the afternoon. Her illness lasted fourteen days, of them six days were difficult; she did not nurse at all, and only drank water. The origin was fever, it appears to be [the] plague."[62]

The genre of plague treatises, discussed further in the following chapter, captures the sense of anxiety that individuals and society felt as they saw loved ones die around them. The rapidity of the death in many instances of the epidemic instilled awe and fear in people's minds and hearts. As time went by, the plague's economic and demographic consequences also took their toll. In addition to this agony that people were going through by seeing the death of their friends and relatives and neighbors, the conditions of economic and social flux also had consequences that affected people's lives.

The social transformations developing throughout the late fourteenth and fifteenth centuries had effects on people's livelihoods and social relations. We can only try to imagine what effects they must have had on individuals living in fifteenth-century Cairo or Damascus or Aleppo. And one can only imagine how it would feel to be a great Mamluk *amir*, falling from glory and from the social circles with which one was familiar to a position of modest means or poverty. This is an aspect that historians have not often addressed, probably because of the nature of the surviving sources. Yet modern trends in historical writing are paying more attention

to the individual and his perceptions and feelings. In fact, the literary production of the period gives us indications here and there of the pressures
individuals were facing. For example, the Damascene Ibn Tawq mentions
that the shaykh, Taqi al-Din Abu Bakr b. Qadi 'Ajlun, "hid at home when
melancholy overcame him or when the demands of the people were too
much for him."[63] Such passing references can be tapped in order to try to
reconstruct how contemporary individuals experienced the difficulties of
their times, which were full of fear and uncertainty.

Indeed, the plague, in addition to the political climate, contributed
to what might be considered a general climate of social malaise. There
were other manifestations of this social anxiety and malaise, including
reports of suicide. In a study of references to "suicide" or voluntary deaths
in the late Mamluk period, Bernadette Martel-Thoumian has counted
some twenty-eight cases reported in the chronicles from 1468 to 1516,
despite the traditional Islamic religious condemnation of suicide as a sin.[64]
Generally speaking, suicides are often associated with times of political
instability and economic hardship. Modern sociological studies associate
a high rate of suicide with troubled societies or societies undergoing critical conditions.[65] It is therefore not coincidental that the numbers in her
study should correspond chronologically to this period.

While current research of the primary sources does not allow us yet
to gauge whether this was an increase in the number of suicides or rather
an increase in references to such deaths (which would still indicate a shift
in the historiography), the information that is provided on most of these
cases gives some idea about the groups in society that were likely to come
under pressure, and often the nature of these pressures. Indeed, out of the
twenty-eight cases discussed by Martel-Thoumian, thirteen were related to
conflicts with the sultan and the ruling authorities.[66] Several were indebted
prisoners. Others were senior officials who were unable to pay up the sums
demanded by the authorities and who preferred voluntary death over possible imprisonment and torture, such as Nasr al-Din ibn al-Safadi, the
nazir al-khass and *wakil bayt al-mal*. According to Ibn Iyas, when the *nazir
al-khass* died suddenly on 4 Dhu al-Hijja 907/9 June 1502, it was said that
he had poisoned himself because he was unable to pay the sum demanded
by Sultan Qansuh al-Ghawri.[67] These are the exact sort of pressures we saw

with the rise and fall of Abul-Khayr al-Nahhas. Al-Safadi, by contrast, is an example of one official who did not bounce back, and could not endure the pressures associated with the fall from administrative grace. Many of the people committing suicide had suffered a drastic social fall.

These pressures were not only a concern for administrators. We have discussed previously how additional taxes and extortion were applied to merchants and craftsmen, and this might explain the apparent suicide of one Ibn Mas'ud, a wood merchant, in 903/1498.[68] The fear of torture in prison was another apparent cause for suicide, such as in the case of a servant at a garrison in 890/1485.[69]

We have seen how the economic challenges the late Mamluk state faced led it to resort to numerous policies including confiscation of property and constant demands for extra-legal taxes from various groups in society. In many cases, persons whose properties were confiscated were also imprisoned and tortured until they paid certain sums to the state and sultan. That some would resort to voluntarily ending their lives gives us an idea of the sort of real pressure this placed on people, especially administrators. In fact, the confiscations came to be so common as to lead the elite to devise mechanisms to safeguard themselves and their households against them, with limited degrees of success. These included creating *awqaf* and using female members of households as custodians of property.[70] Although the period witnessed the meteoric rise of some individuals from rags to riches, there was also a high risk associated with such prospects.

Protest as Manifestation of Malaise

The social anxiety is also acutely reflected in the frequent protests, especially on the streets of important cities. These will be discussed in more detail in chapter five. But it is important to mention here that the tremendous changes and transformations that were occurring in society left many uneasy, and with limited tools through which to express this unease and try to ameliorate their situations. Protest was one of those tools. For example, the rise of individuals of lowly backgrounds to positions of state was resented, partially, we must assume, because it represented a breakdown of the social order, and partially of course because it came in the context of exorbitant levies and taxes. The refusal of this state of affairs led to frequent attacks on government officials. Some of these attacks also took on a sectarian form as non-Muslim officials were targeted.

The protests, as we shall see, reached deep down in society and involved people from various walks of life: tradesmen, artisans, skilled and unskilled laborers, Sufis. This malaise reached the lower strata of society as well. The reports of the protests, especially from the Egyptian and Syrian cities of Cairo, Mahalla, Damascus, and Aleppo, indicate that the dissatisfaction was widespread. It also indicates that different people reacted differently to the difficult circumstances they were living through and to the transformations occurring in their societies. Many tried to channel those transformations in their favor and to manipulate the circumstances—with varying degrees of success.

Conclusion

The late Mamluk period was one in which Egypt and Syria and their regimes faced a number of important challenges and crises, from the plague, to the decimation of the population, to decreased agrarian production. We saw in the previous chapter the various policies to which the Mamluk regime resorted in order to deal with those challenges. Some of the challenges, some of the policies, and some of their repercussions combined to produce deep social transformations as well. Thus new social groups rose to the fore. The Bedouin expanded and rose in authority, the composition of the Mamluk army changed, and Coptic conversions to Islam continued, leading to a change in the placement of Christians within the population. Furthermore, some of the policies of the time precipitated a degree of social mobility, both upward and downward. All these transformations altered the social order and created a sense of anxiety and social malaise. This was reflected in the increased rates of violence and voluntary deaths, and in increased forms of urban protest. These changes were also reflected in the cultural production of the times. As society changed, people came to express themselves differently—both in their writing and in their behavior on the streets.

4

POPULARIZATION OF CULTURE AND
THE BOURGEOIS TREND

Mamluk culture has been often associated with ceremonials, royal patronage, high-quality artistic production, and luxury goods that museums have collected, such as large-format Qur'ans, carpets, glass, and metalwork of the highest quality. This production continued well into the fifteenth and sixteenth centuries, although the quality of various products went up and down. For example, as Blair and Bloom have argued, despite the economic distress caused by the repeated plagues of the fourteenth century, artistic production of metalwork continued to be of high quality, although it declined in quantity. The absence of metalworkers and the shortage of silver and copper might have been reasons for this.[1] Glass manufacturing and painting, on the other hand, witnessed a decline, and some royal objects came to be imported from Europe.[2] However, during the reign of Qaytbay many of the economic problems were overcome. This improvement was reflected in a distinct revival in many arts, including metalwork, manuscript illumination, and carpet-weaving.[3]

The mainstream narrative of Mamluk culture usually ends here. In discussing art during the later Middle Ages, the focus often rests on the courts, and literature is often ignored. Yet there is another layer of culture that has for the most part been left out. If these cultural products are viewed as expressions of their time rather than as museum pieces, a different picture of this period emerges. As discussed in the previous chapters,

71

social and economic transformations that were taking place during the late Middle Ages, and in particular during the fifteenth century, allowed room for social mobility. We have seen how the fortunes of some members of the Mamluk class were depressed and how some artisans and tradesmen, like al-Nahhas, rose up tremendously. While some fields suffered because of the decimation of the population caused by the recurrent plagues, others benefited because of funds being released and because of changes in patterns of world trade (carpet-weaving being one example). Thus textile production declined as the plagues killed off skilled workers of the Alexandria workshops, so that the number of weavers in the city reportedly declined from twelve or fourteen thousand in 1394 to only eight hundred in 1434. Furthermore, the Mongol invasions disrupted trade routes and made the dyestuffs normally brought from Iraq and Iran very scarce. Various factors, including technological stagnation, probably led to European textiles becoming cheaper, so the dumping of European textiles became an established reality in the region.[4] On the other hand, carpet production seems to have flourished in the fifteenth century, as the continuous warfare in eastern Anatolia led to workmen immigrating to Cairo. This continued well into the sixteenth century, as Italian inventories of the large "Cairino" carpets testify.[5]

Surviving examples of artistic artifacts and architecture tend to be examples of royal or elite patronage, as vernacular production is less likely to be preserved. While this illuminates the social and economic issues related to artistic production, it is still limited in that it is biased toward elite production and consumption. Other forms of artistic production, including literature, religious studies, and historiography, allow us to study changes in the cultural production of the period in relation to a wider section of the population. Although this is still also limited, it allows us to see that the social, economic, and political transformations of the late Mamluk period paved the way for some social mobility and allowed for an element of popularization in the cultural production of the times—that is, elements of popular culture came to permeate and influence mainstream and high culture. The blurring of the boundaries between popular and educated literature is one of the main characteristics of Mamluk production.[6]

This chapter will not discuss the trajectories of individuals so much as the collective experiences of urban dwellers and their cultural manifestations. This social mobility is closely connected to what scholars refer to as the "bourgeois trend" in Mamluk literature and society, which is clearly reflected in the written sources of the period.[7] While it is difficult to speak of social classes and the rise of the middle class in its socioeconomic sense during this time period, and hence difficult to speak of a bourgeoisie in the full sense of the term, there are signs of the rise of middling groups of people whose culture, as reflected in the surviving literary sources, combined elements of both the traditional, literate culture of the educated elite and the popular, vernacular culture of the masses. Middling classes were not only the ones gaining wealth, but the ones whose wealth came to find cultural expression that is distinguished from high culture. The production of these groups of people survives in some of the literature of the period; this is what can be referred to as a "bourgeois trend." It reflects a growing sense of awareness and consciousness as well as a widening space in society and in culture for a class of ordinary people who made their voices heard through documented literary production, and politically through protest. Their political participation will be discussed in the following chapter, while this chapter focuses on the popularization and vernacularization of culture.

Factors behind Popularization

A distinction between popular and high culture in the Arab–Islamic tradition goes back to the Abbasid period at least.[8] However, from the thirteenth century onward more sources of Arabic popular literature and especially popular narrative, survives. Whether this is evidence of increased production or better survival conditions is still open for debate.[9] Yet, more important than the sheer number of popular works that survive, is the growing tendency for popularization of cultural production. This includes new popular genres developing during the post classical period as well as elements previously associated with popular culture becoming mainstream and included in high cultural productions. A number of reasons could be suggested for these apparent processes of popularization and vernacularization of culture in the late Mamluk period. The first of

these is decentralization. The postclassical, or the post-Seljuk, period witnessed a change in the production of culture in various parts of the Islamic
world and the former lands of the caliphates. As Abbasid Baghdad gave
way to a number of regional courts headed by various, often rival, regimes,
regional styles developed. A consequence of this political decentralization of the Middle Ages is that, as Thomas Bauer explains, "the courts
of caliphs, princes, sultans and governors gradually lost their central role
in literary communication. Instead, urban, bourgeois milieus increasingly
participated in the consumption and production of literary texts."[10] This
development crystallized during the Mamluk period, and its consequences
and the possibilities it created were visible by the fifteenth century.

Furthermore, as we have seen in previous chapters, the late Mamluk
period witnessed a gradual diffusion of power and decentralization of politics to a certain extent. This is a development that would continue more
clearly during the Ottoman period, especially as the main Egyptian urban
center, Cairo, moved from being an imperial capital to a provincial one on
the periphery of another empire. Nelly Hanna has referred to the effect of
this state decentralization in the Ottoman period on cultural production,
arguing that the ruling class is more likely to play a dominant role in culture
at a period when the state is centralized, and, vice versa, that cultural production is likely to be less polished and refined, with more room for cultural
forms and patterns to emerge from below, when the role of the ruling classes
is reduced and the state is decentralized.[11] Her comments with respect to
the seventeenth century could partially apply to parts of the fifteenth. The
beginnings of such developments are discernible in the late Mamluk period
and could account for much of the popularization of the cultural production
of the period. One of the consequences of this process is an increasing popularization and vernacularization of written texts. This is a development that
took different forms in various provinces of the Islamic world, and appears
clearly in material surviving from Egypt and Syria.

Changes in Mamluk Culture

Not only were there new middling classes rising, creating a bourgeois
trend, but the elite of the time were also different. At least two cultural
trends can be discerned among the elite. The first is that the courts of

the Mamluks were not uniquely invested in classical Arabic culture. The background and education of the Mamluk military officers must have affected their literary tastes and their willingness and ability to patronize classical Arabic literary genres.

The Arabic of the first-generation Mamluks was usually weak. This might have been a contributing factor in making them cultural and literary outsiders and might partly explain the ambiguous attitudes expressed toward them by the ulama of the time, since religious culture continued to be articulated in classical Arabic.[12] Thus the court culture of the Mamluk sultans and officers was not exclusively focused on Arabic in the tradition of the caliphates. Instead, Turkish culture was also expressed and supported by the Mamluk court. In fact, Haarmann points to the period after 1400 and especially after 1450 as one in which a Mamluk Turkish literary school developed and flourished, with numerous literary and didactic Turkish works written or commissioned at Mamluk courts.[13] Despite this, however, Turkish never completely replaced Arabic, which continued to enjoy pride of place as the main language of court, but obviously classical Arabic was not as enjoyed and appreciated as it had historically been in other courts such as those of the Umayyads or Abbasids. While surviving books suggest that Arabic remained the dominant language for educated Mamluks, as a smaller number of books in Turkish survive, we also find references to royal patronage of works in Turkish, such as the Sira of the Prophet written in Turkish by Mustafa ibn 'Umar al-Darir, a blind Mawlawi Sufi from Anatolia, which was written for Sultan Barquq.[14]

In addition to the inclusion of Turkish as a court language and the rise of a Turkish literary school, popular cultural forms came to be included within court culture during the Mamluk period. Even *qasida*s (long poems in the classical style) composed for official purposes tend to include vernacular language and to be more conversational in style. Court culture itself came to be more open to vernacular forms, which were perhaps easier for the non-Arab rulers to understand and appreciate.[15] Even Arabic poems eulogizing powerful sultans or describing the wars of the Mamluks carry a popular, even pedestrian, air that is closer to the language of popular epics than to the *qasida*s of classical Arabic poetry. However, unlike the first-generation Mamluks whose Arabic was generally poor, the children of Mamluks, the second-generation *awlad al-nas*, were usually more embedded in local Egyptian and Syrian societies and versed in both Turkish and Arabic, which made them potential sponsors and patrons of literary production in the vernacular in particular.[16]

Various Forms of Patronage

Aside from the changes in the culture of the ruling court, and its openness to different forms of literary production, in the Mamluk period, due to the political and social factors discussed earlier, the ruling elite played a much more limited role in setting cultural standards. The decentralization and diffusion of power was reflected in society and in cultural production. New forms of patronage emerged; patronizing cultural production was no longer the monopoly of the ruling sultan's court.[17] As the elite came to play more limited roles in setting the cultural standards and literary taste in the Mamluk (and post-Mongol invasion) period, popular poetry, for example, appeared more frequently in written sources of the time.[18] Poetry documented in written sources was no longer of a type associated only with the ruling elite. Furthermore, unlike previous regimes such as the Abbasids, medieval regimes such as that of the Mamluks did not rely so much on classical poetry in their legitimation mythology. This paved the way for popular poetry.

Indeed, the very social mobility of which we have seen other manifestations elsewhere probably opened the door for new types of patronage and new audiences for popular poetry. Thus the growing numbers of persons of lowly origins in positions of authority and affluence, the rise of a new Egyptianized landed class,[19] and the increasing rates of literacy prompted by the establishment of *kuttab*s probably influenced literary taste and patronage. Similarly, not only sultans but also Mamluk private soldiers acted as patrons of cultural life in their houses, seeking and finding "comfort for a disappointing military and public career in the bliss of piety, poetry, and scholarship."[20] There were thus multiple and relatively decentralized forms of patronage.

What is of interest to us is the rise of such poetry as the *kan wa kan* or the *zajal*, and their inclusion in written manuscripts of an academic nature and by scholarly writers, as this indicates a new form of patronage. Whether or not more colloquial poetry was being produced during the Mamluk period, it was clearly more *recorded* than in other periods and was also being studied theoretically.[21] That in itself is a shift in the discourse and marks an acceptance of a type of poetry sometimes associated with the non-elite. We can also gauge the popularity of some prose forms through the criticism and advice of a scholar like Taj al-Din al-Subki (d. 771/1369). Al-Subki advised book copyists not to copy texts that were a waste of time and useless to religion, which for him include such works as *Sirat 'Antar*, erotic literature, and recipes for intoxicants; he cautioned this even though clients usually paid more for these commissions than for books of religious sciences.[22] Al-Subki's advice is an indirect indication of the popularity of a wider spectrum of written texts during the late Mamluk period, which hints at a wider audience and readership. The Mamluk period also witnessed the rising popularity of the *Alf layla wa layla* corpus and of folk epics such as *Sirat al-Zahir Baybars* and *Sirat 'Antar*.

Popular Sufism

Not only were there new artistic forms and genres developing during the late medieval period, allowing people to express themselves in new ways, but also religious expression witnessed some change. While the main canonical works and dogmatic ideas had crystallized and been established by the classical Abbasid period, prompting some writers to repeat the cliché that after al-Ghazali (d. 1111) the gate to *ijtihad* was closed, various currents within religious thought and practice continued to develop. This is quite clear in Sufism. Sufism was never a monolithic movement, and by the Middle Ages it is possible to speak of two broad currents, one high and philosophic and the other more popular, with many hues in between. It is during this period that Sufi *tariqa*s spread and gained popularity. This is the Sufism of brotherhoods, of holy men, of traveling dervishes, of pious *ghazi*s, of collective rituals. This popular trend of Sufism was also favored by the ruling military regimes. The tolerant and syncretic nature of many Sufi *tariqa*s won them a following among people outside the central Arab–Muslim lands, many of whom were newly converted to Islam. The Sufis themselves are also thought to have helped in converting people on the frontier and border regions of the Muslim world, introducing non-Muslims to a tolerant and accessible Islamic idiom. Many famous

Sufi masters whose followers formed *tariqa*s were themselves originally from Persian or Turkish backgrounds. This is one reason perhaps why Mamluks and other non-Arab Muslim rulers were quite comfortable around Sufis and patronized Sufi shaykhs, endowing their khanqahs with extensive *awqaf*. Sufi holy men were also believed to possess special blessings and supernatural powers that could come to the aid of followers, including princes and officers.

Although Sufism had gained importance, especially through patronage, since the Ayyubid period, it is in the fourteenth and fifteenth centuries that it came to be popular among ordinary Egyptians, including artisans and peasants, and Egypt began to produce its own Sufi intellectuals and saints, who gained importance equal to the émigré Sufis of previous centuries.[23] This is further evidence of the merging of classical and vernacular culture and the mainstreaming of popular culture during the late Mamluk period. While from the perspective of intellectual history it is remarkable that some of the leading Sufis were poorly educated or illiterate, from the perspective of social history it is equally remarkable that increasing numbers of artisans came to be involved in Sufism and to occupy important positions within the Sufi community. Artisan Sufis could enjoy an exalted status within the Sufi community even if they were from lower social classes or if their professions were considered lowly, and they were honored rather than derided for their manual work. They were sought out for their mystical knowledge and teaching. In a report narrated by the sixteenth-century Sufi and scholar 'Abd al-Wahhab al-Sha'rani, a Sufi shaykh used to send his students to study with a pious weaver: "They read to him from the books of the four Sunni schools of law while he wove cotton and wool on his loom."[24] Sabra connects the rise of this combination of illiterate Sufis and learned artisans who became the greatest saints of Egypt in the Ottoman period with the difficult transition from Mamluk to Ottoman rule, a bitter pill for people used to thinking of Cairo as the center of a great empire. In those turbulent times, rumors circulated that the end of the world was near, and in such a tense environment, people turned to "simple commoners like themselves, everyday saints, to sanctify an increasingly fallen world."[25] However, this sense of doom is not related solely to the Ottoman takeover and arguably predates it. The rise of Sufi artisans could also be interpreted in light of the social mobility of the period as well as the general popularization of culture.

Although Salah al-Din is credited with introducing khanqahs to Egypt, and setting a precedent for rulers' patronage of Sufism, it was not until the Mamluk period that the institution developed fully and was accepted by religious scholars and integrated in Egyptian society, as Fernandes has shown.[26] Sufism was strongly patronized and supported by the Mamluks, perhaps as a cultural paradigm that popularized Islamic religious sciences and made them more accessible to a non-Muslim-born and non-native-Arabic-speaking public, the Turkish Mamluks. Furthermore, at least initially, patronizing the Sufi Khanqahs was one method through which the Mamluks sought to extend their influence over the religious establishment by creating a group of religious-oriented men directly tied, through stipends, to their Mamluk benefactors.[27] This for a while earned the Sufis the antagonism of the more scholarly and at least nominally more independent ulama. Over time, Sultans patronized both the more legally oriented madrasas of the jurists and the khanqahs, *zawiya*s, and *ribat*s of the Sufis. And over time, even prominent ulama held joint positions in khanqahs and madrasas.[28] From the time of Sultan Barquq onward, the ties between the Mamluk court and local Sufi leaders became stronger. Barquq himself was active in trying to harmonize *'ilm* (religious sciences and theology) and *tasawwuf* (Sufism), while later Sultan Khushqadam was known for venerating Ahmad al-Badawi of Tanta and Sultan Qaytbay supported the cause of Ibn al-Farid (d. 1235).[29] When Ibn al-Farid's statements about the mystical behavior of the Prophet were denounced by some ulama, Sultan Qaytbay supported Ibn al-Farid's proponents and granted them immunity, in large part to avoid rioting, as Ibn al-Farid's views enjoyed broad support among the masses as well.[30] The close relationship between Mamluks and Sufis also took other forms: some Mamluks, such as the Sultans Barquq, Faraj ibn Barquq, or Qansuh al-Ghawri, had their mausolea built inside the Sufi khanaqahs they founded hoping that their closeness to the Sufis would benefit them in the afterlife. Others arranged positions for their sons and for retired officers within the khanaqah administration.[31]

'Abd al-Wahhab al-Sha'rani's advice to Sufis on how best to approach and deal with government officials, while cautionary in tone, is also indicative of the close ties that connected the communities in the late Mamluk and early Ottoman periods. It was a reality that needed to be taken into account and managed in the best interests of the Sufis, from al-Sha'rani's point of view. The issues about which al-Sha'rani cautions the novice and naive Sufis are quite indicative of these relationships, in which it was possible for aspiring officials to seek a shaykh's assistance in obtaining government posts.[32] The *amir* was also expected to confess the sources of his income to his shyakh even if they were ill-gotten, and "if he cannot return the ill-gotten gains to their rightful owners, he should ask the shaykh to intercede with God and with those he has treated unjustly on his behalf."[33] The power of the shyakh to pray for the government official was perceived as real and immediate.[34] Many *waqf* documents established by Mamluk officers and sultans even specified that prayers should be offered in perpetuity for the soul of the founder.[35] In a world where so much was uncertain, as we have seen already, the meteoric rise and unceremonious fall from grace had almost become the natural life story of individuals in government, so that a pious man's prayers were a real asset. And just as they could make a man, they could break him: "Sha'rani informs the emir that the same shaykh whose prayers may help him obtain a government appointment can also bring about his dismissal."[36]

Even if we were to take al-Sha'rani's statements and injunctions to *amir*s and Sufis alike with a handful of salt, replete as they are with exaggeration and self-aggrandizement, it is still indicative of the ties that bound both groups. This type of spiritual dependency on Sufi shaykhs that Mamluks and other officials developed gives us a sense of the way in which Sufism, popularized in the late medieval period, managed to synthesize different cultural traditions and perhaps bring the culture of the foreign Mamluks closer to that of the local populations. The type of fervent piety that was promoted by popular Sufi shaykhs could also be used to mobilize the masses in support of the regime and against enemies or infidels.[37] This kind of mobilization was a double-edged sword, however, as we shall see when we discuss popular protest in the following chapter.

This elite Mamluk support for particular Sufi shaykhs and orders was paralleled by the popularization of these orders, especially in urban centers. Similarly, within the Sufi movement another popularization of sorts was also taking place: increasingly, local Sufis from lower-class backgrounds, and often without formal education or even illiterate, came to occupy positions of leadership within the community.[38] Sufism thus allowed individuals from modest social backgrounds, and not necessarily highly educated like the ulama, to rise in stature, and occasionally in wealth, within their communities. This is one type of social mobility apparent in this period. This phenomenon also created new types of leadership in the community and new cultural experiences.

Manifestations of Popularization in Written Cultural Production

Throughout the late Mamluk period a wider space opened up for non-elites to express themselves and have a greater presence on the cultural scene. This was occurring at a time when, for a certain number of these non-elites, whether tradesmen or craftsmen, the possibility of learning to read and write had expanded, as we know from the number of elementary schools (*kuttabs*) that were constructed during this period.

The popularization of culture was manifested in the written works themselves: in writing style and language; in the emergence of new genres; and in different kinds of subject matter. Secondly, it was also manifested in terms of the writers and their social backgrounds, as non-elites entered the world of authorship. And thirdly, and partly because of the aforementioned reasons, the point of view of the urban population seems to be more strongly represented in surviving written texts, not only by the non-elite authors, but also by writers from within the established intellectual traditions.

Surveying the literary production and written texts surviving of the period, the modern reader cannot help but notice the increasing inclusion and echoes of colloquial Arabic in the written texts. For example, in his diwan *Nuzhat al-nufus was mudhik al-'abus*, Ibn Sudun (d. 868/1464) mixes classical and colloquial Arabic as well as classical and non-classical meters.[39] Even poetry that followed the classical forms came to employ rhythms and meters associated with popular poetry such as the *ruba'iya*, the *kan wa kan*, the *quma*, the *baliq, muwashshah, muwaliya*, and *zajal*.[40] One sign that the colloquial language was more prevalent in written discourse is that even the manual by Safi al-Din al-Hilli (d. 1349), *al-'Atil al-hali wa-l-murakhkhas al-ghali*, includes non-canonical forms of Arabic poetry and colloquial poetry.[41] Himself a merchant by trade, al-Hilli traveled from his hometown, Hilla, spent some time in the court of Mardin, and traveled repeatedly to Egypt and Syria.[42] He is perhaps the most famous Arab poet of his century. He came to Cairo during the reign of al-Nasir Muhammad and composed poetry in praise of the sultan. In *al-'Atil*, described as "the first poetics of Arabic dialect poetry," al-Hilli lists various forms of non-ca-nonical and non-classical styles of poetry, namely *zajal, mawaliya, kan wa kan*, and *quma*. It is a normative description of each of those genres and their linguistic properties, and at the same time an anthology of exam-ples of such popular poetry, some of which are of his own composition.[43] His text also suggests that there was a demand for popular poetry and compositions during his time even though it was still viewed with con-descension by the literati.[44] It also suggests that some poets specialized in popular forms exclusively. More poems tended to follow these forms and shortened forms in general, such as the *mathnawi, ruba'iya khumasiya*, and *siba'iya*, in place of the classical long odes or *qasida*s.[45] These forms were also considered more fitting for lighter entertainment purposes.[46]

Vernacularization of histories

The popularization and vernacularization that characterizes late medieval and late Mamluk culture is well reflected in the historiography of the period. Historical works written during that period, especially during the fifteenth century, include echoes of the vernacular, reflect an increasing interest in the mundane, and reveal a different sense of self and identity of the authors—many of whom came from popular backgrounds—who include themselves in the narrative. History itself was a prevalent genre during this time period, prompting many learned men to try producing historical material.

There are echoes and examples of the use of the vernacular even in works of a historical nature. Robert Irwin has remarked on various levels of understanding this phenomenon where the writings of historians are concerned. On the one hand, some chroniclers used invented dialogue in their texts to explain policy-making: some put deliberately incorrect Arabic into the mouths of Mamluks while others had them speak flawless Arabic.[47] On another level, and more generally as Irwin explains, some chronicles were themselves "written in an Arabic that was often grammatically incorrect and stylistically poor."[48] Irwin suggests that while a colloquial idiom may have been employed strategically to reach a wider audience, it is more likely that "some historians were unable to write otherwise."[49] The use of language that is closer to the colloquial in its structure, idiom, and even vocabulary is not uncommon in historical works, but at the same time it is not uniform, so that in late Mamluk times we would not find a whole text written uniformly in such a manner. Rather, certain sections, especially those dealing with matters of "popular" concern, the gossip of the city dwellers and the affairs of the common people, matters which were increasingly incorporated into historical texts—these sections would be the more vernacular ones, as in the chronicle of Ibn Iyas.[50] These are subjects that were more likely related orally to the writers in the first place. Irwin seems to give more weight to the explanation that faults the abilities of the writers themselves, rather than to a general development in Arabic writing at the time. However, there is more to the rise of the colloquial and the use of the vernacular in writing history, which is itself part of the popularization of history during the late Mamluk period.

Thus the language used and the material incorporated under the heading of history brought it somewhat closer to genres of story-telling. Increasingly, elements of popular interest were incorporated in the works. Ulrich Haarmann has argued that some late medieval historians increasingly moved away from conventional historiography toward a new "literarized" mode of historical writing. Thus, references to wonders, exotic occurrences, and popular motifs increasingly found their way into the works of historians like Ibn al-Dawadari (d. after 1337), in his *Kanz al-durar wa jami' al-ghurar*, and Ibn Iyas in his *Bada'i' al-zuhur*.[51] It was a tendency that was to continue into the Ottoman period, when popular histories as a genre seem to have flourished. The increasing use of the vernacular reflects an oral link as well as an interest in popular issues. Whereas for a long time the creeping of the vernacular into written texts and poetry was taken as a sign of the "decline of the language"—and of the sorry state of culture, as discussed earlier—the changing perspective also made room for discussions of contemporary, daily events to which the writers were eyewitnesses, or which were relayed to them orally.[52]

New writers, new genres

The late medieval and early modern periods were a time when some form of literacy and education was spreading among a wider sector of the population—if only as a result of the proliferation of madrasas and *kuttab*s patronized and endowed by the ruling classes, as discussed earlier. It is also a period when a considerable number of women scholars are mentioned in the biographies. Scholars have discussed possible reasons for the sudden appearance and later disappearance of women Hadith scholars from the biographical dictionaries. Most biographical dictionaries of the period included entries on notable women of the military and ulama classes, yet al-Sakhawi (1428–97) was somewhat innovative in dedicating a whole volume exclusively to contemporary women: the final volume in his *al-Daw' al-lami'* referred to as *Kitab al-nisa'* (Book of Women).[53] It contains some 1,075 entries, making it the largest surviving collective biography of women in premodern Islamic historiography. In general, however, the biographical dictionaries of this period include a larger percentage of entries on women than earlier or later collections.

Historians who have closely studied the biographical dictionaries remark that although entries on women are included in even the earliest collections, such as the tenth-century *Tabaqat Ibn Saʿd*, the percentage of women included reached its peak in the fourteenth century. It is not clear why this peak occurred, when it did, nor why the number of women in subsequent dictionaries declines considerably, and the matter is open to speculation. Is the apparent increase in the visibility of women in medieval dictionaries a reflection of change in the structure of society that allowed more room for women, or is it a reflection of a bias in the sources, or perhaps a mixture of both? One possible explanation relates again to the demographic crisis of the fourteenth century. As waves of the plague, including the Black Death, swept through the Middle East, the populations were decimated. The intellectual legacy of the ulama, who regarded themselves as the moral guardians of the community, was at stake. To appreciate this threat it is important to recall that oral transmission continued to be important within Islamic religious studies, making the chain of transmission from one reliable scholar to another part and parcel of the knowledge being produced and transmitted. Thus the human resources of the communities and networks that produced these dictionaries gained value. It was important to safeguard and transmit these resources in times of crisis and dwindling numbers. Women of this scholarly class, perhaps, were regarded as reliable custodians and transmitters of this intellectual and spriritual wealth.[54] This might have led to the apparent increase in the number of women teachers and transmitters. The increased number of women Hadith scholars and the impressive number of *ijaza*s (certificates and licenses to teach a particular text) they are said to have issued during the Middle Ages supports this hypothesis. It is likely that the community of ulama, in a time of social and political stress, sought to maximize use of its human resources, including that of its women. It could explain why the dictionaries of the fourteenth and fifteenth centuries included more entries on women; since the dictionaries essentially historicize this class, which was relying more and more on women as custodians of knowledge, they came to include more entries on women. Asma Sayeed, who has studied the repeated fluctuations of women's participation in religious discourse and transmission since the rise of Islam, has recently argued for a confluence of various factors behind this apparent increase of references to women transmitters of Hadith. They include: the canonization of Hadith, the wider acceptance of written transmission of the Hadith, the rise of family networks of ulama, as well as "the promotion of traditionalism as classical Sunni orthodoxy," which allowed for unusual age structures for pedagogy and a preference for the shortest possible chain of transmission of Hadith.[55] The latter two factors encouraged the increasing acceptance of *ijaza*s issued for children, including female children.

It remains difficult to explain why the number of learned women appears to drop sharply from biographical dictionaries in the sixteenth century. A number of reasons are suggested, including a stagnation in Islamic scholarship, which decreases the need to seek knowledge from women, or a reaction to the devaluation of the contact between teacher and pupil, or increased bureaucratization of the scholarly establishment, making official posts, the domain of men, more important than scholarship.[56] Sayeed, on the other hand, connects this drop to increased emphasis on the legal training of scholars as well as the rise of organized Sufism which characterize the Ottoman period.[57] These factors affected the importance of Hadith transmission, the area in which women scholars were most represented.

Other possible explanations for the apparent increase in the number of women included in biographical dictionaries in the Mamluk period relate to the changes in the genre itself. With the rise of centennial dictionaries, more room was made for a larger number of entries and hence a larger number of women to be included by a single author. Furthermore, it could be argued that the criteria for including individuals in a given dictionary had become less strict with time, making room for less outstanding women and women who were related to the authors of the dictionaries in some manner.[58] This is related, as mentioned earlier, to the changing criteria of inclusion in biographical dictionaries in general, of both men and women. Whatever the causes behind this phenomenon, it connects to our theme of a spread of literacy and different types of education and knowledge during the late Mamluk period among wider sectors of the urban population. Certainly not all Hadith transmitters were necessarily literate, but that type of knowledge denotes a certain level of education. Although we do not hear of *kuttab*s for girls, there are indications that girls and women of scholarly families were given an education at home. *Kuttab*s, on the other hand, increased in number, and became available to a wider sector of urban society.

Indeed, there seems to have been an increase in the number of *kuttab*s during the Mamluk period, roughly corresponding to the period when the Mamluks dominated the Red Sea spice trade, as Hanna suggests.[59] Sabra's study of *waqf* deeds between 1300 and 1517 shows that at least forty-six were established to provide basic education for boys in Cairo during that period. Sabra's graph has a total of fifty-two *kuttab* teachers (with typically one teacher per *kuttab* with few exceptions) providing for some 1,176 students.[60] What this suggests is that more members of the population were getting some form of education: more of them could read, and some could write as well. And this growing sector included women. This widening scope of literacy, at least in the urban centers, meant that more people from more diverse backgrounds could pen texts themselves, or patronize and enjoy them. Increasingly, less educated individuals, even some who were not part of either the religious or the military-bureaucratic establishments, also took to writing histories.

Thus, in the late fifteenth and early sixteenth centuries, Ibn Tawq, the Shafiʿi notary in Damascus, thought of setting down his diaries in a semi-annalistic mode: al-Taʿliq. Similarly, Ibn al-Sayrafi, whose father was a money-changer in the market, also wrote a history. Later, in the eighteenth century, another Damascene, this time a barber, Ahmad al-Budayri al-Hallaq, the famous Barber of Damascus, also wrote a history of his own.[61] The popularization trend whose roots are evident in the fifteenth century eventually bore fruit with the popular chronicles of the eighteenth.[62]

This spread of literacy among people from more diverse backgrounds was reflected not only in historiography, but also in the production of literature. Many poets were no longer solely dedicated to poetry as a means to make a living. Many were craftsmen and professionals, including butchers, eye doctors, merchants, and book sellers.[63] Others came from commoner backgrounds, such as the poets Ibrahim ibn ʿAli al-Miʿmar Ghulam al-Nuri (whose father was apparently a builder) and Yusuf ibn ʿAbd al-Ghalib ibn Hilal al-Iskandari al-ʿAllaf (whose father may have been a seller of fodder); the famous dramatist Ibn Danyal (d. 710/1310) was himself also an ophthalmologist (kahhal).[64] The poet Ibn Sudun who, although a recipient of a religious education and at one time an imam, also worked as a copyist and a tailor to make ends meet.[65] This probably also influenced the development of new, more popular forms and genres in written prose and poetry as well. It is perhaps not surprising that, given an opportunity to enjoy and support artistic and literary production, new classes would support different tastes and genres, paving the way for more popular and vernacular forms. These new forms and genres include the muwashshah and zajal forms, which by the fourteenth century came to be widely employed by court poets and others in the Mamluk region.[66] Similarly, the mawaliya (precursor of the mawwal) flourished in Egypt and Syria in the fourteenth to sixteenth centuries.[67] Zajal was a form that appealed also to the educated ulama who composed poetry, such as Abu 'Abd Allah Khalaf ibn Muhammad al-Ghubari (fl. 1341), who wrote during the Qalawunid era.[68] Scholars disagree over why it is that a form like the *kan wa kan* fell out of fashion by the seventeenth century; some blame the use of vernacular itself, as it geographically isolated the literary production in question, with others pointing out that the form was more suitable for moral counsel and thus did not lend itself to singing which would have aided its popularity. However, its existence and popularity in the previous century or two fits in with the general cultural atmosphere we can glean from the sources. In the words of Larkin, the *zajal* by al-Ghubari

> vividly illustrates one type of patronage these poetic arts found during the Mamluk era. Rather than the elite ruling class that constituted the patrons of classical Arabic poetry through the twelfth century and beyond, we have here a representative sample of a virtual petite bourgeoisie—what al-Maqrizi (766–845/1364–1441) referred to in his *Ighathat al-umma bi-kashf al-ghumma* as 'ashab al-ma'ayish.[69]

This is a development attested in other parts of the Muslim world at the time. For example, the popularity of the *Maqamat* of al-Hariri, well into the thirteenth and fourteenth centuries, is sometimes ascribed to bourgeois patronage.[70] Similarly, Hanna has argued that such developments in the written literature, including the interest in local affairs and the use of a language close to the vernacular, are manifestations of the rise of an urban middle-class culture during the period from the sixteenth to the eighteenth century.[71] Some characteristics of popular literature also came to influence classical poetry; thus some vocabulary, expressions, and metaphors from popular poetry appear in the classical poetry of the period as well.[72]

In addition to poetic forms of a popular nature, the late Mamluk period was also famous for the rise of popular prose: the *Alf layla* collections as well as the famous epics such as *Sirat al-Zahir Baybars, Sayf bin Dhi Yazan*, and *Dhat al-Himma*, for example.[73] Indeed, the *Alf layla* stories reflect an urban, mercantile society in which merchants often come to play important and heroic roles often previously associated with kings and princes.[74]

Many of the characters in the embedded stories are artisans and craftsmen: tailors, barbers, physicians, brokers. In many ways these prose collections point to a popular culture of entertainment that patronized new genres. Those collections, which survive for us in written manuscripts, but which were meant to be orally performed in public or private gatherings, also include many references to everyday life and often use the vernacular.[75]

Similarly important is the rise of genres that were used by both common people and the literati, further confirming the development of a popularizing trend in the literature whereby popular elements entered the mainstream. The lines between the ulama and the 'udaba', between the religious scholars and the literati, came to be blurred. Scholars of Hadith often composed poetry, and poets were often ulama; the distinct categorization that allowed for professional poets in previous periods disappeared in this one.[76] But craftsmen and tradesmen also came to participate in the production of culture. Indeed, the lines between high culture and popular culture, like those between the ulama and the 'udaba', became increasingly blurred.[77]

Everyday life and literature

A further aspect of the popularization of the cultural production of the period relates to the subject matters dealt with. Matters of everyday concern were much written about, in literature and also very often in histories and chronicles. Thus, some of the non-classical poetry that survives from the period deals with affairs of everyday life. This includes poems in the *kan wa kan* form which employ one meter and one rhyme.[78] A form that was developed by the common people of Baghdad initially for composing stories, legends, and dialogues, the *kan wa kan* spread to Egypt and was popular in the late Mamluk period before falling out of fashion in the seventeenth century.[79] It was a form used by common people composing poetry as well as by highly educated members of the religious establishment preaching to them. It was also especially used by women in poems dealing with important celebrations, such as a Sufi's donning of the ascetic's wool, or family occasions. They include poems of congratulations on aspects of everyday life, as diverse as a child's teeth coming in, the weaning of a baby, the dyeing of a bride's dress, or the ritual bath a mother takes forty days after giving birth.[80] That is, they are subject matters that are intimate yet common; they are not necessarily the topics of high classical poetry which praised rulers and debated high moral ideals such as bravery and chivalry, but they are matters most people in society could relate to. The short forms and easy meters also probably made them easier for a wide group of people to memorize and recite. Similar subject matter is also found in Ibn Sudun's *diwan*, which covers a wide range of issues such as the delights of hashish, food, and drink, as well as occasions such as birth, circumcision, marriage, death, and Nile festivals.[81]

There are many examples of poems devoted to this subject matter that allow us to imagine, to glimpse very briefly and fleetingly, the settings in which this type of cultural production was appreciated and contextualized. For example, a *zajal* by al-Ghubari which is included in al-Ibshishi's *Mustatraf* (a Mamluk distillation of Arab cultural wisdom and literary taste) also includes the names of various shopkeepers; thus the poultry man, then the spice seller, then the fruit seller are evoked, as are the name of the sponsor of the gathering and the products of these small businesses. This could indicate that al-Ghubari's poem itself might have been commissioned by a group of local shopkeepers.[82] It therefore serves as a clear illustration of one of the forms of patronage that existed during this period, and which allowed new, socially mobile persons a place in the poetic and artistic landscape of the time. Cultural and literary salons were no longer the exclusive domain of royalty, but here we can imagine a gathering of members of the non-elite professional classes, also enjoying literary entertainment. It also reflects some of the interests of a non-elite sector of society. When they enjoyed literature these new middling groups did not necessarily want to hear about the heroic feats of the elite, but, perhaps, wanted to see some reflection of their own lives and concerns in the entertainment they enjoyed. Similarly, in Muhammad al-Bilbaysi's *Maqamat al-mulah wa-l-turaf*, forty-nine members of diverse crafts—and one qadi—are represented as gathering together in a friend's house, exchanging jokes and each giving speeches and poems on wine in the colloquial language of their crafts.[83] Such a scene could very well be a reflection of the social changes of the times that allowed a new class of craftsmen, tradesmen, and shopkeepers, some of whom might have been literate thanks to the spread of *kuttab-sabil*s during this era, both to enjoy

as an audience some leisure and entertainment and to sponsor such popular literary production. In so doing, a new type of literature with new
concerns was produced.

Everyday life as history

The historiography of Mamluk and Ottoman Egypt and Syria is remarkable for its interest in contemporary history, and in the particular aspects
of that history that historians chose to record. Indeed, medieval historians
of Mamluk Egypt and Syria stand out in the degree of attention they
gave to everyday affairs. Tarif Khalidi remarks in his study of classical
Arabic historiography that medieval historiography is notable for its shift
away from narrating the glorious, golden days of Islam to narrating contemporary events, which historians of this generation obviously deemed
just as worthy of recording.[84] Rather than simply chronicle the achievements and fates of their rulers, Mamluk and early Ottoman historians of
Egypt and Syria were also recording their own times in general. Their
societies, in themselves, were deemed worthy of observation and analysis. Khalidi relates this development in historiography to the broader
changes in Arab-Islamic history, including the rise of Turkish military
dynasties and the onslaughts of the Crusaders and the Mongols, which
led to an increasing militarization of Arab-Islamic society. This in itself,
he argues, brought about stricter control over the lives of individuals, as
states, having monopolized political power, set out to interfere in the economic, social, and religious life of their subjects. An increased degree of
bureaucratization and hierarchization resulted from these developments,
with the sultanate at the top of the military-political pyramid, and gave
rise to the concepts of *siyasa* ('rule' or 'governance') and sharia (religious
law). For Khalidi, the new historiography of the Middle Ages, most typically the bureaucratic chronicles, came under the umbrella of *siyasa*.[85] It
was meant to encompass all aspects of governable society.

In so doing, this historiography not only chronicled the affairs of the
rulers and the elite, but also mentioned aspects of everyday life. Thus the
historiography of the period itself was being transformed. This seems to
be a reflection of the general intellectual climate, aided in part perhaps by
the backgrounds of some of the historians. It had crystallized to a large

extent by the fifteenth century. Some historians and scholars/writers of the period themselves came from commoner or artistic backgrounds, like Ibn al-Sayrafi or Ibn Tawq. However, even those historians who were somehow related to the Mamluk establishment (such as Ibn Taghribirdi, al-'Ayni, and Ibn Iyas) did refer to the common people and their affairs repeatedly in their writings. Rather than restrict their writings to narratives of the deeds and misdeeds of the ruling men and their regimes, they chose to include in their histories affairs and circumstances that related to the urban population in general. They were increasingly interested in micro-history.[86] The everyday found its way into histories and chronicles. As discussed already, chronicles and histories of the Mamluk period increasingly included language that was either colloquial or close to the colloquial. This was a style particularly used by historians when recounting events of a popular nature: gossip, market news, marvels, crimes—and protests. In particular, the reader of these chronicles cannot help but notice the references to repeated protests that took place in the cities of Egypt and Syria. It is difficult to determine whether the apparent increase in references to protest is simply a change in the interests and bias of the historians writing about them. But it is significant to note that historians of this period, who wrote about the ruling sultans and their wars, the factional rivalries and coups of the warring Mamluk *amir*s, also referred to affairs of everyday life in the urban centers, to price fluctuations, crimes, and punishment, as well as to popular protests. These were events that were deemed important enough by the historians to refer to and include in their chronicles.

While chroniclers and historians continued to focus on the affairs of the ruling regimes and sultans, often arranging their texts according to the reigns of particular Mamluk sultans, their focus also widened to include interest in the local affairs of their communities. In this a distinction is noticeable between historians based in the capital, Cairo, and historians of the Syrian cities.

Center versus Periphery, Cairo versus the Provinces

Modern scholars have referred to Egyptian and Syrian schools of medieval historiography.[87] There are broad outlines that distinguish the two schools. As might be expected, the Egyptian (Cairene) school during the late Mamluk period tended to focus more on politics of the state and the sultanate. However, the definition of politics and the political preoccupations of the Syrian historians were different, allowing more room for the activities and maneuvers of the urban notables, including the ulama and merchants, hence providing a more local perspective. An interest in local, popular politics is evident in both the Egyptian and Syrian schools, but is more pronounced in the writings of Syrian historians and predates the Ottoman period. That is, historians who were based more closely to the center of power, namely the Cairo Citadel, tended to be writing more in the shadow of its occupants and the ruling elite in general. While their works still broadened to refer to the affairs of Cairo and occasionally the affairs of other Mamluk cities, they were more aware and conscious of the presence of the sultan and the role of the Mamluk *amirs*. Therefore, even when matters of popular protest were raised, historians would often narrate such events in the context of the failings of power and the short-comings of the ruling sultan.

In Syria the attitude was different. The sultans did not cast such long shadows on the historical narratives. Their presence is not heavily felt in the texts, even though they are acknowledged. It was in Syria that works such as Ibn Tawq's *al-Ta'liq* in the fifteenth century and later al-Budayri al-Hallaq's chronicle in the eighteenth century appeared. Ibn Tawq was apparently a notary at a Damascus court and his text *al-Ta'liq*, though it tries to emulate contemporary chronicles, is more of a diary of daily events in the city with comments on some of the author's personal affairs. The history of Ibn Tawq's much more learned contemporary, Ibn Tulun, also gives more attention to local affairs and events happening in the city more generally. Syrian historians of the late Mamluk period, such as Ibn Tulun, were more interested in events from a local perspective, the activities of the particular communities to which they belonged, and their positions within them. The ulama and their affairs and dealings are depicted as more important than the Mamluk *amirs* and their doings. Imperial politics was not their sole focus, so that, for example, the viceroys of Damascus did not occupy the same positions in Ibn Tulun's narrative that the Mamluk sultan and the Citadel did with Cairene historians. The Mamluk sultans often appeared in Syrian chronicles as the distant arbitrators of last resort and the final court of appeal when local politics had reached a deadlock. This is a development in the writing of history, but it must also be somehow a reflection of the social and political history of Syria at the time. Local elites and notables played important roles in the functioning and politics of their cities. And they wrote about it.

In contrast, despite the interest expressed by al-Maqrizi and others in urban and social affairs, none of the writings of the Egyptian historians offer a distinctly grass-roots perspective. We have not discovered an Egyptian equivalent to Ibn Tawq yet, although al-Biqa'i comes close. In fact, Egyptian scholars seem to wean themselves off the genre of chronicles altogether after the Ottoman conquest, unlike their Syrian counterparts. Ibn Iyas's *Bada'i'al-zuhur* remains the last major work in the Mamluk historiographic tradition.[88] Scholars have remarked that after a lull following the Ottoman conquests, a new type of historiography emerged in Egypt in the late sixteenth and early seventeenth centuries combining imperial Ottoman and provincial Egyptian affairs, mostly retaining the formative characteristics of Mamluk historiography by focusing on Egyptian history from an imperial point of view. Thus we get the works of Abul-Surur al-Bakri (d. ca. 1619),[89] al-Damurdashi (fl. 1688–1775),[90] and finally al-Jabarti (d. 1825),[91] the last traditional chronicler.[92] This suggests that there was a strong connection between the Egyptian historians of the late Mamluk period and the regime, even though they were not simply mouthpieces of the regime and several of them were quite critical of Mamluk rule in general. However, the regime still dominated their narratives, even if critically. Some of the historians themselves came from Mamluk backgrounds. Furthermore, at that time period, history was written with a didactic purpose and to provide a moral sermon, as well as for entertainment—hence the references to *'ibra* and *i'tibar* in many of the titles. The lessons that written histories were deemed to carry were also addressed to the statesmen.[93] In all cases they seem to have been strongly influenced by the presence of the regime even when they increasingly wrote about other subjects in their texts. This in turn supports part of Khalidi's thesis that this historiographical tradition, developed under the rubric of *siyasa*, was connected to the rise of the Persian–Turkish military-feudal dynasties of the medieval period.[94]

The Cairo-based medieval historians were meticulous in recording annual Nile levels and floods, for example. They were also keen on recording the changing prices of basic foodstuffs. While al-Maqrizi, for one, included changing prices in most of the monthly entries of his history, al-Suluk, and in the overview at the beginning of each yearly entry, another historian, al-'Ayni, included a special section for the prices of each year in his 'Iqd al-juman. Of particular importance, especially during the late Mamluk period with its increasing economic and financial difficulties, were the fluctuations in the exchange rates of the various currencies in circulation. These too the historians monitored and recorded. The interest in the life of the community at large is probably the reason for including other everyday interests and affairs. The histories record plagues, famines, food shortages in general, fires, crimes, rumors, disputes, "miracles," construction and building works, and maintenance and irrigation works, in addition to the more traditional concerns of the ulama, namely the decisions and battles of the rulers, diplomatic efforts, bureaucratic appointments, and factional rivalries among scholars and soldiers alike. Even the domestic disputes of ulama found their way onto the pages of history.

Most chronicles included a section of obituaries at the end of the records of each particular year. It has been remarked that these biographical entries (in addition to the ones in the longer biographical dictionaries such as al-Sakhawi's al-Daw' al-lami') served as a kind of medieval "Who's Who." It is significant, and perhaps not surprising, that in any given year the names included in one chronicle will differ from those in another, indicating the interests, biases, and social circles in which the writer in question worked and which were the focus of his attention.[95] Similarly, historians who covered the same time periods and years, did not always include the same material or events, as is the case of comparing Ibn Taghribirdi and al-Biqa'i.[96] There was considerable diversity in the materials historians included in their works, in both the biographical entries and the historical events they listed. They were not simply copying from each other.

It is interesting to note that just as historians were recording a wider variety of events in their histories and chronicles, some of which related to the everyday affairs of their cities, common people also increasingly figured in the biographical dictionaries of the period. The biographical

genres of *tabaqat* and *tarajim* are classical in Arabic historical and judi-
cial writing. They are often considered branches of historical writing.[97]
Their beginnings lie in the history of Hadith (Prophetic sayings), *sira*
(Prophetic history), and the Arab interest in genealogy and biography.
By the medieval period, biographical dictionaries *(tabaqat)* had become
the genre through which the Muslim scholarly class historicized itself.[98]
Wadad al-Qadi has argued that through the biographical dictionaries
the ulama were offering an alternative history of the Muslim community.
She reads the biographical dictionary as a counterpoint to the chronicle;
whereas the latter was mainly concerned with the political achievements
of the state, the biographical dictionary would historicize the achievement of the community, through the knowledge of its scholars.[99] The
tabaqat literature typically included biographies of the scholars and
members of a particular *madhhab* (school of law), profession, city, or century. Their rationale was multifold: connected to the need to ascertain
the integrity of religious scholars and Hadith transmitters in particular,
tabaqat were also meant to provide coming generations with role models.
Khalidi ascribes the resurgence of biographical dictionaries during the
medieval period in part to the tensions among legal schools and the
vacuum created by the eclipse of the caliphate, which was increasingly
filled by a sense of mission among the scholars.[100] By historicizing the
ulama, and especially the notable and virtuous among them, the *tabaqat*
worked to confirm their role as guardians of the faith and to simultaneously reflect the power of the Mamluk empire and its institutions to
survey, record and asses the lives of its subjects.[101] Michael Chamberlain
also points out that the dictionaries were designed to record a person's
status in the city, as proved through evidence of religious knowledge,
morality, genealogy, offices held, marriage alliances entered into—a person's network of relations in society.[102] There is an inherent assumption
that the people who were listed in a biographical dictionary somehow
merited their inclusion, by being scholars themselves, teachers of future
generations, or transmitters of important knowledge. The interesting
thing for our purposes here is that by the late Mamluk period, more and
more commoners also came to be included in such dictionaries. Therefore, just as historians such as Ibn Tulun and Ibn Iyas chose to include

events such as demonstrations by silk weavers and glassmakers in their chronicles, others included individuals of less illustrious backgrounds in biographical dictionaries.

This tendency to include a wider cross-section of the urban population in historical narratives appears to be an attribute of late Mamluk historiography, whether chronicles or biographical dictionaries, one which will allow for the development of more popular chronicles in the eighteenth century, such as al-Budayri al-Hallaq's chronicle. The trend is already apparent earlier, in the biographical dictionary of Ibn al-Hanbali (d. 1563).[103] It is worth noting that another Damascene *'alim*, Najm al-Din al-Ghazzi (d. 1651), later criticized Ibn al-Hanbali's biographical dictionary for including unworthy characters who did not belong in history: builders, painters, merchants, singers, and other more "common" people. Al-Ghazzi suggests that Ibn al-Hanbali lacked sufficient entries under specific alphabetic letters and that he perhaps just wanted to lengthen the sections of his dictionary by adding any names, even if the characters were unworthy of such honor.[104] Despite his disdain for the inclusion of non-scholarly and non-elite figures, al-Ghazzi's biographical dictionary and that of his Cairene contemporary, al-Sakhawi, also have room for middle- and minor-ranking ulama, pious men, popular Sufis, and Mamluks of various standings, even though it is the ulama who continue to occupy center stage and have the longest biographies. While most biographical dictionaries of the period included entries on notable women of the military and ulama classes, al-Sakhawi was innovative in dedicating a whole volume exclusively to women. Figures of non-elite backgrounds also appear in 'Abd al-Wahhab al-Sha'rani's famous biographical dictionary of Sufis. Khalidi considers this inclusion of undistinguished "nonentities" as a "summoning of the commoners" and sees it as an indication of "the power of the Mamluk empire and its institutions—military, political, religious—to survey, record and assess the lives of its citizens."[105] I will discuss the theme of surveying and recording the world as the writers know it in more detail later; however, regardless of this quite possible impetus, it is also not unlikely that contemporary writers saw some merit in the lives of the individuals whose biographies they recorded and the affairs of the common people which they narrated in their histories. It fits with a general opening up of both the intellectual and the cultural space, as well as of the political space, as we shall see later. For while the bureaucratization and hierarchization that Khalidi postulates for this period might be fitting as a description of early medieval and early Mamluk written texts, it is arguable that the impetus was different by the fifteenth century and the late Mamluk period.

After the fall of the Mamluk regime the historiography of Egypt changed considerably. The later tradition of Egyptian and Syrian Ottoman historiography is often divided by modern scholars into two distinct schools: the traditional ulama historians and the military historians. One could argue that the all-encompassing gaze of the late Mamluk writers gave way to more focused perspectives in the Ottoman period, a development that gave rise to the military chronicles of Egypt and the popular chronicles of Syria. Both these new types of history writing share common characteristics such as the preoccupation with local affairs and the prevalence of colloquial Arabic, which becomes more pronounced.

With the change in the structure of power under the Ottomans, the reasons for writing history differed and the focus of the historical gaze also shifted. The more local and provincial interests of the Syrian historians do not seem to have been as sharply affected by the change of regime as those of their Egyptian counterparts. Perhaps this is why the popular trend within Syrian historiography continues and bears its more remarkable and well-known fruits in the eighteenth century.

Civic Interest

A common thread that connects many of the late Mamluk and early Ottoman historical writings is what one may tentatively call their 'civic interest,' an interest in cities and their urban communities, including their politics. Urban affairs and politics in their widest senses formed the foreground of most of these histories. Despite the continued interest in recording—sometimes critically—the history of the ruling elite, and the doings of the scholarly community, there was room for concerns of the city and its people. This included food prices, food shortages, grain hoarding and manipulation of markets, crimes, and violence that disrupted public order.

The anxieties resulting from the economic and social transformations were issues of popular concern. This is echoed in the historical writing of the period. For example, al-Maqrizi, one of the master historians of the fifteenth century, had his finger on the pulse of his city. Perhaps because he himself at one point occupied the position of *muhtasib* (market inspector), al-Maqrizi was attuned to changes in the rhythm of city life, picking up on the grievances of common people, their dissatisfaction with particular government decisions, their mumbles and their roars, and sharp and unanticipated changes in prices. In addition to beginning a year's narrative—in the annalistic tradition—with the names of the sultans and senior men of state who were in power, he would also list important events, not only from the point of view of central institutions, but also from the point of view of the people of the city. Prices of basic foodstuffs are often listed in his famous chronicle, *al-Suluk*. He faithfully mentions when their prices rise or fall, when they are available or when they are scarce. It is this palpitating rhythm that also betrays a sense of anxiety. For, as historians have remarked, while famine was relatively rare during this period, food shortages were not, and the threat of dearth was often imminent. The availability of basic foodstuffs on the markets was not something to be taken for granted. Other historians of the period also give similar records and lists; often the Nile flood—of paramount importance to the economy, the state, and society—was also recorded. The same is noticeable in Ibn Taghribirdi's works. This is not a development unique to al-Maqrizi, although he has a special talent for it, nor was it unique to Cairene historians. Historians of Syria also exhibited a similar sensitivity to the changing fates and affairs of their city.

Various reasons have been suggested to explain why it is that histories, including chronicles and biographies, and encyclopedias were prevalent genres in the Mamluk period and were so attuned to recording minute details. Khalidi has considered this attention to details and recording as part of the encyclopedic attitude and broadening of history by Mamluk chroniclers, making the chronicles resemble a feudal or cadastral survey. He reads it in the context of the rise of military-feudal dynasties and the militarization of Arab-Islamic society.[106] This comprehensive overarching control of society is thought to be behind the impetus to survey everything, record everything, include everything—everything with a relation to governance, that is. It is perhaps best represented in the imperial bureaucratic chronicles of the period, but this does not cover all the texts of the time. More recently, Elias Muhanna's study of al-Nuwayri's *Nihayat al-ʿarab fi funun al-adab* as an example of large-scale compilations also stresses the context of the political, demographic, administrative, and institutional centralization of the early fourteenth century.[107]

The broad and encyclopedic compilations of the period have been at times understood as being born out of fear of the destruction of Islamic knowledge, especially in the wake of the destruction and loss of libraries after invasions such as the Mongol invasion of Baghdad.[108] Contemporary religious scholars might have perceived it to be their duty and obligation to record Islamic knowledge and heritage of the preceding and classical period in order to preserve this legacy for posterity. Yet the drive to record and categorize various aspects of contemporary society, not only received canonical knowledge, especially by the later fifteenth century, but also suggests a deep interest in the affairs of these societies, deeming them worthy of study and analysis. It could reflect a sense of anxiety that the world as these writers knew it was changing, and hence a desire to maintain it and safeguard it or else control and understand it by recording it. Scholars have remarked on the social and psychological trauma that the Black Death and the recurrences of the plague caused to societies in the central Islamic lands. People made sense of the calamities that befell them through various scientific, moral, and religious interpretations. They also reacted in various ways to such trauma. The attempt to conceptualize a threatened civilized existence, analyze and record it, could be one such reaction on the part of some intellectuals. We can discern hints of it in Ibn Khaldun's extensive study of human civilization, for example. For Ibn Khaldun (d. 1406), the decimation of the populations caused by the various waves of plague threatened civilization:

> In the middle of the eighth [fourteenth] century, civilization both in the East and the West was visited by a destructive plague which devastated nations and caused populations to vanish. It swallowed up many of the good things of civilization and wiped them out. It overtook

the dynasties at the time of their senility, when they had reached the
limit of their duration. It lessened their power and curtailed their
influence. It weakened their authority. . . . Civilization decreased with
the decrease of mankind.[109]

The sense of insecurity brought about by the consecutive challenges
of the plagues, Crusader and Mongol threats, and deepening economic
crisis might have urged this shift toward contemporary history as society struggled to make sense of and come to terms with the calamities
that befell it. Some of the psychological and cultural reactions to these
challenges can be gleaned from the numerous plague treatises written
during that period.[110] Plague epidemics were traumatic experiences for
the generations that lived through them, especially as large numbers of
people died very quickly. Children and young people in particular died in
large numbers, prompting the appearance of a literary genre lamenting
the untimely death of offspring and consoling bereaved parents.[111] People
struggled to make sense of the calamities that befell them by producing
various medical and religious explanations. The genre of plague treatises
that matured in the fourteenth century reported accounts of historical
epidemics and suffering endured by previous generations in an effort to
provide some form of consolation to contemporary readers, urging them
to bear their grief with patience and fortitude.[112]

Modern historians who have studied medieval plagues have tried to
reconstruct the impact of its detrimental consequences on the psyche of
medieval societies; these are societies that witnessed their populations
being decimated over an exceedingly short period of time, with some villages and urban centers falling to ruin. It is understandable that medieval
Arab Muslims reacted in different manners to such trauma. For example,
Basim Musallam has argued that one of the reactions of the populations
to the plague epidemics might very well have been to practice contra-
ception, already an accepted and religiously sanctioned social practice.
Reacting against the trials and tribulations of "bad times"—plagues, invasions, and economic deterioration—many people might have sought to
safeguard their civilized and urbane lifestyles by limiting the number of
their dependents through birth control.[113] Rather than passively suffering

the effects of plague, famine, and war, Musallam argues that large sectors of the population might have reacted, proactively and consciously, in various ways that ultimately affected their destinies.

The interest in commentaries, encyclopedism, and legal proceduralism has further been explained by Petry as being born out of the circumstances afforded by Mamluk patronage through the *awqaf*. As the *awqaf* afforded the religious establishment considerable autonomy, scholars sought to preserve this and in turn became more conservative. As various financial and economic challenges loomed, confiscation and fiscal intervention by Mamluk authorities became a threat that scholars actively sought to avert.[114] This they did in part by holding on to established legal practices, as well as perceived traditions, customs, and ways of life.

It is within this mindset, one traumatized by successive challenges beyond its control, that late medieval historians were recording the lives of their cities. The interest in the minutiae of mundane urban existence that is so palpable in medieval histories could indicate an attempt to preserve the rhythms of daily life in the face of such challenges, by recording it and hence interpreting it and making sense of it.

Certainly the demographic and economic effects caused by the plague left an indelible mark on the writings of the master historian of the time, Taqi al-Din al-Maqrizi. In many ways it informed his history of the Fatimid period and especially his study of *al-shidda al-'uzma*, the great famine and factional war of the twelfth century, in his *Ighathat al-umma bi kashf al-ghumma*.[115]

The interest in civic matters also extended to reporting on urban protest. Matters of popular concern, as well as references to protest, are surely to be found in earlier Arabic histories. However, my contention is that the discourse itself, the placement of this information within the text, and the logic of the text are quite different in the late medieval/early modern period than in the classical period. A classical historian such as al-Tabari, to give but one example, does discuss uprisings and rebellions, including popular uprisings in Baghdad during the third civil war. But both the uprisings in Baghdad, and al-Tabari's narrative of them, are very different in their logic from the urban political action of Cairo and Damascus in the fifteenth and sixteenth centuries. Al-Tabari includes the uprising in Baghdad in the context of a high-politics struggle for power between the royal troops and the Khurasaniya troops, which in turn was part of the power struggle within the Abbasid household that spilled onto the streets of Baghdad, inducing ordinary residents of the city to take matters into their own hands and carry arms in order to defend themselves. This is a different situation, and a different narrative structure, than that which medieval historians steadily followed. What al-Maqrizi, Ibn Taghribirdi, Ibn Tulun, and Ibn Tawq give us is a living pulse of their cities, including matters that relate to protest.

When protests are referred to in late medieval works, they are not political acts that were about to threaten the regime, nor were they the stuff of high politics and civil war. No one expected the sugar riots of Damascus to displace the Mamluk regime. Yet they were important to the everyday life of the inhabitants of the city and to its commercial network whose business interests were affected by both the policies of the state and the angry reactions on the street. They were also narrated as reflections of bad policy, and of the ordeals that common people were faced with. Similarly, when *julban* soldiers rioted in Cairo and shopkeepers rushed to close down, historians noted this because the safety and security of the common subject were affected. When shops closed, life in the city stopped—and *that* was something worth noting in a chronicle. This civic interest marks the writing of late medieval historians.

Writing the Self into History
By the fourteenth and fifteenth centuries, history had become an established genre in the Arabic scholarly tradition. By that period the tradition had matured to include accepted stylistic and formalistic conventions. As we discussed earlier, the period is also known for long encyclopedic compilations. Indeed, the development of the Arabic bureaucratic tradition, which included formal historiography, had reached an apogee of sorts by the Mamluk period, best exemplified by works such as al-Qalqashandi's *Subh al-'Asha*. However, alongside this formalistic crystallization, new elements were creeping into the writing of history. Just as news of everyday events and matters of civic interest steadily made their way into the historical narrative of the Mamluk period, so too did matters relating to the lives of the writers themselves.

Indeed, one of the changes that are perceptible in the literature of the period is a growing move toward individuation.[116] This is apparent in the historiography produced in the Mamluk period and becomes quite noticeable in the fifteenth century. While throughout the postclassical period, historians increasingly became conscious of their role in the world and their unique contribution, this trend took a more personal turn in the late Middle Ages. That is, historians while writing about the affairs of their times, the high politics of rulers, and the affairs of their cities and urban networks, also wrote about themselves and their own personal affairs. This is evident in different writings of the period that include autobiographical material.[117] This also allowed for an increased representation of domestic history as authors wrote more about their wives, concubines, and daughters, and about the female relatives of their acquaintances as well.[118] As Torsten Wollina notes in a study of Ibn Tawq, "the 'blurring of lines between history and autobiography, and hence the increasing representation of the domestic' which is evident throughout the whole period (with a marked increase in the fifteenth century) may also have led to a different mode of representation of the self than in Ottoman times."[119]

This trend has been fiercely debated in the literature. Whereas earlier scholars had noted the lack of autobiographical material in premodern and medieval Arabic literature, interpreting it as a statement about the importance of communities over individuals and collective identities which were deemed diametrically opposed to European individualism, more recent scholarship has been regarding the matter in a different light.[120] Scholars have been reconsidering material of a personal nature within literary genres other than the autobiography and the memoir. Autobiographical and personal material can be found in places as varied as colophons and introductions to books.[121] In this regard, some of the historiographical material of the late Mamluk period does include indications of an individual awareness and concern. We have already remarked on the interest in everyday life and urban affairs. This extends to matters of personal interest as well, where the authors are often eyewitnesses to certain events, or else are the object of the events being narrated. Even in the relatively classical chronicle of Ibn Iyas, there is material that resembles a diary.[122] In al-Suyuti's (d. 1505) famous autobiographical work, *al-Tahadduth bi ni'mat Allah*, despite its adherence to a traditional Arabic structure of biographical and autobiographical texts, "no reader could leave this work with any doubt about al-Suyuti's vision of himself as a unique individual or the sheer force of his at times overweening personality."[123]

Al-Biqa'i (d. 885/1480), for instance, inserts his own life story as part of his chronicle *Izhar al-'asr li asrar ahl al-'asr.*[124] His messy domestic life with its family feuds and marriages and childbirth is combined with traditional historical narrative.[125] It is in parts personal enough to include an account of a dream his wife had.[126] This personal, individual trend is also quite clear in Ibn Tawq's *al-Ta'liq.* The author includes in his text material relating to his family life, the illnesses of his children, and quarrels with his wife, in addition to matters relating to his income and business dealings. He records when his wife and children visit the public bath and enumerates the sums spent on the visit.[127] He records, diligently, the times when his patron shaykh fights with his "Egyptian" wife. And while some of the records, such as those accounts of public bath visits, or accounts relating to his chicken-raising business or sums related to court business, make the text at times resemble a personal book of accounts, other reports do not seem to have this practical function and are closer to a diary. For example, Ibn Tawq seems very conscious of illness and when it hits. He records, for instance, that he caught a cold, accompanied by shivering and fever.[128] He also records the various stages of the illness of his baby daughter in 891/1486, which sadly culminated in her death.[129] These are matters of a very personal nature, relating to the author's own family and sometimes his own body, yet he saw fit to include them in a work that in terms of structure is arranged as a chronicle.[130] The imminent threat of the plague meant that every fever was a cause for worry, even panic—and that was worthy of record. Personal matters are also reflected in the poetry of the times, so that it can be said that this is an outlook characteristic of this generation.[131]

This interest not only in their own times, but also in their own life stories, very much characterizes the writers of the late Mamluk period. This could be a reflection of the turbulent times they lived through, and their perception that theirs was a difficult time that made their personal experiences worthwhile. It could be one way in which people of their generations made sense of the calamities they faced and expressed their vulnerabilities: calamities such as the recurrent plagues, the Crusades, and the Mongol invasions and subsequent wars.[132]

These and other references suggest that late medieval writers exhibited a different awareness and consciousness of their societies, themselves, and their roles. Certainly much has been written about the self-consciousness of western man in the modern period and the way in which this development, reflected in autobiography and the novel, shows the rising consciousness of the self. While lately scholars have revised some of their assumptions about an essentialist Islamic culture in which individuality is subsumed within or in tension with the collective spirit, this is still an area of ongoing study. Much of the current research centers on the modern period and the transition to modernity, but the transition is viewed as a rather late one, so that historians of literature tend to focus on nineteenth- and early twentieth-century biographies, rather than classical and medieval texts. Yet, as we have seen, while biography was already an established genre by the medieval period, the biographical dictionaries proliferated and took on some newer concerns in the Mamluk period. Furthermore, historians were increasingly historicizing themselves in their works, providing a rather personal narrative. The authors are more visibly present in their texts. I believe this is a qualitative difference. One of our dominant figures, al-Sakhawi, is infamous for his scathing remarks on people in his biographical dictionary. He also includes many members of his family in this dictionary, including otherwise unexceptional women. This enhanced sense of self is part of the changes that were developing during the fifteenth century, and they inform the attitude toward public life which saw increased participation in politics by the non-elite.

New Audiences for Written History

The various factors that we have discussed, including the social transformations in society that allowed for the spread of literacy, for the rise of middling classes, for the popularization of written literature, for a broadening of the pool of people who produced such literature, are all interconnected with the rise of new audiences for this new literary production. This also applies to those who might have been enjoying historical texts as well. Scholars have often commented on the prolific output of Mamluk historians. Indeed, history was a popular genre in the Mamluk period. However, the very popularity of history has also been cited as indicative of the lack of innovation and creativity—a presumed intellectual stagnation—of the scholarly output of the medieval period.[133] This is questionable, to say the least. Within the historical realm new and interesting sub-genres were developed, including encyclopedias, universal histories, and biographical dictionaries. Indeed, the very paradigm of intellectual stagnation after the golden age of Arab-Islamic scholarship has been questioned in later years, with historians of science and thought revising their views of the later period.[134] That more histories, or works with a historical bent, were being written during the Mamluk period suggests that there was then a broader audience for it. History has often been a favorite with rulers. Especially when historical works were mostly concerned with the political history of past elites, they were also meant in part to educate rulers on governance, and to offer moral counsel. In the Mamluk period we see the concerns of the written histories broadening to include other subjects, including matters of civic interest and even of personal interest to the individual historian. This could be connected to the social transformations that were occurring and would suggest that, by this time, there were new audiences and more people interested in histories.

Indeed, history as a genre was quite popular during the Mamluk and Ottoman periods. The profusion of surviving manuscripts of historical works is one indicator of this.[135] Probate deeds and inheritance records of the Ottoman period show that history was among the genres often included in private book collections.[136] The majority of the historical titles listed go back to the Mamluk period; the titles that recur frequently in probate records include al-Maqrizi's *Khitat* and *Ighathat al-umma*, al-Suyuti's *Tarikh al-khulafa'*, Ibn Khaldun's *Muqaddima*, al-Sakhawi's *al-Tibr al-masbuk*, local histories of Jerusalem and Mecca, and works of the contemporary Ottoman historians al-Bakri and al-Ishaqi, in addition to the works of al-Tabari and Ibn Khillikan and some Turkish and Persian histories.[137]

While it is impossible to tell exactly who were the audiences addressed by the historians, there is reason to believe that they included the scholarly class as well as the newly literate members of urban communities.

This would include soldiers and merchants, but also perhaps more learned artisans and craftsmen. As discussed earlier, the patronage of the religious establishment and the founding of *kuttab*s actually produced a growing number of literate individuals with some form of education, who could very well have been part of the targeted readership regardless of their professions, as the general literary production of the period suggests. How far the audience for history spread beyond the literate circles remains unclear. However, some modern historians have suggested that the echoes of a vernacular language that appear in later histories, such as for example Ibn Iyas's *Bada'i' al-zuhur*, reflect a link with oral recitation,[138] and therefore possibly a more popular and less educated audience. Similarly, an earlier text such as Ibn Sasra's, which is an account of Damascus during the reign of Sultan Barquq, was written in the colloquial around 1390.[139] Didactic, moralizing, and laden with fables and proverbs, Ibn Sasra's text was meant to educate and moralize its public.[140] Writing it in the colloquial could have been a strategy to ensure that it reached its intended, wide, popular audience more easily. It would not have been written in the colloquial if it were meant for the elite or the highly educated alone. Furthermore, it is quite possible that written histories were read out loud at private assemblies or, by the beginning of the sixteenth century, at coffee shops.[141] Indeed, the habit of reading books out loud was well established and widespread.[142] We know of literary salons where books were read out loud and discussed, we know that folk epics, some of which are historical in nature, were also read out loud and narrated in public. Alternatively, some of the written texts themselves could have evolved out of delivered lectures and "history-telling" sessions, or even gossip sessions. Ibn Zunbul al-Rammal's account of the Ottoman conquest, for example, was one of the more frequently copied histories and was part of popular entertainment.[143] The title of Ibn Tulun's chronicle, *Mufakahat al-khillan fi hawadith al-zaman* (Entertaining friends with stories of the times), itself hints at the idea that history might be a form of entertainment—amusing anecdotes to discuss with friends on a warm summer night, perhaps. The later, seventeenth-century chronicle of al-Damurdashi, one of the leading examples of an Ottoman soldier's chronicle, carries heavy echoes of the vernacular both in discourse and in structure; one can almost hear it being dictated.

Folk epics that incorporated historical events, such as the *Sirat al-Zahir Baybars*, were another form of popular history whose recitation was part of the entertainment culture in Mamluk and Ottoman times and up to the nineteenth century.[144] In fact, tales of a historical nature, stories of the ancients, were a favorite topic among storytellers in the Middle Ages in general.[145] If written histories had another—oral—life, then that would mean that history was even more popular and reached a wider audience.

It is therefore arguable that common people were part of the process of historiography, at least by being part of its intended audience and sometimes part of its producers. The "popularization" of history—if we may use that term—has several manifestations, chief among which is a sense of diversity, among the producers and the consumers of history and among the subjects covered by historians and constituting history.

Who Wrote History and Why?

In a previous section I have argued that the spread of literacy and the rise of middling classes meant that people from various backgrounds were expressing themselves in writing by the Mamluk period, some through literature and others through history. I would like to return here to this issue of who the historians of the late medieval period were, in order to better understand why they were writing histories in the first place.

As one would expect, the biases, personal characters, social positions, and intellectual backgrounds of the authors of written histories differed greatly and influenced their writings. With the exception of *al-Ta'liq*—the "diaries" of the fifteenth–sixteenth century Damascus author Ibn Tawq, which are an early example of the overlap of several genres despite their apparently annalistic structure— most late Mamluk and early Ottoman historians were writing to voice their opinions about current politics and perhaps to shape, influence, and participate in those politics. This is important to keep in mind, for even the inclusion of matters of popular and civic interest which is increasingly prevalent in their writings is not divorced from the question of power. The ruling elite remained the center of political power in their narratives.

It is important to recall here that these historians had varying relationships with the existing power structure. Some of the historians of the time were established ulama who were close to the ruling circles and enjoyed the patronage of powerful *amirs* and sultans, for example, Badr al-Din al-'Ayni (d. 1451), who occupied the positions of *muhtasib* (market inspector), qadi, and *nazir al-ahbas* (inspector of pious foundations).[146] Al-'Ayni was himself a Turk, and his knowledge of Turkish was perhaps one reason he was closer to the Mamluk sultans, attracting their friendship and favor.[147] Historians report that al-'Ayni was a regular at Sultan Barsbay's court, reading him histories of kings, in Turkish, in the evenings.[148] Even closer to the ruling elite was Ibn Taghribirdi (d. 1470), a student of al-'Ayni's who was himself also a Turk and a son of a senior Mamluk officer, and perhaps therefore less critical of Mamluk policies than his contemporaries.[149] However, even Ibn Taghribirdi, in certain sections of *al-Nujum al-zahira*, was critical of Mamluk corruption and factionalism. Similarly, in his *Hawadith al-duhur* he was "so critical of Qaytbay and Yashbak al-Suduni that he was bastinadoed for criticism of the latter."[150] Yet other historians, like al-Maqrizi (d. 1442), bridged the gap between religious scholar, civil administrator, and historian. Coming from a wealthy scholarly family and occupying posts of teacher, preacher, and *muhtasib*, when it came to history, al-Maqrizi was an independent scholar.[151] He started writing history after his career as a public official ended. His works, which attracted attention even during his own time, were not commissioned by the ruling sultans or any of the *amirs*. In fact, if anything, al-Maqrizi's works often express sharp criticism toward rulers like Sultan Barquq, for example, or even the whole political establishment under Sultan Mu'ayyad Shaykh.[152] Indeed, he accused the Mamluks of setting aside sharia in favor of the *yasa*, the pagan law code of the Mongols. He also reported the violations of *waqf* provisions by Mamluk authorities and criticized their financial and monetary mismanagement.[153] Similarly, the Hadith scholar and historian al-Suyuti was very critical of Mamluk rule in principle. He clashed with Sultan Qaytbay several times, obstinately refusing to go up to the Citadel on the first of every month in order to present himself to the sultan and collect his salary as shaykh of Barquq's tomb.[154] Later on he refused Sultan al-Ghawri's offer to direct his madrasa.[155] In general, in his writings the fifteenth century is presented as a century of intellectual decline and military catastrophes.[156]

The historian Ibn Iyas (d. ca. 1524), whose *Bada'i' al-zuhur fi waqa'i' al-duhur* remains an indispensable source for the waning days of the Mamluk sultanate and an eyewitness of the Ottoman conquest of Egypt and Syria, does not seem to have been firmly established in scholarly circles. He is not mentioned in the biographical dictionaries of his time and does not mention such personal details about himself as his actual occupation. However, he was a descendant of Mamluks and a holder of an *iqta'*. His writing suggests a certain familiarity with the daily events at the Citadel, perhaps through his brother, who served in the artillery division under Qansuh al-Ghawri, and his sister, who was probably married to a Mamluk *amir*.[157] Ibn al-Sayrafi (d. 1495) came from more humble origins; his father was a money-changer at the mint.[158] Ibn al-Sayrafi himself joined the ranks of the ulama and rose to the position of deputy Hanafi qadi, which afforded him some opportunities to witness the machinations of the Mamluk state. His chronicles report many incidents that occurred in courts and at the audience sessions in the Citadel. Ibn al-Sayrafi might have hoped to win the patronage of some senior Mamluk officers, such as the *dawadar* Yashbak min Mahdi, but all we know is that he often had to make ends meet by copying manuscripts to supplement his income and by occasionally working in the jewelers market.[159]

Ibn Tulun (d. 1546), who lived in Damascus, was more the traditional *'alim*. He was also quite a prolific scholar and writer in a variety of subjects, his works not limited to history. He was a scholar of Qur'an, Hadith, and *fiqh* who occupied a number of teaching and administrative positions, although none of very high rank. Hence he was not part of the political elite of Damascus. Ibn Tulun says in his autobiography, *al-Fulk al-mashhun fi ahwal Muhammad ibn Tulun*, that he occupied thirty different posts during his lifetime, including teaching positions at the Umayyad Mosque and at the Shaykh al-Islam Abu 'Umar (the 'Umariya) madrasa in al-Salihiya in Damascus.[160] He was offered the position of *khatib* at the Umayyad Mosque and that of Hanafi mufti of Damascus later in his life, but he declined both, citing old age.[161] Ibn Tulun, who was of Turkish descent, studied with a number of leading scholars from a young age, making such progress that he is said to have practiced *fiqh* at the age of eleven and begun teaching at the age of fourteen with his paternal uncle, the qadi and mufti of Dar al-'Adl, Jamal al-Din Yusuf ibn Tulun, who supervised his education.[162] He also studied under a number of leading ulama of his time, including Muhiyy al-Din 'Abd al-Qadir al-Nu'aymi and Jalal al-Din al-Suyuti.[163] Thus Ibn Tulun enjoyed an interesting median position within the community of scholars of Damascus; he was highly educated in a number of the important disciplines of his time, involved in and familiar with affairs of the scholarly community, while at the same time maintaining a sufficient distance from their politics to be an insightful observer.

Ibn Tawq (d. 1509), Ibn Tulun's contemporary, is by contrast a much more elusive historical figure to trace. He seems to have been a Shafi'i notary, and he recorded some of the proceedings related to his work and earnings in his text al-Ta'liq. He was hardly the court historian. Ibn Tawq was quite immersed in the local affairs of the Shafi'i circles in Damascus to which he belonged. He was close to the famous 'alim Taqi al-Din ibn Qadi 'Ajlun and probably served as his clerk. The viceroy and the dawadar appear only in the background of his narrative. Indeed, to the extent that there is one domineering figure in his text, it is Ibn Qadi 'Ajlun.

These and other historians therefore came from different social backgrounds, which is reflected in the texts they composed. However, even in the writings of those more connected to the ruling establishment we can trace a certain civic interest and an awareness of the plight and circumstances of the urban population. They did not simply write approvingly about the power structure; on the contrary, they were often critical. In fact, these historians recorded the frequent acts of protest in their communities, sometimes sympathetically. In some way, their very writing of history was itself a form of protest.

Historiography as protest

It is arguable that the very historical discourse used to narrate those events and to speak of popular politics was in itself a way of protesting the dominant political order.

Although the increased number of educated and literate members of society was in large part a product of the militarized social order that patronized the religious establishment, this did not translate into straightforward identification with the regime. And while many of those educated men were employed in the regime as administrators and judges, the educational system still produced even larger numbers who might not have been incorporated into the system. Indeed, several of the personalities who figure in historiography are learned men who do not seem to have been in the employ of the state, at least not for the majority of their careers. Furthermore, Petry has debated whether by patronizing the religious establishment through the institution of *waqf*, the regime and the elite were also creating opportunities for this establishment to be autonomous, for by relying on the incomes from *waqf*-endowed salaries, scholars could retain a certain degree of autonomy from the state apparatus.[164] Even though officials did not interfere in the content of scholarship or what professors taught, as the government's economic and financial difficulties increased, the vast amount of wealth held in *waqf* by the various religious establishments was under potential threat of confiscation and financial intervention by the state. This threat, Petry argues, might be another reason that prompted scholars toward proceduralism rather than creative production. This threat was also, perhaps, at the heart of the tension between scholars and sultans in the late Mamluk period. As the ulama struggled to maintain their autonomy and their financial benefits, they were critical of many of the policies of the rulers that could have had negative impacts on their interest group. This might be one reason behind the critical attitude of some scholars toward contemporary rulers.

Konrad Hirschler, in his study of the thirteenth-century historians Ibn Wasil and Abu Shama, has argued convincingly that their texts were not simply biased by "generally unproblematic representations of the past," but rather that through their texts the authors discussed various issues of relevance to their times, "most prominently the question of ideal rule."[165] The two authors had considerable room for maneuver so that, despite writing within the same genre, during the same period, and relating more or less the same events, their texts are characterized more by their differences than their similarities.[166] This pattern can also be seen in later chronicles and even panegyrics. A study of the representation of al-Zahir Baybars, for example, shows that historians of the thirteenth, fourteenth, and fifteenth centuries and the creators of the popular epic *Sirat al-Zahir*

Baybars presented very different perceptions of the sultan, and that they used these varying and often contradictory accounts to make various political arguments.[167] Hirschler rightly takes issue with Rosenthal's claim that "history was not used as a means for the propagation of idea, or, more exactly, historians as a rule did not consciously intend, in writing their works, to reinterpret historical data so as to conform to the ideas they might have wished to propagate."[168] Indeed, the writings of late Mamluk historians not only reveal their varying political positions, but also carry a deep protesting streak.

One set of questions worth posing with respect to this historical material concerns what each of these authors was doing in writing such histories. This involves both the intentions of the authors (which some of them declared), and the statements they were making by writing such histories.[169] The question of the legitimacy of the Mamluk sultanate and its rule is a continuous theme within the historiography of the whole period. However, in the writings of the fifteenth century it is possible to discern a protesting trend not simply at the rule of the Mamluks per se, but more poignantly at the particular policies they were following in the fifteenth century in response to the deep changes taking place.

Aside from the official historiography represented by the handful of panegyrics that survive from this period, most chronicles do not set out to glorify any particular reign or ruler. The main exceptions are al-'Ayni's biographies of the sultans al-Mu'ayyad Shaykh and Tatar.[170] The vast majority were not commissioned court histories. In fact, rather than praising the ruling Mamluk elite, many historians and ulama are seen to have been quite critical of the Mamluks, and the Turks in general. Some modern historians have suggested this might reflect dissatisfaction on the part of the scholars as a collectivity after having lost some of their authority and prestige with the rise of the Turks in medieval Islamic lands.[171] Indeed, even though many individual Mamluks were singled out for praise, an underlying argument remained that their rise to power was a subversion of some sorts. A general disdain of Mamluks and Turks and a condescension toward them are clear in al-Subki's *Mu'id al-ni'am*, where they are represented as weak in faith and education.[172] This attitude is reflected in, among other sources, al-Maqrizi's introduction to his history of the Mamluk state, *Kitab al-suluk li ma'rifat duwal al-muluk*, where he begins by praising Almighty God who in His power gives power to those who are weak and raises them from humble origins, thereby subversively highlighting the humble origins of the Mamluk Turks.[173] It is the corruption of the Muslims and their deviation from the true path, he implies, that led them to fall under the authority of former slaves.[174] A similar note is struck in a book by al-Maqrizi's disciple, Abu Hamid al-Qudsi, in his *Kitab duwal al-Islam al-sharifa al-bahiya wa dhikr mazahar li min hikam Allah al-khafiya fi jalb ta'ifat al-atrak ila al-diyar al-misriya*.[175] While al-Qudsi's book seeks out the (hidden) wisdom in being ruled by the Turks, thereby highlighting many of their good services to Islam, it is not free from criticism, especially of the behavior of later Mamluks, his contemporaries.[176] The book also suggests that it is not "normal" or "acceptable," for the Turks to have risen to power; this is not the way things should be, or the "natural order of things." Thus while the author uses a rather traditional structure for his time—beginning in the usual manner, and using religious language in the form of prayers and invocations—he does so in a manner that carries multiple new meanings, and that is subversive. The use of this structure also urges us, as modern historians, to reconsider some of the dominant assumptions about the stasis of this period. It shows that traditional genres were being used in novel ways.

In fact, a sense of doom, disappointment, and nostalgia pervades many of these works. The glorification of earlier regimes, both Fatimid and early Mamluk, as well as the events related about their contemporary societies, suggest that historians like al-Maqrizi, Ibn Taghribirdi, Ibn Iyas, and Ibn Tulun were writing in part to lament their own times. Thus when al-Maqrizi comments in *Ighathat al-umma* that the misfortunes that befall people because of famine, plagues, and inflation are the fault of rulers and their preoccupation with things other than the interests of the people, he is clearly blaming contemporary rulers for contemporary conditions.[177] It is a note that is echoed in his history of the Fatimid state, *Itti'az al-hunafa'*, which nostalgically glorifies the reigns of the Fatimid caliphs.[178]

Similarly, al-Maqrizi's *al-Suluk* is replete with the historian's criticisms of Mamluk rule. In reporting a violent protest which occurred in Damietta in 820/1418, al-Maqrizi firmly relates it to the corruption that allowed for the sale of senior government posts in late Mamluk government.[179] This is not simply divine will, not at all.

Al-Maqrizi was aware of the effects of Mamluk politics on the population at large. His gaze was wide enough to incorporate various sectors of society; the poor and the weak are given voices in his narratives. In a vignette reported under the events of the year 821/1418, al-Maqrizi demonstrates the injustices that government policies placed on common folk and the abuse of these policies by officials.

And in this month [Sha'ban 821/September 1418] the son of a trades-man drowned in the canal. His father got him out [of the canal] dead, but was not able to bury him without the permission of the *amir* 'Ala' al-Din 'Ali ibn al-Tablawi, the governor of Cairo—as was the custom. When he sought his permission, [the governor] ordered him to be sent to prison; so he was imprisoned. He sent people to tell him that there was no way for him to be released until he paid five dinars. They kept discussing it with him until he promised to pay. He was released on parole. He sold the merchandise that he and his family lived off, and that brought in three dinars. Then he took all that his wife—the drowned boy's mother—had and sold it; it brought in one dinar. He borrowed another dinar to complete the *wali*'s five dinars. He then borrowed more money to pay the parole officers—the *wali*'s assis-tants—and some to pay for the boy's shroud and to pay the caretaker. He then left his wife and ran away. *This is part of what the governors and rulers do in those strange times* [italics added for emphasis].[180]

As we can see, al-Maqrizi made several decisions in narrating this episode, in what purports to be a chronicle of changing regimes *(duwal al-muluk)*. He decides that such a relatively unusual affair, a boy's drowning in the Nile, merits inclusion in his chronicle, and uses it to highlight a cru-cial aspect of state–society relations, namely the extortion that state officials imposed on the subjects, and to show the reactions of those subjects (the man flees, a non-confrontational form of everyday protest, not dissimilar to peasant flight). And he ends this vignette with a statement that makes his purpose very obvious and clear: it is corruption that does this to people.

The common people often enter the narrative in order to highlight aspects of the rulers' achievements or failure; their fate is a reflection of the elite's. History remains the outcome—good or bad—of the rulers' politics. Yet, unwittingly perhaps, these same historians present us with the evidence that things were not that simple.

Despite their varying relations with the ruling regimes, many historians seized opportunities in their historical writing to criticize the ruling authorities. The historian as critic and as pedagogue is one of the subtexts of medieval historical writing. History was meant to teach future generations lessons. However, direct criticism of the basis of Mamluk or Ottoman power was rare. More prevalent is criticism of particular government policies and certain government officials, even sultans, the latter naturally criticized after their demise.

Excessive taxation and the procedures that the late Mamluk government followed in collecting dues were occasions for criticism by historians. For example, al-Maqrizi is sharply critical of the taxation campaigns of the *ustadar* (major domo of the sultan's household), the *amir* Fakhr al-Din ibn Abi al-Faraj, in 816/1414 in Upper Egypt. In fact the historian compares the *ustadar* to a gang leader:

For he did in Upper Egypt as gang leaders do when they attack a village by night and control it; he would descend on a town and plunder all the grain and cattle in it, and steal the women's jewelry and clothes and would not depart from the town and head to another before leaving it more deserted than the insides of a donkey. By these doings he has ruined the towns of Upper Egypt, with dangerous consequences.[181]

He was also critical of the excessive dues the state levied from its subjects under various guises, including the death/burial tax discussed earlier. Al-Maqrizi's recounting of the story of a man walking out on his family, which one might assume recurs in many societies across history, and his decision to include it in his chronicle, shows the historian's sensitivity to social realities in his time. He uses this simple everyday story as an occasion to comment on what he considered an unjust tax by first putting before the reader the difficult consequences such a levy forced on simple people. He is critical of the excessive levies that the *ustadar* collected in Rajab 822/July 1419: such unjust, excessive taxation could only lead to economic ruin in the long run, he argues.[182] Al-Maqrizi's text is replete with such vignettes, which allow us to glimpse the pace of life in late Mamluk Egypt and Syria. Such vignettes are also a hallmark of Ibn Tulun's chronicle. Functioning as they did as news bulletins of their lives and times, they also provided their writers with literary formats through which they could criticize their ruling regimes and societies. This too was considered part of history.

Taxation was not the only cause for al-Maqrizi's criticism of government policy. He referred critically to the sale of various offices of state and considered it a corruption of the system which led government officials to levy extralegal taxes, to make up for the bribes they paid to secure their positions in the first place.[183] The corruption of the system also led, in the historian's view, to the appointment of individuals not suitably qualified to government positions. Hence we read his scathing criticism of the *muhtasib* Sharaf al-Din Muhammad ibn ʿAli al-Hibri in the man's obituary. Ibn al-Hibri is described as a former sugar trader and a convicted felon of bad repute.[184]

Not only al-Maqrizi, who might have had an ax to grind with Mamluk administrators, but also al-ʿAyni, who continued to enjoy good relationships with Mamluk sultans, writing panegyrics for al-Muʾayyad Shaykh and Tatar and occupying positions of state throughout his career, was occasionally critical of government policies in his writing. Thus he comments that the taxation imposed on the people of Aleppo in 822/1418 during al-Muʾayyad Shaykh's reign was a heavy burden to bear.[185] He was also critical of the appointment of an unfit man to the position of *wali* of Cairo.[186] In fact, throughout his text he repeatedly criticizes the appointment of disreputable men to positions of state through bribes, a tacit criticism of the ruler's decisions.[187]

Some historians indicated their disapproval of state policies indirectly through formulaic phrases. Phrases invoking God, such as "God is our refuge" or "There is no power except unto God," recur in the chronicles. They usually come as concluding sentences to reports on some of the atrocities committed by state officials and the burdens endured by the common people. Such phrases indicate the author's critical opinion while at the same time implying that nothing could be done before such oppression except to turn to God and endure. Despite the apparent passivity of such a stand, it is still implicitly subversive. Ibn al-Sayrafi concludes a section on the various unjust practices by men of state against the believers with a prayer that God may destroy the unjust and those who work for them against the welfare of the Muslims.[188]

Even the last of the traditional Mamluk chroniclers of Egypt, Ibn Iyas, whose *Bada'i' al-zuhur* continues into the Ottoman expansion, is "fiercely anti-Mamluk and his obituaries of sultans are often laced with sarcasm,"[189] despite his Mamluk relations (he seems to have been a grandson of a Mamluk officer).

Ibn Taghribirdi took the same attitude. As Irwin notes:

> Ibn Taghribirdi and other historians writing in the fifteenth century were fiercely critical of their own times, while they looked back on the early decades of the Mamluk regime through a haze of nostalgia. Thus Ibn Taghribirdi could write of Baybars' mamluks that "they were well endowed with courtesy, humility and obedience to their superiors, and good manners and courtesy towards their inferiors," in defiance of the facts.[190]

Irwin, however, does not question this nostalgia or explain what lay at its roots. I have argued in this chapter that this sense of nostalgia itself stems from a dissatisfaction with the authors' own times, their criticism of their contemporary rulers, and their protest of some of the policies followed by late Mamluk sultans and *amir*s. This attitude on the part of the writers, as recorded in written texts and histories, is part of the general cultural climate of the period.

Conclusion

The late Mamluk period, and the fifteenth century in particular, was a time of deep political, economic, and social change in Egypt and Syria. These substantial though gradual transformations naturally involved, and were reflected in, the cultural production of the time. A growing popularization of literature and of historiography is discernible in the surviving writings. The language of writing changed as it came to include more of the vernacular; popular forms of prose and poetry that included colloquial words and expressions spread; and new genres developed. These changes are also visible in the historiography of the period, which saw a similar change in language and content. Contemporary historians were interested in aspects of everyday life, historicized their own selves and some aspects of their private lives, and exhibited a civic awareness of the concerns of their urban communities. They also used their history to comment on and critique the rulers of their times.

This popularization and vernacularization is itself indicative of the changes some social groups were undergoing, and of the opening up of new social and political space, allowing room for new, middling social groups to express themselves differently. The 'bourgeois trend' also had its effects on the politics of the time. While it would be anachronistic to speak of public opinion having developed at such an early period, there are indications that some forms of communal awareness and communal politicking and maneuvering were beginning to take place. Increasingly, different social groups participated in politics in a variety of ways; the historians through whose works we learn of those developments were themselves writing to express opinions about, and sometimes to protest against, the politics of their times. They also report urban protest; riots and negotiations are some of the most visible acts of popular politics in the surviving sources.

5
BETWEEN RIOTS AND NEGOTIATIONS: POPULAR POLITICS AND PROTEST

The previous chapters have argued that throughout the fifteenth century the Mamluk state and society of Egypt and Syria were undergoing tremendous change and development. They have explored theses changes in economic policy, in government administration, and in society. These changes affected the way the state was structured, with power being increasingly decentralized; the mechanisms to which the rulers resorted in order to obtain and maintain power and control society left power more diffused than in earlier times. This created new opportunities and social and political space for members of the non-elite and non-Mamluk classes. It also supported the rise of new social classes and created opportunities for social mobility within existing social groups. These changes are reflected in the surviving cultural and literary production of the times. New social groups and new ruling conditions paved the way for more popular forms of expression, and allowed individuals from more diverse—and lowly—social backgrounds to produce literature that was not only popular during their own lifetimes but, quite importantly, came to be recorded and survived to our times. This chapter argues that changes in state and society were also reflected in the politics of the time. It deals with a sector of society that has often been left out of political histories, the non-elites. It will show how they too were affected by the deep transformations occurring and what roles they played in shaping some of those changes. It will also show how the general conditions affected ordinary people and how the acts of the mostly anonymous groups and crowds affected the decision-making process.

The bourgeois trend of the fifteenth century, which scholars and historians of literature have identified in the surviving sources and manuscripts, is also reflected in the politics of the time. Just as people and individuals from more diverse social groups and backgrounds were expressing themselves in literature, historiography, Sufi thought and practice, and the arts, they were also increasingly participating in politics. This is expressed in the references to popular protest that survive in the literature. This chapter will show that the protest acts of the non-elites, sometimes successful and sometimes not, were not haphazard or impotent, but on the contrary can be analyzed in a more sophisticated way: for instance, by looking at the alliances they made with other social groups, by the negotiations that they undertook, and by the indirect forms of resistance to which they also resorted. In short, the non-elite—especially in the cities—were as much part of the deep transformations of the century as were those who in fact held power, the Mamluk class. This analysis explores the ways in which those who in fact did not have direct access to power could manipulate various tools in their hands, including protests and demonstrations, to make their voices heard. Faced with many burdens resulting from the policies the rulers followed in order to face the tough challenges before them, and without a formal system of representation, people often took to the streets.

Even a casual reading of the surviving chronicles and histories of the late Mamluk period reveals increasing references to instances of popular protest, particularly in urban centers. Rather than cite these instances as further examples of the decline and corruption of an ailing Mamluk regime, this chapter will show that they were instead signs of a new civic awareness and vitality, one which allowed the non-elites increasing roles in the management of their cities and their affairs. Rather than silently endure perceived injustices by the Mamluk order, the non-elite often protested and negotiated better outcomes for themselves. While these new directions did not come to be formalized in political institutions, the surviving narratives suggest that certain social contracts were implied, negotiated, and upheld. In place of the image of the urban non-elite as one lump of people that stoically endured the harsh and corrupt conditions of Mamluk rule, a reading of the protest narratives will show that various groups found ways to negotiate their way into the equations of power.

Reports of protest also connect what we know of the fiscal policies of the late Mamluk sultanate with life on the street. Previous chapters have referred to the various attempts by Mamluk sultans to generate income and cash flow and bring more resources under the control of the sultans.[1] Mamluk fiscal policies ranged from increasing customs duties, to monopolizing certain commodities (including, most famously, spices and pepper since the days of Barsbay), to attempts to manipulate the agrarian production of Egypt and Syria through the *iqta'* system and through restructuring the *iqta'* system. We know of the sultans' attempts to put their hands on as many resources as they could by establishing such specialized governmental departments as the *diwan al-mufrad*, and the competition this generated between the sultans and their *amir*s. However, scholars often fail to consider how this played out on the streets, and how it involved other players in politics—players who were not part of the Mamluk caste. We also forget sometimes, when we study the decrees and rules issued by rulers, that policy does not work only in one direction, from the top down. The narratives of protest can be linked to this grander narrative of power, much as the study of law in practice adds a dimension not apparent when focus is exclusively on the normative discourse.[2] In short, if one broadens the definition of political participation in such a way as to include those acts of protest, it is possible to discern a role for the common urbanite in the transformations of the late Mamluk period.

This chapter argues that there was a role for the non-elite, more sophisticated than mere violence and impotence. It places the urban populace within the transformations taking place, rather than presenting it as a submissive and static mass. One aspect of popular political participation, especially in urban centers, that is more evident in the sources is protest, but the reports that survive of those protests suggest a more nuanced balance of power, with shades in between violence and impotence. This development in the urban political landscape will be situated within the context of Mamluk history in general to see where this leaves the non-elite and how it adds to our understanding of the period, of Mamluk politics, and of what we call the Mamluk state.

Even though there are many references to urban protest in the surviving historical narratives of the late Mamluk period, these reports have not attracted sufficient scholarly attention. In his pioneering book *Muslim Cities in the Late Middle Ages* Ira Lapidus titled his penultimate chapter "The Common People: Between Violence and Impotence."[3] When the non-elite are mentioned in the discussion of Mamluk politics, they typically remain a footnote to the larger drama, with the options available to them limited to either violence or impotence. While this must in part reflect something about the realities of the premodern military rule of the Mamluks, it is also in larger part a reflection of the bias of the sources from this period that survive for us: the windows through which we look at medieval Egypt and Syria. Lapidus also makes the argument that since common people had no intermediary bodies, such as guilds, to resort to in order to express their economic and social interests, and since there were no fully responsible authorities to hear complaints from the people, demonstrations became an important form of economic protest.[4] Indeed, Lapidus gives prime importance to the protests arising from economic grievances. However, in the final analysis he finds that the violent outbursts of the markets were "dissipated into all but fruitless protests."[5] This is because the Mamluks managed to ally themselves with the notables, thereby consolidating their control over the populations and channeling all popular protests into actions that ultimately did not seriously threaten Mamluk hegemony. "Rebellions and crimes never sought to change the government but only to ameliorate specific wrongs," he writes.[6]

Similarly, Poliak, in an early article on the topic, focused on the economic causes behind popular protest.[7] Based primarily on examples derived from the chronicle of Ibn Iyas, Poliak's analysis would later inform the works of such historians as Lapidus, for whom urban revolts and protests in medieval Egypt were always caused by direct and local hardships and aimed at limited gains, namely the redress of the hardship in question. The same approach is at the heart of Shoshan's analysis when he adopts E.P. Thompson's term and argues that a "moral economy" governed the Cairene crowd, who rose to protest any corruption of that economy with the aim of restoring it to its traditional balance.[8]

However, despite the importance of the arguments made by Poliak, Lapidus, and Shoshan, there are other perspectives that need to be included. First, economic grievances did not automatically lead to protest; second, the protests were often sophisticated acts of negotiation; and third, there are a number of other causes of protest that are discernible in the surviving narratives. Finally, as this chapter will argue, the protests can better be understood as part of a larger framework of transformations and as an opening up of the social and political space, rather than as (failed) attempts to overturn the Mamluk regime.

Negotiations

One way to place non-elite groups in the context of the broader changes taking place is to examine the various alliances that were forged, dismantled, and reforged between different urban groups. Artisans and ulama, traders and *amir*s, formed temporary alliances for a variety of reasons in order to confront particular situations and challenges. Reports of protest allow us to see how these different social groups could occasionally work together to consolidate their positions or maximize their gains. This approach to street protests aims to go beyond the dichotomy of impotence and violence. Closer examination of reports cited in the surviving literature suggests that urban popular politics were more nuanced than that. Certainly by the fifteenth century, there had developed in Egyptian and Syrian cities certain repertoires for protest that paved the way for negotiations over power. These were sometimes successful, indicating that the diffusion of power allowed new urban actors to negotiate their interests and occasionally reach favorable settlements with authorities. Quite frequently, alliances were formed with religious scholars.

The negotiations involved various urban actors, including different types of ulama. Of course the study of ulama and their social and intellectual history is at the core of premodern Islamic historiography in general. As various scholars have pointed out, the ulama played fundamental social roles during this period. However, they were not one cohesive or homogeneous group and did not constitute a class in the modern sense of the term. The variations between the different ulama are also reflected in the roles they played in urban politics and popular protest.

Ulama and religious men of different social and intellectual standing played political roles and occasionally interceded in popular politics.
There was a justification for this on the theoretical level. Political activity
is one of the duties of religious scholars, according to the advice of 'Abd
al-Wahhab al-Sha'rani in his *Kitab irshad al-mughaffalin min al-fuqaha'
wa-l-fuqara' ila shurut suhbat al-umara'*. A Sufi shaykh should intercede on
behalf of ordinary Muslims, both with God and with political authorities.[9]
Al-Sha'rani himself saw his role in this light.

However, relations between religious scholars and figures, on the
one hand, and powerful rulers and *amir*s, on the other, were often quite
complex. There was a traditional wariness on the part of scholars about
working with government officials. It had been frowned upon by some;
staying away from rulers was commendable, as al-Ghazali, for one example, had advised.[10] Dating back to the *mihna* of the ninth century, the
ulama had obtained a certain degree of independence from the rulers and
established themselves as the guardians of the faith and of the welfare
of the community.[11] By the medieval period an uneasy peace had been
reached between scholars and sultans, best embodied by the vast patronage of the religious establishment by military regimes. The non-Arab
and often non-Muslim-born rulers needed the support and legitimiza-
tion of the ulama, whose implicit approval helped maintain social order,
and the ulama came to depend in part on the patronage of the rulers.
Officials competed among themselves for obtaining the support of repu-
table shaykhs whose prayers and prestige would aid them in their careers.
Similarly, scholars, including Sufis, competed with each other to gain the
patronage and support of powerful officials. A close relationship with
authorities brought gifts and access to power to a Sufi shyakh and his
followers, allowing them an edge over rivals.[12]

Ulama of various social and intellectual standing were involved in the
affairs of their societies and integrated with other social groups—merchants, artisans, Mamluk officers, common people—which allowed them
to play political roles. Indeed the ulama acted both as agents of protest
occasionally and, perhaps more often, as mediators between the state and
the crowd. There is a recurring pattern of a negotiating delegation that
is sent to intercede between a rebelling crowd and the· authorities, which

suggests a local mechanism for dealing with urban crises. The delegation typically included both officials and ulama.

By allying themselves to the ulama, ordinary urban dwellers could better confront the exploitative acts of the ruling class. For example, in 886/1481 when the *ustadar* Ibn Shad Bek imposed a forced purchase of sugar at a price higher than the market rate (the common fiscal tactic of *tarh*), the people of al-Tawwaqin and Jaqmaq markets in Damascus resorted to various means in response to the decree in order to negotiate the price. They complained to local authorities, rioted, negotiated, and used the ulama's network of contacts in the imperial capital to intercede on their behalf with the relevant authorities to repeal the *tarh*.[13] First they complained to the *na'ib* of Damascus, but when this avenue proved futile, the protesters, possibly under the organization of the Shafi'i scholar Taqi al-Din ibn Qadi 'Ajlun, eventually dispatched Shaykh Ahmad al-Dahinati to Cairo with formal complaints and letters to a number of senior officials and qadis. The process bore fruit, for al-Dahinati returned from the capital with three decrees addressed to provincial authorities allowing further negotiation of the price of the sugar in the *tarh*. Rather than simply acquiesce to the fiscal demands of the agents of the state, this network of merchants and scholars used their social capital to negotiate a price that would be more favorable to them. Their practice did not result in an abolition of this particular *tarh*, nor did it restructure the Mamluk economy. Instead it resulted in an alleviation of some of their burdens, safeguarding some of their profit, while at the same time, perhaps unwittingly, confirming the authority of the ruling regime, based in Cairo. This type of protest cannot be categorized as either senseless violence or stoic impotence.

The Mamluk authorities, too, ruled in alliance with the ulama, and in times of crises, such as during urban protests, they could sometimes rely on ulama to relieve the tension and mediate with the dissenting crowds. During a riot in Damascus on Thursday 14 Jumada I 907/25 November 1501 following the imposition of excessive levies, the viceroy of Damascus sent a delegation, including the four qadis and Taqi al-Din ibn Qadi 'Ajlun, to negotiate with the rebel leaders.[14] The crowd, which included people from the neighborhoods of Harat Maydan al-Hasa and Harat al-Shaghur as well as *zu'ar*, had rebelled and set out to kill the *na'ib*. The crowd demanded that the *na'ib* surrender three officials to them: the *usta-dar*, Ibn al-Fuqaha'i, and the brother of the *muhtasib*'s *naqib*. The crowd gathered once more the following day, a Friday, preparing to fight the Mamluks. The Friday prayers were suspended as fighting ensued and a number of Mamluks were killed. Canceling the congregational Friday prayers would have been a decision laden with meaning, and the historians who report such an action must have been aware of it. It was a rare occurrence in a city under Muslim rule. It was possible only because the qadis were themselves involved in this protest. The riot escalated on Saturday. Ibn Tulun, however, is clear that the evil of the common people increased because of the many injustices that befell them. In his interpretation, their behavior was not haphazard or senseless. After further confrontations, in which the *na'ib* almost lost his life, he sent out a delegation including the *na'ib al-qal'a*, the three *hajib*s, the four chief qadis, and Taqi al-Din ibn Qadi 'Ajlun to meet the crowd at the open space designated for the communal Eid prayers. The delegation met with the leaders of the riot, who presented the crowd's demands: abolishing the *mushahara* monthly market levy as well as extra levies on poor people (further *mukus*), and, more elusively, renouncing injustice. The delegation agreed to their demands and the crowd dispersed. Thus the aim of the riot changed from the first day to the last, at least according to Ibn Tulun's narrative; whereas earlier the crowd was mainly seeking revenge against government officials and Mamluks, including the *na'ib* himself and the *ustadar*, the negotiations that followed with the military and civilian elite of the town resulted in different demands, aimed at redressing the injustices rather than punishing the officials. The negotiations resolved some of the grievances and averted further unrest.[15] The mediation of the elite, including the ulama, was crucial in resolving the protest.

Notwithstanding the nature of the historical narrative of Ibn Tulun, readers can still discern that there was considerable organization behind this riot, there were leaders (though they remain unnamed here) with whom authorities could negotiate, and there were particular demands raised—and subsequently met. The involvement of the ulama in the negotiations was very important. There were ulama who occupied official positions, the chief qadis, as well as Taqi al-Din ibn Qadi 'Ajlun, who, though not an official, was a respected *'alim* and member of the community. His connections with the leading ulama and politicians of the time in Cairo confirm his clout and standing, even though he is not known to have occupied an official judicial position. The Awlad Qadi 'Ajlun, Taqi al-Din's brothers, sons, and cousins, were a large family of jurists and scholars who were renowned during the late Mamluk period and who seem to have been quite involved in urban affairs. Biographies of Taqi al-Din indicate that he had a traditional *'alim*'s education, occupied several teaching posts in Damascus, and was renowned for his fatwas. His son Najm al-Din Muhammad occupied the position of chief Shafi'i qadi of Damascus. Taqi al-Din's renown rested on both his scholarship and his position within the community; Najm al-Din al-Ghazzi comments, based largely on Ibn Tulun's chronicle, that people resorted to him to solve their problems and that he represented the welfare of the common people before rulers.[16] This helps elucidate how the urban community navigated this protest and utilized its social resources to find a satisfactory solution. The final resolution of the conflict suggests that there were certain perception of particular injustices shared among the rioters, reminiscent of the notion of a "moral economy" famously espoused by E.P. Thompson for early modern Europe.[17]

The strength of the alliance between the populace and the religious establishment is further manifested by the fact that it touched not only on the high-ranking ulama but also on lesser known, more modest ones, sometimes pious men known only within the contexts of their local neighborhoods. Indeed, religious figures enjoyed some prestige and an aura of respectability, even if they were of humble backgrounds, that allowed them to play roles in their communities. It was not only ulama of an official or senior standing who took part in the politics of the city; more humble figures, especially of Sufi inclinations, also participated. Years earlier, in 895/1490, also in Damascus, a riot broke out protesting the injustices of a tax collector. It started with the chanting of *takbir* (Allahu Akbar: God is Great) at the Umayyad Mosque in Damascus following the Friday prayers which were attended by a number of dignitaries, including the chief qadis, the *hajib al-hujjab* (grand chamberlain), the *amir al-hajj* (commander of the pilgrimage), and the viceroy's *khazindar* (treasurer), as well as the *muhtasib*.[18]

As the Damascene historian Ibn Tulun describes it, the crowds were first roused by a "pious man" from the neighborhood of Maydan al-Hasa called Yusuf al-Bahlul. He cried out in the name of Muslim righteousness against the *khassaki* Qarqamas, who was confiscating people's properties and assets. He was shortly supported by the followers of a certain Shaykh Faraj, apparently a popular Sufi shaykh. The group managed to rally more crowds to their cause, to the extent that the dignitaries present had to retire to chambers within the mosque, in fear of facing the "commoners" on the streets. Qarqamas himself had fled the scene early on and hid in his house. Later the grand chamberlain advised him to remove his precious possessions and take them to the citadel for safekeeping, to protect them from a possible break-in and impending arson. The crowds gathered again the following day, Saturday. This time Shaykh Ibrahim al-Naji was persuaded to ride out leading the crowds. They chanted "Allahu akbar" all the way from Maydan al-Hasa to the Umayyad Mosque, in a reversal of the previous day's march, and cried out slogans denouncing Qarqamas. The crowd then headed to the gates of Qarqamas's residence, which was close to the mosque, crying out *takbirat*. At this point the soldiers attacked the crowd, causing "a lot of evil," as Ibn Tulun put it.

The contemporary Damascene writer Ibn Tawq also mentions the riot and refers to the *takbirat*.[19] Although his account is briefer and less clear than Ibn Tulun's, it centers on the *takbir* against the *khassaki*. According to Ibn Tawq, Shaykh Faraj was arrested following the afternoon prayers and brought to the residence of the *khassaki*, who asked him whether he had chanted *takbirat* against him. Despite his denial, Shaykh Faraj received a beating of sixty blows. 'Isa al-Qari, a leading merchant, went over to the *khassaki*'s residence to intercede on Shaykh Faraj's behalf, but to no avail.[20] The following day, Saturday 11/Jumada II, people rose in rebellion against the *khassaki*, this time because of the treatment meted out to Shaykh Faraj; they chanted *takbirat* and "raised banners, Damascus was upside down, some people were killed, others wounded."[21] The raised banners could be the banners of Sufi *tariqas* indicating a procession in protest. In Ibn Tawq's narrative, the riot ended not coercively by the soldiers but diplomatically through the intercession of dignitaries, including the qadi, the *hajib*, the *amir al-hajj*, and 'Isa al-Qari, who calmed the people down.[22]

Despite the differences between the two accounts, what we know of this incident suggests that neighborhoods formed urban social networks, with some form of local leadership, possibly with a Sufi bent, that could be tapped in times of crisis. It is the people of Maydan al-Hasa and of al-Qubaybat who are specifically mentioned in the arrest decree.[23] On Saturday, the crowd led by Shaykh [Burhan al-Din] Ibrahim al-Naji headed out from Maydan al-Hasa to the Umayyad Mosque. When the decree first arrived calling for the arrest of those responsible in the incident, the soldiers sent to al-'Azqiya to carry out the arrest were wounded and returned empty-handed and humiliated. This suggests that neighborhoods and perhaps Sufi groups had their own armed gangs as well, or that at least the residents of neighborhoods had enough weapons to fight and intimidate a group of soldiers. Despite the authorities' use of coercion to put down the rebellion, the intercession by notables of the ulama to calm the crowds suggests the rebels did enjoy some leverage against the Mamluk officers and that the rebellion's resolution involved some negotiation. Not only the ulama, but the reference to the merchant 'Isa al-Qari, further alludes to a wider urban network with interconnected interests. This was no senseless mob. This is confirmed by the subsequent details: when a royal decree arrived soon after for the arrest of some of the participants in the riot, the soldiers who were sent to carry it out were attacked and defeated. When another decree arrived later, the qadis and senior state officials decided to ignore it—in effect, to disobey central authorities by not implementing a royal decree—for fear it would reignite *fitna* (civil strife).[24]

In the urban social networks that negotiated power, the ulama who were integrated in their neighborhoods played important roles. So too did merchants, as some of the examples show. Indeed, merchants in particular were more likely to rely on their networks of allies and partners in order to complain to authorities. This was not exclusive to the Syrian urban scene. After an attack by soldiers on markets in Cairo in Muharram 916/ April 1510, the merchants of the Ibn Tulun Mosque market and the Taht al-Rab' market complained to the sultan about the soldiers' behavior and described the damage and losses they incurred.[25] It is not clear whether the sultan compensated any of the merchants or whether the soldiers were made to return any of the loot, since Ibn Iyas remarks that "most" did not retrieve their stolen goods. However, the complaint itself illustrates the expectations the merchant community had of state authorities, suggesting that in some cases merchants might have been compensated for soldiers' unruly behavior, and indicates the responsibility the latter were expected to bear. Of course such attacks by soldiers, the new recruits or *julban*, are one of the issues that repeatedly challenged Mamluk sultans in the later period, especially by the fifteenth century. The system of recruitment changed considerably, allowing for older recruits and requiring, with the fiscal changes, a longer time for recruits to be fully integrated into the Mamluk system. The imbalance and competing demands for financial resources necessitated violence at times, and brought in society at large. This is how one of the major changes in the composition of the Mamluk army, and hence of the elite caste, was reflected on the streets in relations with the population.

The more successful negotiation attempts between authorities and urban networks were, not surprisingly, the ones resulting from collective complaints. Even though there are no clear indications of the formation of craft guilds in Egypt or Syria before the Ottoman period, there are reports of groups of craftsmen or tradesmen of the same trade coming together for collective action for a common cause. This suggests some form of organization and leadership, although it was most probably not a stable or institutionalized organization as would develop later. Thus, in a previously mentioned example, when Sultan Qaytbay imposed a levy of 40,000 dinars on the notable merchants of Cairo in Rajab 892/June 1487 to finance the army, they refused and negotiated the sum down to 12,000 dinars.[26] Again, in Dhu al-Qaʻda 894/October 1489, a delegation of merchants of Alexandria met with the sultan. They complained of the injustices they faced at the hands of the governor of their city, especially repeated confiscation of properties.[27] Ibn Iyas says that the sultan sent an official letter warning the governor to desist. We do not know whether the warning was heeded in this particular case. However, the reference suggests that merchants had access to the sultan, and while reports of court ceremonials assure us that symbolically his elevated position was uncontested, the actual negotiations that such delegations conducted with the sultan simultaneously reveal a more nuanced type of despotism. The Mamluk sultan was First Merchant perhaps, but he was, also, a merchant.

Not only merchants were capable of successful negotiations with Mamluk power. The complaints by Cairene shoemakers of 1471 about a forced purchase of leather led to tax relief, as previously discussed.[28] The riot that the shoemakers of al-Saliba staged was a way to make their complaint heard to Sultan Qaytbay. It resulted in negotiations that ultimately left them triumphant. In Ramadan 875/March 1471 Mamluk authorities forced a sale of leather at double its market value on the shoemakers of Bayn al-Qasrayn[29] and al-Saliba, both central market districts in Cairo close to the Citadel. It is important to note that this came at a time when Mamluk troops were preparing another expedition to fight Shah Suwar, the Dhu'l Qadrid prince. Such preparations placed additional burdens on certain craftsmen and tradesmen, many of whom were compelled to provide gear and commodities to the Mamluk army with delayed or no payment. The shoemakers of Bayn al-Qasrayn, as historian Ibn al-Sayrafi explains, weighed out their share of the leather, paid the money, and patiently endured the injustice, trusting in God's ultimate reward. The shoemakers of al-Saliba, on the other hand, proved more ingenious. They took the leather and promised to pay soon, perhaps to avoid direct confrontation with low-ranking officials. The following day they gathered together and went up to the Citadel to complain to the sultan, but the royal guards refused them entry and sent them back. This treatment is of course noticeably different from that accorded to senior and elite merchants. The shoemakers did not despair; they decided to gather on the mountaintop facing the Citadel, a place where they expected the sultan to be able to spot them while sitting in his courtyard holding his *mazalim* session. The group of shoemakers started crying out for help at the top of the hill. The tactic worked; Sultan Qaytbay noticed the commotion and investigated. Qaytbay directed his anger at his *wazir*, Ibn Gharib, who had ordered the *tarh*, which prompted the *dawadar*, Yashbak min Mahdi, to intervene and cancel the levy. The shoemakers were summoned to the *dawadar*'s residence and asked to return the leather.[30] This is one instance of a totally successful protest: not only did the shoemakers of al-Saliba negotiate the price of a forced sale of leather, they managed to avoid it completely. It is not clear what other mitigating circumstances helped those particular shoemakers get off the hook: did they have more ingrained interests with the royal court, perhaps? Months later (Jumada II 876/November 1471), (another?) group of shoemakers stopped the sultan on a processional ride back to the Citadel and presented him with a written complaint involving the same *wazir*, Ibn Gharib, who had raised their monthly dues from 400 dirhams *fulus* (a currency of account) to 3,000 dirhams *fulus*. The sultan ordered a return to the old rates, but Ibn Gharib only decreased them by half, to 1,500. The shoemakers complained again to the sultan and succeeded in having the monthly dues, the shoes tax *(maks al-akhfaf)*, abolished completely.[31]

Unfortunately the historians rarely give us the detailed information that we find, for example, in Ibn Tawq's or Ibn Tulun's accounts, that include the names of the individuals involved in a certain protest, often referring to them instead as groups. However, despite the usual failure to identify individuals, women sometimes appear in the sources as leaders of the negotiations with authorities. These narratives indicate other forms of protest beyond violent rioting; they sometimes involved negotiations, and often appealed to the sultan against other officials. The motif of the woman who stops a ruler or an official along his way in order to complain of an injustice she has suffered, usually a private injustice, is a recurring one in the sources. In some cases, the complaining women are representatives of a family or a network. It is conceivable that some women attempted to manipulate their protected status in society to their advantage. Carl F. Petry has argued on the basis of narrative sources and surviving *awqaf* documents that during the fifteenth century Mamluk women were used by the system as custodians of property.[32] Their higher life expectancy compared to Mamluk men and their relative immunity from the harsh liabilities men of their class suffered encouraged their role as guarantors of continuity in family structures and elite coalitions.[33] Thus women were often assigned as custodians over properties and endowments. While these women were not immune to a certain degree of confiscation, there are no references to Mamluk women suffering the recriminations that were so common among the men and which included total confiscation of property leading to destitution, imprisonment, torture, and, quite often, death.[34] The references to women presenting cases related to the rights and properties of their social network can be interpreted as an extension or manifestation of that role. By standing up to complain to an official in a public space undoubtedly dominated by men, the women were daring to enter into this domain and to use their assumed weakness to gain a benefit. In a way it was a manner of shaming the men in question by highlighting their failure to safeguard the rights of those whom they were in charge of protecting. It was also a way of stretching the customary rights of women to protection within a patriarchal system to gain benefits, thereby simultaneously negotiating their position within this system.

This tactic was used by women of various social standing, but the narratives almost always refer to individual women, not delegations. Thus we see the mothers and wives of imprisoned *amir*s and state officials intercede on their behalf, using the symbolism of their position to gain favor with a ruling sultan and secure the release of their men.[35] There are also examples of women further down the social scale who complained to sultans.[36]

In 876/1471, an unidentified woman, possibly of Mamluk background, stood up at the *mazalim* session in the Royal Stables to complain to Sultan Qaytbay. She and her siblings, she explained, had a stipend of forty *ardab*s of grain per year from a storehouse in Akhmim, in Upper Egypt, which in itself indicates something of their social status and connections to the Mamluk order. Yet for three years they had not been paid. The grand *dawadar*, then away in battle, was deemed responsible.[37] The sex and occupations of the woman's siblings are not indicated, but it is interesting that it is she, rather than any of the men in her household or social network, who represents her family's cause before the sultan. The possible challenge to the men's honor that is at play here is hinted at by the reaction of the *naqib al-jaysh*. Ibn Abi al-Faraj stood up and pulled off the woman's head cover. He walked down, possibly pulling her by the hair, among the rows of soldiers in attendance and pointed out the depravity of such embroidered head covers (*muqanzaʿ* and *saryaqus*) that had become fashionable. The sultan duly ordered the *wali* to have the town criers announce that women were prohibited from wearing such headwear. Women were frightened by this announcement, Ibn al-Sayrafi comments, and complied.[38] (In fact, we also learn that the sultan decreed that only a particular type of headwear, produced in the sultan's workshops, would be allowed.) It is interesting that this is the only reaction the historian recorded to the complaint. It is as though in reaction to her subtle attempt to shame the senior men of state for denying a woman her customary right (here, the yearly share of grain), the *naqib al-jaysh* upped the ante and attempted to shame her as a woman by declaring her dress immodest, thereby also confirming his patriarchal authority. The historian also falls into the distracting tactic of the *naqib al-jaysh* and fails to follow up on this narrative.

In 895/1490 another woman complained to Sultan Qaytbay of Badr al-Din ibn al-Qarafi, a deputy Maliki judge. Ibn Iyas reports that following several sessions between the qadi and the woman, the sultan ordered that the qadi be beaten and fined a considerable sum of money.[39]

Therefore, it was not that unusual for women to negotiate their rights within public space. Social historians of the Ottoman period who have studied the surviving court records extensively have remarked on how women appear quite independent in negotiating private legal matters such as divorce, alimony, and remarriage arrangements. Women resorted to qadis to demand payments due to them and to ensure fulfillment of favorable clauses they had inserted in their marriage contracts. That the character of the "argumentative woman," who has some knowledge of the legal regime and discourse, extended to negotiating power with the rulers does not, therefore, seem unlikely, even within a patriarchal social order.

Currency Devaluation

Protest as a form of negotiation is reported frequently in relation to issues of currency fluctuation. As discussed in previous chapters, the economic crises that the Mamluk rulers faced in the fifteenth century affected the supply of metals and coinage, and thus the authorities repeatedly devalued currencies. This disrupted markets and was also a frequent cause for protests. Some of the surviving reports offer us a nuanced understanding of how such a matter was translated on the streets and how power was practiced. While it would be anachronistic to speak of the development of 'public opinion' or a conceptualization of the 'economy,' some of the reports suggest that there were common and shared understandings of what fair prices and fair exchange rates should be, and that these were upheld to a certain extent. When they were threatened or transgressed, protest could be expected. This is not far removed from the concept of the "moral economy," coined by E.P. Thompson and used by historians of early modern Europe to explain protests against changes to customary rights. In the "moral economy" paradigm, riots did not occur simply because of scarcity or price rises, but were rather the consequence of sudden and suspicious price rises and shortages.[40] Pre-industrial crowds were informed by the belief that they were defending traditional rights or customs against a perceived injustice.[41] Indeed, this pattern of behavior in early modern European history is taken as evidence of a reforming rather than a revolutionary popular culture, in which protest was a method of complaining about a certain grievance rather than an attempt to subvert it or enforce an alternative policy.[42]

One of the main elements of the economic crisis that the Mamluk sultanate faced during the late fourteenth and fifteenth centuries was a shortage of bullion and cash, which resulted in the repeated devaluation of the currency. This crisis was reflected on the streets of Egypt and Syria— which were cash economies—especially in their cities, and resulted in considerable disruption in the markets. One of the recurring motifs in the literary sources is the minting of new coins and the protests and revolts that issued from repeated devaluation and debasement. In some cases merchants refused to trade and closed down their markets to protest changing currency rates, which they deemed unfair to their interests.[43] Often the negotiation process that followed allowed for a compromise.

As we saw in a previous example, when in 1481 crowds complained to Sultan Qaytbay about the currency, he ordered a meeting of senior men of state to be convened in the Salihiya Madrasa, in the heart of the city, to discuss this matter. The semi-public nature of the meeting is further emphasized by Ibn Iyas's report of how, in the middle of the deliberations, the common people pelted the *nazir al-khass* with stones when he suggested a certain compromise.[44] This suggests that the intermediate discussions were public enough to be followed somehow by the crowds, who intervened partway through, thereby affecting the final result. It also suggests that there were shared ideas among the urban population of what fair rates and fair prices should be, and that communities were at times able to collectively negotiate and bargain to enforce these ideas.

In 813/1410, a new exchange rate for copper *fulus* was met with wide opposition in Cairo and markets shut down, making bread and other foodstuffs unavailable. Sultan Faraj threatened to ride out and attack the common people by force, but his *amirs* dissuaded him and managed to convince him to first lower the new rate and then return to the old exchange rate.[45] In his account, al-Maqrizi regarded the new rates as the result of the sultan's greed for money—an attitude that many contemporary writers took toward Mamluk fiscal policies, but which we, with the benefit of hindsight, can question. Already unpopular and facing an insurgency since his enthronement, Sultan al-Nasir Faraj was not yet in a position to force his will on the markets or on the rest of the Mamluks, whom he desperately needed to maintain his position. Two years later, Faraj would once again face strong opposition when imposing a new copper exchange rate. On 16 Dhu al-Qaʿda 814/29 February 1412, when new exchange rates for copper coins were announced, a "disturbance" occurred in the markets and again the shops closed down. Bread was unavailable. The sultan was angry and "almost let his *julban* troops go down into the city to put the common people to the sword and burn the markets," but the *amirs*—once more—dissuaded him. Instead, some people were arrested and beaten. It is not clear who the scapegoats were, but most probably they were market traders. On the day following the disturbances a man was executed, and rumor had it that this was because of the copper issue.[46] However, public pressure worked in this instance: the old exchange rate was reinstated on 5 Dhu al-Hijja/19 March.[47]

Such examples reveal some of the machinations of politics and economics in Mamluk society. While they reveal the extent and importance of negotiation, even on the streets of the city, they also show the links between merchants and Mamluk officers. The protest described here featured the participation of both: we see the Mamluk *amirs* involving themselves in this particular devaluation and perhaps allying themselves with merchants in order to negotiate a more favorable exchange rate. The merchants' involvement in such economic policies meant that they were also involved in politics, albeit not in a formal or institutionalized manner.

In Damascus in Shawwal 885/December 1480, changes in the currency rates sparked protest all over the city; markets shut down and meat became scarce. Negotiations between the *na'ib al-qal'a* of Damascus and the qadi led to a revised exchange rate that was acceptable to the population.[48] Similarly, in 907/1502, when new coins were introduced, the markets of Cairo stopped trading until a favorable exchange rate was worked out.[49] When new coins were issued in 922/1516 in the last days of the Mamluk regime, Cairene markets were naturally destabilized; products had dual prices depending on the currency used. Markets shut down and bread was scarce.[50] Thus, rather than suffer by accepting royal decrees, merchant communities and the urban population at large resorted to various tactics in order to resist and negotiate state policies, including refusing to trade and shutting down markets. Similarly, negotiations took other forms, rather than senseless rioting by mobs.

A similar disturbance occurred in Cairo after the Ottoman conquest. In Ramadan 923/October 1517, when new coins introduced by the Ottomans initially disturbed the markets, shops closed down. When the *muhtasib* al-Zayni Barakat, who had previously occupied the same position under the Mamluks, tried to resolve the crisis through what would appear to be traditional methods—negotiating a new exchange rate that would be more acceptable to the public—the Ottomans rejected it and so markets closed down again. When rumors spread that the new viceroy, Khayir Bek, would punish some tradesmen by impaling them, markets immediately reopened out of fear, and trade continued at the imposed exchange rate.[51] Having just conquered Egypt, the Ottoman authorities were bound to want to impose their authority on their new subjects; the currency was—and remains—one of the most important symbols of sovereignty. Hence the manner in which this new, strong government dealt with currency fluctuations was firmer than previous Mamluk reactions. More importantly, the Ottoman empire in the sixteenth century was fiscally strong and Ottoman rule initially brought more fiscal stability to the provinces of Egypt and Syria.

Taxes and Levies: Paying Up, Evading, and Protesting

Most of the policies resorted to by Mamluk rulers to deal with their economic and financial crises were geared toward collecting cash and dividends. We saw this previously in references to the forced sales *(tarh)*, the sale of offices, and the compounded customs and market taxes. Taxes in premodern times in Arab-Muslim states were diversified and numerous. An individual urban dweller, depending on his occupation, would have paid taxes several times a year, to a variety of government officials and under a number of different rubrics. Different people, in different places and working in different crafts or trades, were taxed differently.[52] It was often unpredictable as well; in addition to annual and seasonal levies there were arbitrary ones. This division and distribution of the fiscal burden over time is one reason why protest was harder to organize; it was rare that a levy would be imposed on a whole town at the same time. However, people did protest extra levies, especially when the burden they imposed increased as the state's economic crisis deepened. In the process, officials who were charged with collecting extra levies were often the targets of protest. In addition to *muhtasib*s, other officials were also charged with collecting levies and were at times the target of popular protest. Thus members of the *khassakiya*, the Royal Guard, and agents of the sultan who were sent to Damascus to confiscate properties and levy taxes were often targets of protest.[53] Protesting tax collection by such senior officials suggests a certain daring on the part of the people of Damascus. More importantly, perhaps, it hints at a resentment of taxes being levied from Damascus to finance the royal treasury in Cairo.

Similarly, town criers who bore bad news, especially news of newly imposed taxes, were often the scapegoats for the state's decrees. In Damascus in 885/1480, when the state announced new currency exchange rates, crowds stoned the crier.[54] Other bearers of bad news faced similar fates: an announcer of new taxes was burned to death by the common people, also in Damascus, in 893/1488.[55]

Unlike the exchange rates, which were announced in public and were visible to urban dwellers (including our historians), taxes, levies, and extortions were diffused and less dramatic. It is therefore difficult to reconstruct how the various members of the community reacted to them, whether they acquiesced, circumvented, negotiated, or protested the levies. Occasionally the sources give us hints of the less confrontational forms that did not make headlines and so would not often appear in the chronicles.

Less confrontational forms of protest more likely included people further down the social scale, and involved less or unorganized resistance. James Scott has written extensively on what he termed "the weapons of the weak" in reference to everyday forms of resistance that fall short of collective outright defiance among peasant communities in Malaysia. Scott's anthropological observations provide insight for the historian as well, for many of the traditional forms of behavior among peasant communities, which Scott reads as types of resistance, can be imagined in other communities and in times past. Scott points out that while such weapons of the weak are unlikely to do more than marginally affect the various forms of exploitation that peasants confront, they are not trivial: they often have cumulative effects with broad implications. Desertion from and evasion of conscription and of corvée labor, he writes, have limited the imperial aspirations of rulers in Southeast Asia and in Europe. However, everyday resistance tends to steer away from public and symbolic goals. "Where institutionalized politics is formal, overt, concerned with systematic, de jure change, everyday resistance is informal, often covert, and concerned largely with immediate, de facto gains."[56] This makes it difficult to survey and catalog at a distance. As Stilt argues in her study of the *muhtasib*'s practical enforcement of law, common people—especially women and religious minorities—often resorted to passive resistance by refusing to comply with a *muhtasib*'s order.[57] Some even resorted to claiming madness in order to resist particular decrees or judgments.[58] In 841/1438, during the time of a plague epidemic, the Sultan, on the advice of some ulama, issued a decree forbidding women of all ages and classes from going out in public.[59] These ulama had argued that the plague was a divine punishment for improper behavior. Ibn Taghribirdi, who narrates this, implies that it was recognized as an excessive decree which caused grave injustices to many women in society. He also reports how the *muhtasib* faced resistance in implementing this decree:

During that time Daulat Khuja, the market inspector of Cairo, was following up the women and putting them under restraint by punishment and chastisement, until one day he seized a woman and was about to beat her, when from fear she went out of her mind and was in a hopeless state; she was carried home insane, and continued so for months.[60]

It is likely that the woman feigned insanity in order to avoid a punishment by the muhtasib. We can surmise that passive resistance was more frequent in practice but less often recorded than direct attacks on officials.

Tax evasion is sometimes alluded to in literary sources, but would be more readily traced through archival sources, which do not exist for medieval Egypt and Syria. The literary sources that occasionally hint at this sort of common practice include Ibn al-Sayrafi who reports in passing that in Muharram 874/July–August 1469 a group of grape vendors were beaten up for evading the grape tax. Another man who worked for them was also beaten because he helped a man flee from the authorities.[61] There is nothing unusual about the narrative, which suggests that it was common enough. As with other types of evasion, it is impossible through the surviving sources to estimate how effective it was: how much profit could vendors make by evading taxes, for example? How effective were corporal punishments, such as beating, in keeping vendors from evading taxes? Can evasions be construed as a method of negotiating dues to the state? By simply not paying some of the *mukus* (the additional taxes, levies, and customs duties, other than *zakat, jizya,* and *kharaj*) levied by state authorities, were tradesmen in effect negotiating with financial authorities? It is worth noting that "abolishing the *mukus*" is one of the virtuous deeds that good sultans are reported to have performed in the literary sources, which confirms that they were not perceived as "legitimate" by the general population and which would in turn explain attempts to evade them.[62] The famous contemporary scholar Jalal al-Din al-Suyuti even penned a short treatise against the *mukus,* in which he collected all the Hadith condemning it and promised eternal damnation to all officials who levied them[63]—this despite various legal rationalizations of such levies that allowed rulers to continue using them. Indeed, al-Maqrizi claims that *mukus* had increased by his period and that Coptic officials in particular were the ones who unjustly benefited from them.[64]

These extra taxes varied widely in nature. For example, in an incident dating to 876/1471 (discussed in chapter 2), Qaytbay issued a decree specifying a certain type of long headwear for women to wear in public, one which included a royal stamp on both sides. Such a stamp would be the emblem of the sultan's textile workshops, meaning that the decree would result in an indirect form of taxation: by making those head covers the only acceptable ones to wear in public, the sultan was in essence taxing women's clothes or, alternatively, monopolizing a type of textile. Women who did not obey were publicly punished and humiliated, as we saw happen to the woman in the sultan's court. The decree was effective for a while, due to repeated public announcements, but women soon ignored it and reverted to their usual attire, as Ibn Iyas reports—a form of passive resistance perhaps.[65] Besides trespassing upon matters of taste and personal preference, the royal headwear was also an attempt to monopolize a particular product—a typical economic policy of the fifteenth century. As with other forms of evasion, it is almost impossible to evaluate whether such actions had a cumulative effect on Mamluk economics. Was the power of the state curtailed by such acts? Were attempts by Mamluk sultans to manipulate the economy and control the necessary fiscal resources sabotaged by such evasion? What about state power: how was it affected by such acts if they were frequent? Scott points out that "the success of de facto resistance is often directly proportional to the symbolic conformity with which it is masked. Open insubordination in almost any context will provoke a more rapid and ferocious response than an insubordination that may be as pervasive but never ventures to contest the formal definitions of hierarchy and power."[66] Could such acts of evasion have been frequent enough to contribute to the diffusion of state power in late Mamluk times?

Injustices and Perceived Corruption of Officials

We have discussed in previous chapters the challenges that Mamluk sultans and rulers faced and some of the ways in which they responded to these challenges. These policies spurred reactions on the streets, especially in important cities. That is, frequent irregular taxation and levies, sales of offices, and bribery were not meekly accepted by all among the subject populations. Certain government officials were occasionally targeted for censure or attack, and the reports that survive of these incidents show that some logic is discernible behind the protest. Mamluk officers, tax collectors, or agents of the sultan were sometimes targeted by rebelling crowds. And while during the Mamluk period, ulama and qadis were rarely the target of protest themselves, this occasionally occurred in cases when they occupied the public office of the *muhtasib*—a position that attracted frequent attacks because of the *muhtasib*'s role in the market and involvement in the grain economy. So in 828/1435, during a period of bread shortage, crowds in Cairo rose up against the *muhtasib*, the qadi and historian Badr al-Din al-ʿAyni, who fled to the Citadel for fear of being stoned. (Indeed, Ibn Taghribirdi confirms that he was in fact stoned.[67])The sultan ordered his troops to put down the riot by force.[68] In 894/1489, the Hanbali qadi Shihab al-Din Ahmad al-Shini (later to be appointed chief Hanbali qadi) was attacked for issuing a fatwa permitting the state to collect two months' rent on certain properties. The common people of Cairo rioted against him and set out to kill him, but he managed to hide and later fled to Mecca.[69] A century or so later, in 999/1591, when extra taxes were levied at a time of grain shortage, the people of Damascus attacked the chief qadi. The riot occurred after special prayers for rain convened by the authorities.[70] The congregating of a large crowd and the presence of the ruling authorities and notables of the city thus provided an opportunity for the general population to voice its grievances. In all those narratives, the rioting targets particular state officials deemed responsible for particular injustices.

Even though attacks on *muhtasib*s were not infrequent, other reports show that this was not haphazard and was usually connected to a certain understanding of how the markets were working—or not, as the case may be. Protests did not occur only because of additional burdens imposed on the markets, as an episode in Cairo in 877/1472 illustrates. On 3 Rabiʿ I/8 August crowds stopped Sultan Qaytbay at Bayn al-Qasrayn, a busy market, and al-Rumayla, beneath the Citadel, to ask him to appoint a *muhtasib*. They complained that since the post had been vacant, they had suffered at the hands of traders who were selling their commodities at higher prices and cheating in the weights they used. The quality of bread in particular, they complained, had deteriorated. The sultan ordered an investigation into the state of bread and appointed an acting *muhtasib*.[71] Ibn al-Sayrafi explains that raw materials were readily available on the market at reasonable prices; there was no excuse for the tradesmen's cheating. The urban population was aware of that and of the need to have proper supervision over the markets.

We saw how in 895/1490 the riot which occurred in Damascus to protest the confiscation of properties carried out by the *khassaki* Qarqamas threatened to turn violent, so that the official had to flee the crowds to save his life, but the riot continued the following day.[72] In 902/1497, at the beginning of Qansuh al-Ghawri's reign, when another *khassaki*, Tanam al-Jardun, was sent to Damascus to tax the *awqaf*, the people of the city denounced him from atop the minarets of the Umayyad and other mosques, rallying a crowd.[73] While such methods of fund raising by the Mamluk administration were essentially directed at specific groups, merchants and ulama for example, they were expected to affect wider sectors of the population with whom the merchants and ulama were allied and connected, which explains the popular protest. Furthermore, merchants and ulama were well placed with significant social networks in their cities, which could be rallied in times of need.

Indeed, while mediation and negotiation were common enough, they were, understandably, not guaranteed. It is still difficult to determine when a protest could lead to negotiation and when it would have led to violence. The threat of violence is always palpable in any form of protest, or else it would be completely impotent. But it is more likely that even though the fifteenth century in particular was a time of transition, during the reigns of long-ruling sultans, in which a modicum of stability was established, the repertoire of protest by the non-elite allowed for more room to negotiate power and ameliorate some of its burdens. By contrast, there are periods of time, including interregnums, in which the balance of power was not stable and coercion was more apparent. Even during the more stable reigns of Barquq or Qaytbay, we find instances when certain red lines were crossed, especially in provincial cities, and where either the crowds resorted to excessive violence or the 'authorities' put down the protest by considerable coercion.

This might explain the trouble in Damascus during the early years of Jaqmaq's reign. In Ramadan 843/February 1440, a riot broke out in Damascus against its *na'ib* Julban because he had granted his *bardadar* (bailiff), 'Ubayd ibn al-Aq'ad, a monopoly over the slaughter and sale of fresh meat. There are various, complementary reports on the riots, each highlighting different aspects. In Ibn Shahin al-Zahiri's account, the common people had earlier complained to the *na'ib* of the suffering this policy had caused them, as it increased the price of meat. Julban ignored them, so they waited until he went out in a procession and attacked him and his companions. He fled through Bab al-Jabiya to Bab al-Nasr until he reached his headquarters in Dar al-Sa'ada, with the crowd in pursuit. The *na'ib* managed to hide inside his residence but the crowd headed to his *tablkhana* (storehouse of the equipment of the military band), wreaking havoc and kicking the drums and equipment with their shoes. The noise was loud enough to attract more crowds to the riot. They were about to set fire to the place when the *amir*s and qadis interfered and calmed the rioters down by offering to write a formal complaint to Cairo, explaining the crowd's grievances to the sultan. The complaint did not go down well with Sultan Jaqmaq, however. He was extremely angered at the news of the riot and insisted on punishing the people of Damascus. A royal decree was sent to Damascus and proclaimed from the pulpit of the Umayyad Mosque: it threatened the common people with harsh measures if they did not comply with the sultan's orders, thereby also confirming the authority of Julban. In al-'Ayni's account Julban had ordered cattle traders from the village of Qabun to supply him with three hundred Damascene *ratl*s of meat every day, on the understanding that they would be paid later, after he sold the meat. The merchants first responded by cutting off the meat supply to Damascus for three days, which caused much furor in the city. This paved the way for the riot that eventually took place.[74] In this case, the complaints, rioting, and negotiation did not result in a successful resolution, and the sultan was able to force his will and maintain control of the meat market.

In many historical reports of attacks on officials, the desire for retribution is what permeates the narratives, concealing other demands that the crowds might have called for. People did not rebel simply because new levies were imposed, but because these burdens were perceived to be excessive. It is the perception and awareness of injustice that more often led to protest. In a famous attack in Damascus in the late fourteenth century, an angry crowd killed the administrator and broker Ibn al-Nashu for hoarding grain.[75] Similarly, in 843/1439–40, also in Damascus, the crowd raided the governor's residence and attacked his Mamluks. The reason was that he had forced merchants bringing sheep to the city to sell to them at a price below their market value, promising to excuse them from taxes. When he later failed to keep his promise, the merchants reacted by cutting off the meat supply, which in turn angered the people of the city and led them to go and punish the governor themselves.[76] In Jumada II 880/October 1475 a riot broke out in Damascus protesting additional levies imposed by the sultan's agent, Burhan al-Din al-Nabulsi. As Ibn Iyas described it, al-Nabulsi's policies were perceived to have exceeded the limit.

> In Jumada II news arrived from Damascus that Burhan al-Din al-Nabulsi, the sultan's agent, when he had entered Damascus, had committed evil deeds against the people of Damascus. They could not bear that and rebelled against him, stoned him, threw arrows at him, burned down his house, and attempted to murder him. The *na'ib al-qal'a* rode out in person to intercede with the common people until the *fitna* cooled down somewhat. Damascus had almost gone to ruin in these incidents, all because of the injustices of al-Nabulsi. He had exploited the people.[77]

In such violent attacks on senior officials, no direct demand was requested by the crowds, not even the removal of the targeted official; instead, it was retribution that was the goal.

Food Shortage and Protest

Despite the ubiquity of urban protest in the late medieval period, and despite the economic crises and challenges that characterized the period, it is noticeable that food shortages that resulted from natural disasters are not reported to have automatically led to violent protests.[78] That is, low Niles and bad harvests in themselves did not invariably lead to urban protest. Protest is reported when governments failed to manage an impending crisis, and when middlemen and state officials were known to have been profiting from the crisis at the expense of the population or were refraining from carrying out their duties of providing for the general population. It was expected that sultans and *amir*s would open up their grain stores and sell grain at market or fair price during a crisis, or even distribute grain freely to the poor. In 819/1416 when prices were exceptionally high, al-Mu'ayyad Shaykh ordered *amir*s to sell grain from their stores.[79] There are several historical examples of former rulers having done that in al-Maqrizi's treatise *Ighathat al-umma*. Studying grain riots of the fourteenth and fifteenth century reveals that common people had certain assumptions about what economic roles authorities should play.[80] Since the system of *iqta'* allowed the sultans, Mamluk *amir*s, and senior officials to control and amass large quantities of grain, they came to be the chief grain suppliers for urban markets.[81] Therefore, there was some sense in holding them responsible for manipulation of the grain market, especially in years of dearth. Furthermore, there was a paternalistic trend in the Mamluk system, whereby sultans were expected to provide for the populations. When unjust manipulation was suspected, riots were likely to arise.

Therefore, when in 892/1487 the price of grain increased, and the size of a loaf of bread shrank and it was hard to find on the market, a Damascus crowd stoned the *muhtasib*, 'Abd al-Qadir. They considered him responsible for the scarcity of bread because he was also a miller and a baker, was involved in the grain trade, and on top of it he collected the monthly *mushahara* levy from each trade in the market.[82] Thus, not only was 'Abd al-Qadir not fulfilling his duty of providing grain and foodstuffs at fair prices on the market, he was also perceived to be unfairly profiting from the crisis. The profit he made was perceived as immoral. This necessitated his punishment, from the point of view of the crowd.

George Rudé has observed a similar trend in English and French eighteenth-century pre-industrial protest where "bad, or even abysmal, economic conditions were not an automatic 'trigger' to disturbance."[83] He observed that in England strikes and trade-union activity tended to occur on the upswing of a boom and not at the moments of the deepest trade depression. Food riots, though the direct product of bad harvest and trade depression, rising prices and shortages of stocks, did not necessarily occur at the peak of a cycle of rising prices; instead, they tended to arise as a result of a "sudden sharp upward movement leading to shortage and panic buying."[84] It was the political background that gave the economic crises greater intensity—a nuance that is palpable in Egyptian and Syrian protest as well.

Another reason why the grain riots might not have been as automatic as expected lies in the ways in which Mamluk authorities dealt with shortage in times of real dearth. Despite their control and manipulation of the market, and even attempts at monopolizing the grain trade as did Sultan Barsbay, rulers were careful to satisfy the market. They did not allow grain crises to escalate too far so that crowds would be driven to pillage and plunder the grain reserves of the *amir*s or the sultans. They tacitly accepted that there were fair or just prices that ought to be maintained. When this was transgressed, protests were a check that indicated this and urged a different policy. In a way, then, the grain riots were a mechanism by which crowds made their opinions known but also participated in defining and maintaining just grain prices. In fact, Shoshan correlates the increasing frequency of grain riots after 1350 to two main factors which relate to the structural transformations we have been discussing throughout the book. The first is the effects of the plague, and the high mortality it caused, on the grain market. The second is the long-term waves of inflation that hit Egypt throughout the fifteenth century, from 1400 to 1420 and from the mid-fifteenth century to 1517.[85] These were not sporadic outbursts, then. Protest could be perceived as a way of navigating during a time of deep structural transformation.

Mamluks Protesting

Not only the urban crowds and the marginalized, but by the fifteenth century, Mamluk soldiers also joined the ranks of those raising their voices, and their arms, against sultans. In the context of the changing composition of the Mamluk army and the financial challenges that the rulers faced, soldiers repeatedly rose in violent revolt and mutinied. These repeated riots by the soldiers are indicative of the structural changes that the Mamluks armies were undergoing, but they also had repercussions on urban society.

Military mutinies were a part of urban politics. The Mamluk regime was a military regime the majority of whose soldiers were garrisoned in cities; hence any unrest on the part of the soldiery had an impact on the urban population. Despite the sensitivities of the market community to frequent troop rioting and the perils this entailed, sometimes they were not careful enough. While the historical literature is replete with incidents of how rumors of an impending troop revolt led markets to shut down in anticipation, sometimes the markets were taken by surprise. Soldiers' mutinies were a recurrent theme in records of Cairene life, less so in Damascus or Aleppo, for the obvious reason that Cairo was the seat of the sultanate and its Citadel and *tibaq*s housed a host of various and necessarily competing Mamluk factions. Factional wars that took place in Syria were in essence mutinies that aspired to reach the throne in Cairo. It is exclusively the mutiny of soldiers that our historians referred to as *fitna*, which in itself reflects their attitude toward it and suggests that the danger it caused was thought to be the worst. Naturally, a riot by armed soldiers could indeed be more violent than what unarmed masses could threaten. While soldiers' mutinies, frequent as they were, often resulted from the struggles for power among the various Mamluk factions, they were sometimes caused by the economic and financial crises of the regime, thereby reflecting a general crisis that affected the population at large. Furthermore, soldiers' mutinies in their ultimate stages, when they fulfilled their threat, spilled out onto the streets, resulting in direct confrontation with the civilian population.

The most notorious of the regiments were the new recruits, the *julban*. They were particularly troublesome and difficult to control during Sultan Qaytbay's reign as he continued to recruit more new troops in an attempt to bolster his own power vis-à-vis his Mamluk rivals and to fight his recurring skirmishes with the Ottomans.[86] Although a number of historians portray the *julban* as an unruly group repeatedly blackmailing the sultans for more money, several of the incidents they report reveal the intricacies of the Mamluk payment system and its ties to the economy at large. When the regime faced financial crises, it often failed to pay its troops for months on end. Without money, the troops could not buy the necessary food and fodder from the markets, which both affected the market and spurred their rebellion.

The problem of the recruits was acute during parts of Qaytbay's reign. During the 1480s, the Mamluk armies fought several wars in Anatolia in order to defend their areas of control and influence against Turcomans and Ottoman allies. The presence of the troops for prolonged periods of time on the borders had several consequences, including internal destabilization, as

Bedouin tribes, especially in Upper Egypt, found opportunities to reassert their authority. Stretched internally and externally, the sultan was pressed to recruit ever more troops on a continuing basis.[87] This is perhaps one of the reasons why the assimilation of the new troops into the Mamluk system was not immediate nor satisfactory, and why they lacked the discipline of earlier generations of Mamluks. Furthermore, the increase in prices that was to become an important feature of the times meant that their pay was devalued. This was often a cause for their rioting and pillaging.

In 891/1486, a rise in the prices of meat, bread, cheese, and other commodities spurred a rebellion of the *julban*. They attacked the *muhta-sib*'s house and pillaged grain stores. The city was in sufficient disarray to require Sultan Qaytbay to ride down to Bulaq to quell the revolt in person. The *muhtasib* seems to have borne the brunt of the disturbance and to have seriously feared for his life, because his father, who was the *katib al-sirr* at the time, interceded with the sultan on his behalf to relieve him from this duty.[88] In 1489 the dissatisfaction of the recruits was so high that Qaytbay himself made a show of abdicating.[89]

The next sultan, Qansuh al-Ghawri, was able to stand up against troop revolts in the early years of his reign. However, starting from 1511, the state was once more under pressure for resources. Threatened by the European expansion in the Indian Ocean and the Red Sea, and by the Safavid movement in the east, Qansuh al-Ghawri tried to meet the military challenge by fortifying the shores, building forts, and establishing a new corps, the Fifth Corps, which was recruited from outside the Mamluk system. This necessarily required more funds, and Qaytbay was notorious for the ways in which he squeezed levies out of various sectors of the population, including the civilian elite.[90] Despite this, there were delays in paying the troops. With the delays, the rioting intensified.[91]

Ibn Iyas writes that in Muharram 916/April 1510 the *julban* rebelled against Qansuh al-Ghawri, demanding a stipend of 100 dinars per soldier. The cause of their rebellion, he briefly mentions, was related to an interruption in the meat supply and a delay in their meat rations. Ibn Iyas's explanation for the rebellion is ambiguous: "because of al-Mu'allim 'Ali al-Saghir, for he was in prison."[92] He had mentioned earlier, under the events of the previous month (Dhu al-Hijja 915/March 1510), that the sultan had arrested al-Mu'allim 'Ali al-Saghir, one of the meat suppliers, and ordered him to pay 60,000 dinars.[93] Ibn Iyas has only good things to say about this man, whom he describes as a man of morality and charity, and does not explain whether he was being punished for embezzlement or some other misdeed or whether money was being extorted from him, as frequently happened to senior officials.[94] It is also unclear what spurred the meat shortage; demand for meat traditionally increases in Dhu al-Hijja, the month of the Feast of the Sacrifice. It was a time when the sultan traditionally bestowed gifts of meat on his senior advisers, officers, and soldiers.[95] For some reason, meat supplies failed to meet the demand that year. It was perhaps a shortage in meat supplies that led the sultan to cancel some of the customary royal gifts to agents of the state and scholars that year.[96] On the other hand, the tight measures might have been due to financial rather than supply reasons. Yet it is not clear what responsibility—if any—the meat supplier, Mu'allim 'Ali, bore in all this.

The rebelling soldiers first headed to a number of senior Mamluk *amir*s and officers of the State and forced them to ride up to the Citadel and present their demands to the sultan. The Mamluk delegation met with the sultan but he adamantly rejected their demands and almost removed himself from the sultanate, writes Ibn Iyas.

When the sultan refused the soldiers' demand for a stipend of 100 dinars each, they descended from the Citadel and attacked markets and pillaged shops. The rebellious troops attacked the markets of Ibn Tulun, al-Saliba, Taht al-Rab', and al-Bastiyyin. The rebellion lasted three days in all; it escalated to the point that the rebelling soldiers prevented Mamluks from riding out in the city. Markets closed down. The rebels refused to obey the sultan's order to parade in the Citadel. On the third day they went out to Azbakiya, in their full arms, and attempted to declare the *amir* Dawlatbay, the *amir silah*, the new sultan. The *wali* and Tumanbay, who was the *dawadar* at the time, put down the revolt by force and returned some of the stolen goods to their owners. In their turn, the merchants of the Ibn Tulun mosque market and Taht al-Rab' submitted a complaint to the sultan, who ordered al-Zayni Barakat ibn Musa, the *muhtasib*, to go down and investigate. 570 shops were reportedly pillaged in this rebellion and most merchants did not retrieve their goods, worth around 20,000 dinars. Finally, Ibn Iyas mentions that the *nazir al-dawla* was dismissed because of the scarcity of meat that was behind this *fitna*.[97]

Ibn Iyas does not explain here whether the scarcity of meat was something that affected the whole urban population. That the rebels demanded a stipend rather than meat rations might suggest that meat was to be had in the market if money were available, that the real crisis was one of cash flow and funding the army rather than meat supply. However, the sultan's failure to control his recruits left its mark on the city.

A troop rebellion in 921/1515, on the eve of the downfall of the regime, further reveals the links between the livelihood of soldiers and urban society at large. The revolting troops did not demand extra pay but asked the sultan to abolish the levies of *mujama'a* and *mushahara* imposed on market traders, which increased prices "until we can no longer find something to eat."[98] They demanded that he pay them their meat stipends and stop injustices and confiscations of people's properties. They also demanded that he dismiss the *muhtasib* al-Zayni Barakat ibn Musa, the *wazir* Yusuf al-Badri, and the *wali* Kartbay. The soldiers stoned the sultan himself, prevented him from entering the courtyard, and insulted him. Some descended from the Citadel with the intention of looting the houses of *amir*s, but were dissuaded by their colleagues and attacked shops in al-Saliba instead, looting candles, sweets, and bread. The same demands were repeated by the *aghawat* of the *tibaq*. The sultan succumbed to their demands and they confirmed their allegiance to him. However, later he announced that all charges would remain the same.[99] Clearly, despite the hardships these measures caused for both soldiers and common people, and despite the violence of the protests against them, the regime could not come up with alternative policies.

Conclusion

This discussion shows how prevalent protest in various forms was in late medieval Egypt and Syria, and especially during the fifteenth century. It was not unusual, and it seems to have been one of the more common ways in which power came to be redistributed and continuously negotiated—at least in the urban centers. This does not mean that protest was always successful, or that crowds always had their demands fulfilled. In the riot against al-'Ayni in 828/1425, the crowd was quelled by force.[100] The delegation from Mahalla that complained to the sultan of the injustices they suffered at the hands of their *kashif* in 875/1471 were beaten and sent off after failing to provide sufficient proof of injustice.[101] In Rajab 919/September 1513, when a crowd complained to Sultan Qansuh al-Ghawri about the exchange rates of newly minted coins as he rode through the city, the sultan was hardly sympathetic to their plight; his reaction to the protest by his undeserving subjects was to reinstate extra legal taxes, including monthly levies collected by the *muhtasib* as well as taxes on grain and watermelon estimated at 2,000 dinars a month, which he had abolished during his recent illness.[102] During the meat riot in Damascus in 843/1440, the negotiation on the part of the qadis and *amir*s did not lead to the abolition of the monopoly on meat.[103] It simply ended the riot by carrying the complaint to the sultan, Jaqmaq, who did not sympathize with the grievances of the crowd and threatened to put their necks to the sword if they complained again. While historians do not report that any one was actually punished after these riots, it is not unlikely. We know that at least the Shafi'i chief qadi lost his job because of it.

Similarly, the state appears to have stood firm following the grain riots in Damascus in 892/1487. While Ibn Tulun does not report any specific punishments meted out to the crowds who stoned the *muhtasib*, his account indicates that the market strike that followed the riot was ended by coercion rather than negotiation.[104] The government forced shopkeepers to open their shops and stores and sell their grain by force, or else face execution.[105] When the chief silk weavers of the various neighborhoods in Damascus protested in 897/1491 against a newly imposed tax on each loom, the *na'ib* refused to come to their aid and instead changed the tax to a lump sum of 1500 dirhams to be divided among the various *hara*s (neighborhoods) (and presumably further divided among the craftsmen of each *hara*).[106] In 904/1499, when some people from the Damascus neighborhood of al-Qubaybat gathered to collectively complain to the viceroy, during a procession, of a forced sale of camels he imposed on them, the viceroy had the protesters beaten in his presence and then demanded higher sums of money than originally decreed.[107]

Historians did not always report suppression. Therefore, it is left to our imagination to wonder whether in certain cases the state actively suppressed a protest or simply let the crowds vent their anger by demonstrating and shouting slogans or by offering a minor official as a scapegoat. In Damascus in 885/1480, when the state announced new currency exchange rates, crowds stoned the announcer.[108] Ibn Tulun, who reports the incident, does not offer any further details. Unlike other instances, he does not report a negotiation over the exchange rates. Similarly, when crowds chanted "Allahu akbar" from the Umayyad Mosque, protesting a ruling by Sibay, the grand *hajib*, in which he ordered the beating of a man from Madina, no reaction from the authorities is reported.[109]

However, despite the ubiquity of protest, and despite its frequent suppression by force, the data that are available in surviving sources, and the nature of those sources themselves, do not allow us to judge the extent to which the protests affected or aided the downfall of the Mamluk regime. What we can deduce, however, is that the power of the Mamluk rulers was increasingly diffused and that the newly opened space was filled by various newcomers, that the beginnings of a different political scene and urban politics are discernible, indeed that we can speak of urban politics. The fact that protest often paved the way to negotiation suggests that certain repertoires of power sharing had developed and that the participation of the non-elite had come to be ingrained in the way power was practiced by the late Mamluk regime. As we have seen in a number of the examples cited, the final resolution of the conflicts suggests that there were certain perceptions of particular injustices shared among the rioters, reminiscent of the notion of a "moral economy" posited by E.P. Thompson for early modern Europe. This in turn also hints at some form of public opinion in the cities. It shows a vibrant social and political landscape that did not exclude the majority of the population. It shows that at times of deep economic, social, and political transformation, the non-elite were not excluded from the changes their societies were facing. They were very much a part of it, and their roles in the equations of power were potentially changing.

6

PROTEST AND THE MEDIEVAL
SOCIAL IMAGINATION

While protesting against economic burdens and injustices was one way of
ameliorating and negotiating a way out of difficult circumstances, protest
also reveals more nuanced articulations of how the late medieval societies
of Egypt and Syria, especially in their urban centers, imagined the ideal
social order. Some of the surviving narratives about protests allow us to see
ways in which members of the community, including the non-elite, imagined what the ideal social order should be and how they acted to create it
or re-establish it. In some cases, the protests could be understood as ways
by which members of society sought to maintain or restore what they considered traditional rights in a changing world. In other cases, they can be
understood as subversive acts of resistance, which might have had a low ceil-
ing but which nevertheless expressed a form of political participation and
awareness. Protest was also at times manipulated and channeled by those in
authority, to allow for vents that would relieve social pressure. The fact that
this kind of maneuvering was quite common during the late Mamluk period
is testament to the delicate balances both rulers and ruled were negotiating.

Protesting to Maintain Traditions in a Changing Society

Most of the examples cited so far relate to economic concerns: extra levies
and taxes, monopolization, devaluation of the currency. But some of the
most violent protests in medieval urban centers reported by medieval

historians occurred around what we may tentatively label as issues of law and order, public morality, and sectarian strife. These protests in general could be understood as attempts to preserve an established social order, traditions, and customary privileges, in the face of the deep social changes and transformations discussed in chapter three. On the face of it, it seems that moral issues themselves were frequently cause for the population to rise up in protest. Yet it is not always clear why these issues caused protest *when* they did. Presumably alcohol and hashish were to be found on any given day in Cairo or Damascus; what might have differed is the degree to which their consumption was flaunted in public. In a number of reports for Cairo and, even more so, Damascus, the destruction of alcohol and/or hashish by pious, often Sufi, Muslims, as part of their duty to command right and forbid wrong, provided opportunities for direct confrontation with the authorities, especially when these substances were being consumed by Mamluks and soldiers. Construed as a blatant violation of Muslim codes, it might have been a cause for protest guaranteed to garner considerable support on the streets. It also had the potential of embarrassing the ruling authorities by questioning their commitment to upholding Islamic sharia and consequently their right to obedience from the population. The destruction of alcohol is quite literally the textbook example in discussions of *hisba*.[1]

It is important here to remember the function of the duty of *hisba* and its place within the social and cultural paradigm of medieval Muslim societies. Parallel to the duty of obedience *(ta'a)* to God, the Prophet, and those in authority, the *individual* Muslim has a duty "to command right and forbid wrong"—*hisba*. Jurists tried to regulate and restrict the practice of this duty, more commonly by limiting it to government-assigned personnel except in obvious cases that might not require judicial process or reasoning. Understandably, it is the second part of the formula of *hisba*, namely forbidding wrong rather than commanding right, that has the greater potential for confrontation. As al-Mawardi (d. 450/1058) explains it, the individual Muslim, not appointed by the state to practice *hisba*, is not to seek out evil in order to forbid it, is not obligated to come to the aid of whoever asks him to forbid wrong, and is not to exercise his *ijtihad* where matters of *'urf* (or customary practice) rather than sharia are concerned.[2]

Similarly, in his *hisba* manual Ibn al-Ukhuwwa (d. 729/1329) stresses that laymen can only practice *hisba* in blatant, obvious cases that do not require any practice of reasoning or *ijtihad* on their part.[3] Even in such blatant cases the layman in question could only forbid a present ongoing wrong, but did not have the right to punish the offender for an offense already committed or prevent future offenses; these, he stresses, are the prerogatives of rulers, not of subjects.[4] This severely restricts a layman's mandate.

Despite such regulations and restrictions, *hisba* remained a duty incumbent upon the individual Muslim, provided he had the capabilities for it. Ibn Qayyim al-Jawziya (d. 751/1350), for example, insists that it is incumbent only upon the Muslim who has the necessary capabilities; otherwise it becomes a *fard kifaya*, a duty the community in general had to provide for.[5] Likewise Ibn Taymiya (d. 728/1328) did not consider *hisba* a duty incumbent upon every individual Muslim, but rather "a collective duty . . . incumbent upon every human being according to his capacity."[6] Capability would refer to both power and authority. In a sense most jurists maintained a contradictory stance on *hisba*, one that maintained the individual's duty to redress wrongs but made allowance for public order at the same time. Thus, as Ibn Taymiya argued, the *muhtasib*[7] has to weigh the pros and the cons of his deed to determine where the greater good and welfare of the community lies; *hisba* is not permissible if it will unleash a greater evil than the wrong committed.[8]

The canonical text on *hisba*, and the inspiration behind more traditional manuals such as Ibn al-Ukhuwwa's, was al-Ghazali's *Kitab al-hisba*, part of his seminal work *Ihya' 'ulum al-din*. Al-Ghazzali took issue with al-Mawardi's restrictions, in effect arguing for a widening of the scope of *hisba*. Al-Ghazali logically refuted the prevailing views of the ulama of his time regarding restrictions on the practice of *hisba*. Thus he argued against restricting this right exclusively to individuals appointed by the ruler.[9] In essence this means that the state (and its employees) is not the only authority with the mandate to command and forbid; competent adult Muslims could also practice *hisba*, presumably on state officials as well. It is also interesting that al-Ghazali insists on preserving the right of the sinning Muslim (*fasiq*) to practice *hisba*. While he does acknowledge that the forbidding of wrong might not in practice be heeded from someone who is himself a sinner, he argues, that the sinfulness of the *muhtasib* does not alter the evilness of the deed of the (second) sinner. Hence, even a sinning Muslim, the worst imaginable Muslim, has a right and a duty to practice *hisba*. *Hisba* then is not a duty that could be denied an individual Muslim. This legitimizes the *hisba* practiced by laymen who are not part of the religious establishment. It is the circumstances surrounding the deed that dictate the appropriate behavior in response to it, not the identity of the evildoer or the *muhtasib*.

Scholars identify different degrees of *hisba*. Understandably, most of the discussion of the "commanding of right and forbidding of evil" has focused on the "forbidding" part, which could provide more opportunities for challenge, violence, and disorder. The theory distinguishes among various methods of practicing *hisba*, especially forbidding wrong, which vary in degree: an evil may be changed by the hand, or by the tongue, or by the heart. The distinction is based on a Prophetic Hadith:

> He who amongst you sees something abominable should modify it with the help of his hand; and if he has not strength enough to do it, then he should do it with his tongue; and if he has not strength enough to do it, (even) then he should (abhor it) from his heart, and that is the least of faith.[10]

The decision as to which form of *hisba* to employ against a given offense remained largely at the discretion of the *muhtasib*. To be taken into account are not only the severity of the evil act but also the power and authority of the *muhtasib* and his limitations. It is this discourse, however, that is behind the morality campaigns that often turned into sectarian riots in our sources.

Ibn Khaldun was more straightforward in rejecting the morality campaigns against vice with which we are familiar from the historical sources and which were probably the most common practice of non-state *hisba* during the Middle Ages. As part of his discussion of *da'wa*, or religious propaganda, Ibn Khaldun stressed the imperative need for *'asabiya*, or group solidarity and support. Regardless of the righteousness of a deed, it is the degree of force available to uphold it that matters. Even prophecy

requires *'asabiya*. Ibn Khaldun is therefore quite critical of private persons
who attempt to impose a religious order.

> Every mass political undertaking by necessity requires group feel-
> ing. . . . To this chapter belong cases of revolutionaries from among the
> common people and of jurists who undertake to reform (evil) practices.
> Many religious people who follow the way of religion come to revolt
> against unjust *amirs*. They call for a change in, and prohibition of, evil
> (practices) and for good practices. They hope for a divine reward for
> what they do. They gain many followers and sympathizers among the
> great mass of the people, but they risk being killed, and most of them
> actually do perish in consequence of their activities as sinners and unre-
> warded, because God had not destined them for such (activities they
> undertake). He commands such activities to be undertaken only where
> there exists the power to bring them to a successful conclusion.[11]

Ibn Khaldun then cites the famous "hand, tongue, and heart" Hadith to
confirm his point: a Muslim should change such evil with his hand only if
he has the power to do so.

Regardless of the disapproving tone of jurists like Ibn Khaldun, a tone
he shared with the established ulama of his time as the historical evidence
shows, many religious men continued to try to forbid wrongs and overturn perceived evils. Recurrent campaigns against vice typically centered
on destroying drinking houses, alcohol, and hashish.

In the late medieval narrative, as the sources tell us, often a pious man,
a Sufi shaykh or even an *'alim*, would lead a group of followers on a campaign to destroy alcohol and narcotics. Ibn Tulun reports a number of
such instances in Damascus. In Jumada I 885/July 1480 a crowd gathered at the Umayyad Mosque to protest against the toleration of drinking
places.[12] In other cases, these campaigns seem to have enjoyed some form
of official sanction. They might have provided opportunities to members
of the ruling classes to attack their rivals and/or gain popularity with the
population, confirming their legitimacy. They were also a mechanism for
deflecting any criticism away from the rulers and their caste. For example,
Ibn Tulun reports that on 24 Dhu al-Hijja 885/24 February 1481, after

the Friday prayers, Shaykh Taqi al-Din Ibn Qadi ʿAjlun, accompanied by the grand *hajib* Yashbak al-ʿAlay and other shaykhs and Sufis *("wa ghayrihim min al-fuqara'")*, went out to destroy alcohol and other forbidden items. They destroyed a large quantity of alcohol, including a drinking house next to the residence of the *amir* Qarqamas al-Tanami, a *muqaddim*, by the al-Asadiya Madrasa in Harat al-Qasr.[13] In this instance the campaigners had the support of certain factions of the ruling authorities, embodied in the grand *hajib*. Whether it was a factional conflict that urged the campaign to begin with remains open to speculation, but it definitely was an occasion for the authorities to gain popularity and improve their public image. The report stands out because it also mentions a leader of the caliber of Ibn Qadi ʿAjlun, whereas the more established ulama usually kept their distance from this kind of populist attack.

Also in Damascus, in Muharram 890/February 1485, the followers of Shaykh ʿAbd al-Qadir al-Kilani encountered people selling hashish publicly. They seized it and burned it. The shaykh was arrested and asked to pay for the hashish that his followers had taken the liberty of destroying—a common ruling in such cases. He was released on bail and went to the mosque of al-Qasab in the morning and cried out for help. A crowd must have gathered. The group appealed to the Shafiʿi qadi for help, but to no avail. As representatives of the legal establishment, qadis were unlikely to support laymen taking the law into their own hands and practicing *hisba* themselves. The shaykh's supporters and the crowds entered the Umayyad Mosque before prayers, chanting *takbirat* and carrying banners.[14] After prayers the riot developed to denounce the Shafiʿi qadi Ibn al-Muzlaq, who fled to his home. The *na'ib*, meanwhile, was afraid to pray at the Umayyad Mosque because of the crowd and prayed in the Tankaz mosque instead. The following Friday, 18 Muharram, Shaykh Siraj al-Din alluded in his sermon to the riot of the previous week; its crux was that corrupt people are left free to do as they wish.[15] Ibn Tulun concludes his concise version of the incident by mentioning that the *na'ib* appeased people by supporting them in their quest to command good and forbid evil.[16] In such narratives there are very oblique hints of the politics at play behind some of the acts of protest, hints that what appears on the surface is not the whole story.

Later, in 899/1494, a similar confrontation ended more violently. When two Sufi shaykhs went about forbidding the sale of alcohol, they were imprisoned and a crowd stormed into the prison to release them. A violent confrontation ensued with the viceroy's Mamluks, leaving 150 dead.[17] Thus morality campaigns could result in damage that, in the eyes of some, far outweighed their benefits. This explains the attitudes of contemporary scholars such as Ibn Khaldun who were adamantly opposed to such exercises. This intellectual position obviously influenced the Shafi'i judge Ibn Muzlaq as well. And while occasionally state agents were lenient in allowing or even prodding some groups to practice this type of *hisba*, the violent crackdown that more often ensued indicates they recognized the social and political threats such acts carried. Unlike riots that demanded the repeal of particular taxes, or reconsideration of exchange rates, violent acts of forbidding wrong left little room for negotiation. They did, however, award the rioters a certain moral high ground. During times of deep changes and social anxiety, holding onto traditional norms and values gained added importance, and fit in with the conservative outlook of some of the mainstream ulama of the time.

Crowds also occasionally gathered to take the law into their own hands or protest the administration of justice, particularly rulings by police or qadis. We have already discussed the diffusion of power during late Mamluk times in the context of the multiplicity of state actors who carried out judicial functions. Another aspect of this diffusion of power is that urban crowds also occasionally carried out justice. Thus in Safar 889/March 1484, common people called out from the minaret of the Umayyad Mosque against the *hajib al-hujjab* in Damascus, Sibay, because he had unjustly beaten a man from Madina.[18] In Muharram 887/February 1482, the common people of Aleppo attacked their viceroy because one of his employees had murdered a man. The crowd got the accused man out of prison, killed him, and stoned the viceroy, thereby taking justice into their own hands.[19]

A more serious riot erupted in Damascus in 910/1504 when the temporary *na'ib* executed a young man of the *ashraf* (notables who traced their lineage back to the Prophet Muhammad), the son of al-Sayyid Ahmad al-Sawwaf, allegedly without due cause. Crowds rioted and attacked the neighborhood of Harat al-'Abid, killing many of its people and pillaging their houses and other houses close to the residence of the *na'ib al-ghayba* (who was also the *hajib*).[20]

In Dhu al-Hijja 911/May 1506, around the days of the annual pilgrimage and greater feast, the people of the Damascus neighborhood of al-Qubaybat and others marched to the Umayyad Mosque, chanting the name of God and carrying banners; again the reference to the banners might indicate the participation of members of Sufi *tariqa*s. They went up the minaret of the mosque and shouted *takbirat* denouncing the *mutassalim* (who was away from the city at the time, along with the *hajib*) because of the collective fines they imposed on neighborhoods as punishment for murders. They demanded that individual criminals be punished for their crimes. The *na'ib al-qal'a* and the second *hajib* agreed to their demands and released those who had been imprisoned, presumably in connection with the crimes and fines in question.[21]

Thus when a perception prevailed within the city that state officials were not judging rightly, common people took it upon themselves to right the wrongs. These were cases that involved crimes and were usually referred to the police and state officials, and not to the qadis. This dynamic is evident in both Egyptian and Syrian cities, including the capital, Cairo.

Restrictions on Non-Muslims and Sectarian Violence

Similarly, sectarian violence was not infrequent in the Mamluk period, which was often perceived, especially in Egypt, as a period of social transition in which non-Muslims were clearly becoming a numerical minority in society.[22] The fourteenth and fifteenth centuries seem to have witnessed increased pressures on Egypt's Coptic community and were decisive in the community's history, as many members of its elite reportedly converted to Islam at this time.[23] The pressures that the non-Muslims, especially the Coptic community of Egypt, faced are considerable, and have been the focus of a number of studies, including Tamer El-Leithy's dissertation on Coptic conversions.[24] Our general understanding by now is that this was a time of pressure on the community, and that the Mamluk period in general was one in which conversion accelerated.[25] The changing demographics are reflected in some reports of sectarian violence. The delicate, sometimes ambiguous roles of the authorities highlight the challenges. This transition, along with the ongoing economic and social transformations of the period and the political pressures during the reigns of particular sultans, created increasing opportunities for sectarian strife and resistance, which sometimes took the form of urban rioting. The rioting and protests could be understood as attempts by some Muslim members of the community to preserve what they perceived to be their traditional privileges and customary rights, including the "right" to confirm their hegemony over non-Muslim members of the population. In that vein, it is related to the practice of *hisba* as well, to forbidding or undoing a perceived wrong.

The idea that non-Muslims living under Muslim rule should be humbled and subjugated dates back to the Arab conquests of the seventh century. As conquerors, the Arabs were the only Muslims in the societies of the Middle East, and many of the treaties and agreements that were reached with the conquered populations confirmed their authority and hegemony. They were partly meant to distinguish between rulers and ruled, Muslims and non-Muslims, and curtail assimilation.[26] These ideas are at the heart of the famous rules referred to as the Pact of 'Umar, *al-shurut al-'Umariya*. While these rules developed in the context of a post-conquest society, they came to be included in the corpus of Islamic law. They resurfaced and gained renewed importance in the Middle Ages, at a different historical moment and when Muslims had become the majority of the population in most provinces and were no longer vulnerable. Despite this differing social context, the ideas inherent in the Pact of 'Umar remained traditional and customary regulations that were expected to be upheld by Muslim rulers. Failure to do so was a cause for protest. Some scholars have argued that the warfare and military threats of the Middle Ages, especially the Crusades but also the Mongol invasions, provided a pretext for the resurfacing of the Pact of 'Umar (as well as for anti-Christian propaganda in general).[27] It is also conceivable that the deep social transformations, including the waves of Coptic conversions (themselves at least partly a result of subjugation and pressure), that we have been discussing also prompted a backlash that aimed at preserving customary order in a changing society. Furthermore, the recurrent epidemics of plague prompted a heightened sense of religiosity and zeal, part of which was expressed in trying to uphold God's law, including the restrictions on non-Muslims that were part of the Pact of 'Umar and that were perceived as *shar'i*. Failure to do so was considered by some to be a cause for the plague. As Stilt explains, by acting on visible issues such as enforcing dress codes on Christians and Jews (or indeed prohibiting women from going out in public), the ruling authorities could assure the public that all measures to stop the spread of the plague were indeed being taken, while simultaneously implying that the rulers themselves were not responsible for any wrongdoing that could possibly induce divine wrath.[28] It was a tactic that helped deflect criticism or responsibility away from the rulers.

Thus, specific discriminatory restrictions regulating the behavior of non-Muslim subjects were repeatedly reinstated throughout the fourteenth and fifteenth centuries. It is not clear whether enforcing them had always been the duty of the publicly appointed *muhtasib*. While regulating the behavior of non-Muslims is not listed in the texts of the sultans' appointments of *muhtasib*s, it does appear in *hisba* manuals. Indeed, medieval *hisba* manuals include a number of restrictions and conditions not included in the classical Pact of 'Umar.[29] In the spirit of the Pact of 'Umar, restrictions were meant to both distinguish and subjugate non-Muslims and to assure that Muslims were given social privileges and special stature. Naturally, they were not accepted easily. Thus, Christians and Jews were prohibited from riding certain animals—even the less prestigious donkeys—within cities that had been the garrison towns of Arab-Muslim conquerors; they were to move on foot. They were to wear small turbans and cloaks with narrow sleeves. In public baths they were to wear bells around their necks. Christian women were to wear blue cloaks, while Jewish women were to wear yellow cloaks.[30] Al-Maqrizi reports that on 8 Sha'ban 820/20 September 1417, after hearing a case against a Copt, the assembled *fuqaha'* and the *ustadar* Fakhr al-Din 'Abd al-Ghani ibn Abi al-Faraj discussed the contemporary behavior of Christians in general. They ordered an announcement prohibiting Copts from wearing turbans and headwear that was similar to those of Muslims, or robes with wide sleeves similar to those of Muslim qadis, riding horses, and employing Muslims in their service.[31] It is in this context, in which the restrictions were revived and sometimes upheld by those in authority, that some sectarian riots occurred. These riots were therefore part of the reaction and consequence to the social transformations taking place at the time.

In Rabi' I 822/April 1419, al-Maqrizi reports that the *muhtasib* and *wali* of Cairo reinstated restrictions on *dhimmi*s.[32] This particular year was a year of plague in Cairo and the provinces of Egypt. Al-Maqrizi writes of the large number of dead registered in the *diwan* and of extraordinary measures taken to come to terms with the epidemic, including collective prayers led by the sultan and the senior ulama at the outskirts of Cairo and generous almsgiving and sacrificial meat distributed by the sultan. In times of epidemics a general perception prevailed that the plague was a form of divine punishment for deviating from the straight path.[33] During the morality campaign of 822/1419, the sultan ordered the *muhtasib* and the *wali* to eradicate vice, including destroying alcohol and preventing women from lamenting the dead. It is in this context that the mandate extended to enforcing customary restrictions on the public behavior of non-Muslims.[34] In this difficult year of 822/1419, circumstances combined to lead to a riot against foreigners in Alexandria.[35]

The plague induced a commitment to command right and forbid wrong, hence the zeal of the *muhtasib* in enforcing customary regulations. The revival of restrictions on *dhimmi*s could be read within this context, an attempt by an alien political order to assure the population of its religiosity and legitimacy during a time of crisis. The legitimacy of the Mamluk officers as good Muslim rulers had remained questionable, a point that led many rulers and sultans to overcompensate by displaying their good Muslim credentials through a variety of means. Defending Muslim lands from foreign invasions, patronizing the religious establishment, and supporting religious learning institutions were some of these tactics; enforcing what were perceived to be *shar'i* regulations was another. What better way to enforce these than against the Other within, namely non-Muslim subjects?

During the fourteenth and fifteenth centuries, several decrees were issued banning *dhimmi*s from working in the bureaucracy. Modern historians have argued that various official and scholarly pressures led many Coptic bureaucrats to convert to Islam during the fourteenth century in particular. However, the fact that the decrees were repeated again during the fifteenth century suggests that the bureaucratic establishment continued to employ Copts for at least two generations after the initial bans, and consequently that some Copts continued to find ways to circumvent the restrictions. On 8 Jumada I 825/30 April 1422, a decree was issued prohibiting Jews and Christians from serving in the *diwan*s of the sultans and *amir*s.[36] The year 825/1422 was not particularly stable either, and the decree came in the very early months of Sultan Barsbay's reign. Perhaps the administration of the newly installed sultan wanted to prove its credentials and bolster its legitimacy through such measures. Al-Maqrizi comments that this decree was not implemented; people found ways to ignore it. Although the reinforcements are mentioned repeatedly and at closer intervals during the fifteenth century, most historians relate them as traditional rules to which people had failed to adhere strictly.[37] The moral attitude that the writers themselves represented was in support of the restrictions, which confirmed a certain hierarchical order in society which was to their own benefit as guardians of the now hegemonic religion (most historians somehow belonged to the ulama class). Still, their narratives also suggest that individuals found ways to circumvent and ignore these restrictions.

In Rabi' II 843/September 1439 a sectarian riot broke out in the Egyptian coastal town of Damietta. Ibn Shahin al-Zahiri explains that it started with the death of a pious man from Damietta, Shaykh 'Abd al-Rahman, a man who was probably a Sufi and who had followed his uncle in leading a *zawiya* in the city. The members of the *zawiya* went out on a ship to fight the Franks off the Syrian coast. 'Abd al-Rahman and a group of other zealous fighters from the city died in battle. When news of their martyrdom arrived in Damietta, people flocked to 'Abd al-Rahman's home to pay condolences to his family. Rumor had it that a Christian resident of the city, Jirjis ibn Daw, was joyfully celebrating the news by holding a party in his house while the families were mourning. The historian explains that the man was already rumored to be spying for the Franks before this incident. A crowd attacked his house and brought him before the qadi, with enough evidence against him to warrant a death sentence (or so Ibn Shahin al-Zahiri reports, without giving any details of the evidence). However, the *na'ib* of Damietta, Muhammad ibn Ahmad ibn Salam, dissuaded the qadi from issuing the sentence right away. He warned him of the sultan's possible anger and urged him to imprison Jirjis until the sultan was consulted. According to rumor, Jirjis had even offered the *na'ib* a bribe. The crowd waited eagerly outside the qadi's quarters, expecting a death sentence. When they heard the verdict they rioted. Jirjis, fearing for his life, pronounced the Muslim *shahada* but the crowd did not pay much attention to his conversion: they killed him and burned his corpse. They then attacked the churches in the city. Ibn Salam reported the events to the sultan and tried to blame the people of the city for the events. The sultan was angered and sent a Mamluk *amir* with troops to punish them. Instead, the people of the city convinced the *amir* of their case. Ibn Salam was duly removed from office.[38]

Decades later, in 876/1472, a sectarian riot broke out in Cairo after a group of Christians from Giza murdered an *'alim* and Qur'an reciter whom they accused of encouraging their children to convert to Islam. At a time when communities were facing the pressure of conversion or dwindling numbers, such rumors would cause exaggerated alarm. The murderers, reportedly six, severely mutilated the corpse before attempting to dispose of it and failing.[39] Tensions were high in the city. The *wali* arrested the men in question and brought them before the *amir akhur kabir* (chief fodderer and supreme commander of the army), Janbak min Tatakh al-Faqih. Janbak's political faux pas was seemingly that he took his time, deciding against putting the men to the death right away and instead ordering their imprisonment until they could be brought before the sultan—the same decision Ibn Salam had made. Why Janbak decided to do that is not clear, but he was possibly trying to avert civil strife in the city by bringing such a heinous crime before the sultan. (Ibn al-Sayrafi begins his report by stating how horrible, strange, and rare such a crime was.) After all, the reigning sultan, Qaytbay, particularly enjoyed playing the judge,[40] and this was a crime that would attract public opinion and hence strengthen the sultan's legitimacy. It was possibly the prudent choice to make if Janbak also feared public disorder as a result of a death sentence. Rumors were apparently faster than the Mamluk judicial machine: crowds gathered below the Citadel and intercepted the accused men before they reached the prison. They were stoned to death. Only one of the accused was saved; he managed to utter the *shahada* during the riot and was duly removed and taken to prison.[41] Ibn al-Sayrafi does not relate many details. We do not know what information reached the common people—for example, whether they assumed that the murderers might get off with imprisonment and avoid the death sentence.

Understandably, the state was quite averse to such instances where crowds of common people would take the law into their own hands. After the 876/1472 incident in Cairo the Mamluks complained to the sultan that such behavior on the part of the common people should not be accepted: they were "killing with their own hands, holding the reins of the royal Mamluks and ruling for themselves."[42] The sultan ordered the *wali* to send out a crier announcing that no one was to rule for himself or "hold back the reins of [the horse of] a Mamluk."[43]

The two reports have remarkably a lot in common, despite the differences in time and place. Both involve sectarian tensions between pious, most probably Sufi, groups and Christians. In both cases the rioting crowd would not accept anything less than an immediate death sentence. In both cases the governors decided to wait. This raises the question of how frequently such instances recurred in cities and whether a repertoire of behavior had been established, so that when governors failed to follow a custom of applying the death sentence immediately, the rioters took the law into their own hands. This might be one of the thin red lines that separated obedience from protest in medieval cities.

The fact that the restrictions against non-Muslims were repeatedly reinstated throughout the late Middle Ages suggests that these communities often resisted the law through various means. In Rabi' I 822/April 1419, al-Maqrizi reports that when the *muhtasib* and the *wali* of Cairo reinstated restrictions on *dhimmi*s, only some people followed the old decrees, while others did not.[44] Two months later, the same decrees were repeated. In addition, non-Muslims were prohibited from working in government and Mamluk bureaus. Al-'Ayni explains that Christians refrained from riding their horses within the city but used to ride them once they got outside the city, while others, tired of the insults and humiliation, "pretended to convert to Islam" in order to be able to ride their horses and return to their jobs.[45] Similarly, al-Maqrizi writes that many *dhimmi*s tried to pay bribes in order to evade the restrictions, to no avail, while others converted to Islam, which allowed them privileges such as employing Muslims and riding horses.[46] Others refused to obey the decrees and protested by refusing to go to the public baths or to let their women go out to the markets, preferring to stay at home rather than go out in public in what they considered humiliating attire.[47] We can only begin to imagine the anxiety such decrees would have caused to the Coptic community, especially among its elite who served in the top bureaucratic positions. It is normal that they would try to circumvent such decrees by bribery, or, if that did not work, by succumbing to conversion.

Even some of the reported causes for protest inform us of methods used by the non-Muslim communities in order to resist the restrictions imposed on them. While increasing restrictions, including on employment opportunities, drove many Copts to convert to Islam during the late medieval period, many converts may have continued to practice their Christian faith in private. Restrictions on building new churches and synagogues were probably circumvented by holding prayers in converted residences, as an example from al-Sakhawi's *al-Tibr al-masbuk* demonstrates. In 846/1442 a complaint was filed with the Shafi'i Qadi against a group of Karaite Jews, accusing them of turning a house, Dar Ibn Samih at Harat Zuwayla, designated as a school and lodging for Jewish children, into a synagogue.[48] The legal deliberations all centered on this being a new establishment, which would be against the customary regulations imposed on non-Muslims, who were granted protection over their existing houses of worship but not allowed to build new establishments after the conquests. However, just as the legal proceedings throw light on the discriminatory tactics imposed by the state and members of society, they also allow us to glimpse the maneuvers that the urban population devised in order to circumvent these laws. By gaining approval for a primary school for children, the Karaite community was able to establish a place of worship in a central part of Cairo.

Furthermore, as Tamer El-Leithy has shown, many Copts manipulated Islamic sharia law itself in various ways in order to safeguard their interests—another form of resistance. Thus many resorted to single-generation conversion, whereby a convert's offspring remained Christian and were allowed to inherit directly from their grandparents.[49] Others resorted to legal ploys and exploited the differences between Muslim *madhahib* to their advantage.[50] Finally, others actively sought martyrdom by declaring themselves apostates and reverting to Christianity, thereby symbolically resisting the imposed order and defying Muslim hegemony.[51]

Just as a certain perceived social order that distinguished Muslims from non-Muslims was reinforced in times of crisis and occasionally upheld by protest, so too did distinctions between genders. The periodic morality campaigns that usually coincided with plague epidemics included restrictions on the behavior of women. Occasionally the sources allow us to imagine how urban women resisted these restrictions. In Dhu al-Hijja 822/January 1420, one of the moral decrees of the zealous *muhtasib* Ibn al-'Ajami prevented women from passing through the mosque of al-Hakim, the main mosque in Fustat. Men were ordered to take off their shoes when they went into or passed through the mosque, but women were banned completely.[52] Al-Maqrizi's report and Ibn al-'Ajami's decree suggest that the demarcation between the mosque and the surrounding market was rather blurred and that what bothered the *muhtasib* and morally upright public opinion was the association of men and women in this public space. The flip side of this decree is how common it was for men and women to associate in public on normal days, behavior attested in numerous sources.[53]

In Dhu al-Hijja 824/December 1421 a public decree was announced, forbidding women to go out to the cemeteries—a pre-Islamic custom. The *hajib*, Jaqmaq, was quite strict in applying it. Al-Maqrizi explains that large numbers of people had been falling ill that month and so women were going out in droves on Fridays, holding mourning gatherings at the cemeteries.[54] The decree was perhaps meant to control not only the public association of men and women, but also the anxiety and hysteria that pervaded the city. It was certainly an extraordinary measure, and one that must have been ignored soon after. Indeed, *ziyara*, visiting family

cemeteries and Sufi shrines, was one of the more important social practices in medieval Cairo. The Qarafa (the cemeteries to the east and south
of Cairo) played an extraordinary role in the social and moral economy
of the medieval Cairene urban space, providing opportunities for social
mixing between genders, classes, quarters, ethnic groups, and occupations
in a traditional society defined by complex social boundaries.⁵⁵ Less than
a year later, in Ramadan 825/September 1422, on the eve of the Lesser
Feast, women were again prohibited from going out to the cemeteries.
Al-Maqrizi comments that many women complied, which also suggests
that others did not.⁵⁶ It remained a custom until the twentieth century.

In Rajab 825/July 1422, the *muhtasib* forbade women, as was their
custom, from staying out on the streets and in shops to watch the procession of the *mahmal*, the palanquin carrying the *kiswa* (brocaded covering)
of the Ka'ba, which traditionally was at the start of the pilgrimage caravan
leaving for Mecca every year. According to custom, the women spent two
days and a night out on the streets. Al-Maqrizi, who disapproved of this
custom, reports that they soon returned to it.⁵⁷

In Ramadan 841/February–March 1438, during an outbreak of plague,
Sultan Barsbay consulted the ulama on the possible causes for it. Some
argued that the plague spread with adultery *(al-zina)*, and complained that
adultery was widespread in Cairo because women went out to the markets
in their fancy attire day and night. They advised that women, except the
old and women who had no one to care for them, be prevented from
leaving their homes. Policemen kept women off the streets, which, historians explain, caused immeasurable injustice to widows and craftswomen
who needed to support themselves. A few days later the restrictions were
relaxed; slave girls were allowed to go out to do shopping for their households, women were allowed to visit the public baths during the day, and
elderly women were allowed to go out and attend to their business.⁵⁸ In
some neighborhoods of the city, women might have ignored the decree.
In others, however, it seems to have been implemented by force. When a
month later, in Shawwal 841/March–April 1438—that is, a few weeks after
the decree was issued—a woman's son died of plague, she was kept back
from joining his funeral, out of fear of the sultan's troops. The woman
went up to the rooftop of her house to watch the procession pass by,

but then threw herself off the roof. Another woman was actually arrested when she joined her son's funeral.[59] However, since historians also refer to the disruption this caused to the markets, it is also probable that some form of protest was expressed.

The modern historian can only guess, but it is unlikely that such decrees were fully enforced for long. Yet they betray the fear and anxiety that drove rulers to issue such drastic measures to begin with. The fact that similar decrees were reissued three years later, in 844/1440, indicates that state authorities were not always vigilant in applying these orders and that people often ignored them.[60] As we have seen, in 876/1471, Qaytbay issued a decree specifying a certain type of long headwear for women to wear in public, one which included a royal stamp on both sides. Women who did not obey were publicly punished and humiliated. The decree was effective for a while, due to repeated public announcements, but women soon ignored it and reverted to their usual attire.[61] Compliance was probably associated with times of crisis, after which the decrees were forgotten by all. In general, however, vice campaigns often spurred clashes with sectors of the urban population. The repeated announcement of such decrees relating to public morality suggests that their implementation was short-lived and that the people found ways to circumvent them.

Crowds did not only interfere to impose customary rights, or to protest injustices; occasionally they also gathered to call for certain legal outcomes in particular cases. In some cases the crowd did not—and could not—seek to punish the perpetrators of evil but instead brought the grievance before the ruling authorities. In 875/1470, a crowd of people from Bulaq, Cairo, marched into the headquarters of the *dawadar* protesting the abuse of a girl from their neighborhood at the hands of a soldier to whom she had been married. Ibn al-Sayrafi, who reports this case, was also involved in the marriage proceedings of the girl to the soldier. However, perhaps because of his involvement, his account of the events is rather sketchy.[62] The facts he tells us are these: an "ugly" child of twelve *(dhamima min jihat al-hay'a)* was abandoned by her parents who left the city. She was destitute and appealed to the Hanafi qadi to find her a suitable match to save her from "begging." Ibn al-Sayrafi, the deputy qadi in charge, nominated three suitors. A Mamluk soldier was chosen from

among them and a marriage contract was concluded.[63] Ibn al-Sayrafi stip-
ulated that the man should not consummate the marriage, presumably
because the girl was a prepubescent minor. The chronology of what happened next is not clear. The soldier did consummate the marriage against
the stipulations of the contract. His Mamluk master may also have raped
her.[64] The husband filed a complaint against her with some *naqib*s and she
was fined a dinar. He then divorced her and, it would seem, coerced her
to forfeit the marriage gift he owed her by having her maternal aunt write
him a promissory note for seven dinars, perhaps in return for the divorce
settlement. At this point, the girl's maternal aunt rallied the people of
their neighborhood to the girl's cause. The people of Bulaq gathered,
carried the young girl, and headed for the residence of the *dawadar*. The
dawadar summoned both the husband and his patron, a member of the
royal Mamluks called Faris, had the soldier flogged one hundred times,
and ordered that he be paraded through the city as an example to anyone
who rapes girls *(yaftah al-banat)*. He was also ordered to pay the girl four
dinars. Only then does Ibn al-Sayrafi, who wholeheartedly approved of
the *dawadar*'s ruling, say that the soldier was essentially a thug. He explains
that both the soldier and his master had caused innumerable offenses to
the people of their neighborhood, Harat Baha' al-Din Qaraqush.[65]

This case has been analyzed by Petry, who read it as evidence of the
prerogatives of the military elite, which took precedence over conjugal
rights.[66] For Petry, the *dawawar*'s final ruling was a compromise that
restored only some of the rights of the girl (four dinars out of a liabil-
ity of eight) and left her eligible for another marriage, while punishing
the husband and his patron but allowing them, as members of the ruling
caste, to walk free.[67] However, this does not give sufficient attention to
the roles played by the other characters, namely the girl's maternal aunt
and the people of Bulaq. When the sharia courts could not offer justice,
the aunt resorted to an age-old tactic: she raised a riot in order to attract
the attention of the ruling authorities to what was perceived as a blatant injustice committed by a member of the military class: imagine the
Bulaq crowd marching to the *dawadar* carrying the girl. Could the people
involved have had other previous grudges against this soldier, which they
now had an opportunity to finally avenge? Ibn al-Sayrafi's comment that

"there was a clamor for her in the city" suggests that her case did garner considerable public support. Whether this was due to the case at hand alone or to other grievances the crowd shared with the girl and her aunt, or indeed whether it resonated with general grudges against the military class, remains a mystery.[68] On the face of it, a crime against a child of their own quarter and the financial burden it placed on her (the reader will recall that the marriage was pursued in order to provide for her in the first place) was enough of a motive to cause the people of Bulaq to riot. The force of the crowd in saving the fate of this girl and restoring some of her rights is unmistakable. Regardless of their motives, the image Ibn al-Sayrafi draws of a crowd carrying a girl and marching into the *dawadar*'s headquarters to complain about a member of the military throws light on the ways in which the common people suffered from the military system and the ways in which they resisted its injustices.

Protesting against Rulers and Middle Officials

Despite, or perhaps because of, the prevalence of protest, rulers had devised mechanisms to channel such anger and dissent. When the anger was directed at middle officials, it could be allowed to escalate into violence. Thus protesting directly to Qaytbay or later to Qansuh al-Ghuri was one thing; protesting to and against his subordinates was another. It is therefore not surprising that *muhtasib*s and agents were often the target of stoning in the Mamluk period, a fate that shifted to qadis later on in the Ottoman period. Sultans, on the other hand, were considered above the fray, the judges of last resort. This channeling of protest was also one way that crowds attempted to right perceived wrongs, by punishing the persons they deemed responsible for particular injustices and by taking the law into their own hands at times.

We have seen how *muhtasib*s often bore the brunt of popular dissatisfaction, as happened with al-'Ayni in 828/1435.[69] The function of the post of *muhtasib* underwent a gradual transformation during the late Mamluk period, one that brought to the fore the administrative and financial duties of the *muhtasib* at the expense of the responsibility for regulating public morality.[70] The interference of *muhtasib*s in the economy became deeper and more arbitrary. This transformation is related to the state's attempt to extract more revenues from a shrinking economy; it is part of the general transformation in the practice of power that we have been discussing.[71] A *muhtasib*'s duties included supplying the main urban centers with food and controlling the prices of the main commodities as much as possible, a function that complemented the Mamluk rulers' expanding monopolies. Thus, it is perhaps understandable that the occupants of the post would be the target of public and scholarly censure. Indeed, a striking pattern that emerges from the chronicles of the period is the relatively short tenure of *muhtasib*s during most of the late Mamluk period, averaging three to six months at times.[72] It is only during the final decade of the sultanate that the exceptional *muhtasib* al-Zayni Barakat ibn Musa occupied the post for a longer period of time.[73] The short tenure of *muhtasib*s reflects the instability of the post and the pressures, both official and popular, exerted on the occupant. Some scholars blamed "corruption" and the growing interference of military officers for this instability.[74] Yet as we discussed, the instability itself could also be understood as arising out of the challenges that the Mamluks faced and their attempts to make ends meet. In the process, the functions of rule and governing were changing.

The increasing role of the *muhtasib*s in collecting revenues for the state provided lucrative opportunities for amassing wealth, a situation which the state authorities were quite aware of. They ensured that appointees paid the state a considerable sum on their appointment[75] and periodically confiscated their properties, as they did with other middle-ranking and senior employees. The *hisba* was subject to sale, as were other posts discussed previously. The pressure the state imposed on its servants was translated into pressure on the markets. In Rajab 823/July 1420, when Sarim al-Din Ibrahim ibn al-wazir Nasir al-Din Muhammad ibn al-Husam al-Saqri was appointed to the *hisba* of Cairo, he was asked to pay the treasury a thousand dinars, which, al-Maqrizi commented, he would duly collect from the tradesmen.[76]

The intricacies of the post and its relationship to the common people are elucidated by al-Zahir Tatar's decree in 824/1421. While in Damascus the sultan canceled the annual dues of 1500 dinars that the *muhtasib* of Damascus was obliged to pay the *na'ib* and compensated the *na'ib* for the loss of revenue. This was meant to relieve the common people of the pressures of the *muhtasib*'s levies. In fact, the sultan ordered the town criers to announce that should the *muhtasib* ask them for (extra) levies they should stone him! This decree, posted on the walls of the Umayyad Mosque, throws light on the system. It shows that popular punishment of unjust officials was not only expected but also sanctioned or channeled in some manner; common people often acted as checks on the system of government through their protest. It also shows that rulers and senior officials occasionally deflected blame onto less senior employees, who became scapegoats.

During the Mamluk period, the *muhtasib*s were also deemed responsible for the grain supply. It was therefore a sensitive post to occupy, even if a potentially lucrative one. As Sabra and others have pointed out, the common people, unlike the Mamluk elite and state officials who were paid stipends in kind, had to buy their grain and foodstuffs from the market. During times of food shortages, when the poor failed to draw the attention of the state to their plight by other means, they resorted to disturbances such as direct physical attacks on *muhtasib*s.[77]

In 818/1415–16 the Nile was slow to rise, which caused panic on the market, a grain crisis, and eventually a grain shortage. According to al-Maqrizi the overall circumstances were also difficult; everything that could possibly go wrong did. The low Nile led to a low harvest, rats attacked grain stores, the Bedouin in Buheira rebelled, and troops went out to fight them, destroying more grain reserves in the process. Furthermore, troops went out to Upper Egypt during harvest time and plundered without arresting the rebelling Bedouin, who continued to threaten various provinces.[78] It was also a year of plague. Al-Maqrizi's account states that with the sultan in Syria fighting insurgents, local officials took advantage of the crisis to achieve personal gains. Instead of opening state stores of grain to the public, grain was hoarded; prices of grain and fodder continued to rise.[79] People clamored for bread at bakeries and opposition to the *muhtasib* was brewing, so much so that he feared for his life and asked to be removed from office. His replacement failed to relieve the crisis and soon resigned. Bread continued to be so scarce that people started queuing for it from midnight; men and women walked to the banks of the Nile and spent nights there awaiting grain-laden boats from the provinces.[80] The behavior of both *muhtasib*s confirms their fear of the crowd's anger, particularly in difficult times. Though outright protest is not reported during that crisis, al-Maqrizi's account shows both the perils and opportunities that the job of the *muhtasib* entailed.

Al-'Ayni's own testimony confirms this. When offered the position of *muhtasib* of Cairo by al-Mu'ayyad Shaykh in 819/1416, he at first demurred, arguing: "O master, these are strange times and the *hisba* is difficult these days; for the people of this city, especially its commoners and its market people, ascribe everything that relates to commodities and prices to the *muhtasib*, especially bread."[81] And indeed, as previously mentioned, al-'Ayni himself was attacked during one of his tenures as *muhtasib* of Cairo during a bread shortage.[82]

On 29 Rajab 853/17 September 1449, another *muhtasib* of Cairo, 'Ali ibn Iskandar, was stoned by an angry crowd.[83] Much later, in Rabi' II 894/March 1489, some people presented a written complaint to the sultan accusing the *muhtasib*, Kasbay, of neglecting his duties, leading to an increase in prices.[84] The same dynamics occurred in Syrian cities.[85]

However, as argued earlier, because of the divided nature of premodern taxes, the officials who were related to the process were numerous, making the targets of popular censure also numerous. As we have seen, in addition to *muhtasib*s, other officials were also charged with collecting levies and were sometimes the targets of popular protest. Thus members of the *khassakiya*, the Royal Bodyguard, and agents of the sultan who were sent to Damascus to confiscate properties and levy taxes were often targets of protest.[86] Similarly, town criers who bore bad news, especially news of newly imposed taxes, were often the scapegoats for the state's decrees.[87]

Qadis, on the other hand, were usually assigned positions overseeing the management of *awqaf*, which on rare occasions made them targets of protest during the Mamluk period.[88] Thus Sharaf al-Din Abu al-Ruh 'Isa al-Ansari al-Khazraji al-Maqdisi, of Jerusalem, is reported to have "devoured" the money belonging to the pious endowments, which led the people of the city to complain against him several times to the sultan.[89]

Ibn Tulun's account of an event in 885/1480, the murder of Sultan Qaytbay's agent Muhammad ibn Hasan ibn al-Sawwa in Aleppo, offers interesting insight on provincial urban politics.[90] Ibn al-Sawwa had advised the grand *dawadar* to tax the people of Aleppo and to recruit troops from among them in order to attack the castle of Mardin and confiscate the properties of the deceased Hasan Bek, Uzun Hasan of the Ak Qoyunlu, obviously upon the sultan's orders. The taxation was harsh on the people of Aleppo, a crowd of whom rose in protest and set out to kill the *dawadar*. Interestingly, the grand *dawadar* did not try to calm the masses, but instead deflected their wrath toward Ibn al-Sawwa, the representative of the sultan and hence of the central government, who, he argued, was the one truly responsible for the taxation. Since the late Mamluk state had increasingly interfered in the economy, instituting monopolies on various goods including sugar, the sultan's agents were important officials, often Royal Mamluks.[91] The crowd duly tracked down Ibn al-Sawwa, dragging him by his feet to the gates of the Aleppo citadel, where they burned him to death. It is impossible to imagine such a riot taking place in the city, right at the foot of the citadel, without the acquiescence, if not the outright encouragement, of local troops and authorities. Ibn Tulun's narrative suggests that the *dawadar* practically urged the agent's murder, and that provincial authorities were not simply representatives of royal power but were power players in their own right. It also reveals the type of political negotiation that could take place in a provincial city between a crowd of the urban population and city officials. Here the negotiation was not simply to reduce or abrogate the tax, or to overturn a policy perceived to be unjust, but rather to punish those responsible for the injustice.

Another incident involving a state official, which Ibn Tulun reports for Rajab 893/June 1488, is equally brutal. Ibn Tulun does not mention the official's name or his position: he is simply a man sent to Damascus with a royal decree ordering a levy on the grain middlemen and preventing them from inspecting loads of grain. Such measures would have led to an increase in the market price of grain and consequently of bread. The crowd pursued the man, who sought refuge at the tomb of Zakariya in the Umayyad Mosque. The move did not provide him with much safety: he was stabbed to death and his corpse later dragged outside the city and burned.[92] Once more, the centrality and the sanctity of the site of the murder—the central mosque of the city—suggest the compliance of provincial authorities. There is no mention in Ibn Tulun's narrative of local authorities or troops interfering to safeguard this man's life. This raises the possibility that provincial authorities might have occasionally offered scapegoats to angry masses in the form of expendable minor or middle-ranking officials..

In another instance, when the state assigned excessively high taxes to raise troops to fight Tamerlane, it was the *ustadar* (the majordomo), Yulbugha al-Salimi, who was the target of public censure, even though he was following the orders of the sultan.[93] Al-Salimi was quickly arrested and fined, although al-Maqrizi, who reports the incident, does not explain whether this was to appease the angry population or because the sultan felt he was embezzling more than his share of the levies—the common rationale behind fines and confiscation of property.[94]

Even more violent and gruesome are the events al-Maqrizi reports for Damietta in 820/1417. The historian reports the lynching and murder of the governor and deputy-governor of the city.[95] In Dhu al-Hijja 820/ January 1418 a group of people from the fishing village of Simnawa, situated close to Tanis and around Lake Manzala, fed up with the injustices of the *wali* of Damietta, Nasir al-Din Muhammad al-Salakhuri, attacked his deputy and then laid siege to the *wali*'s residence, pursued him as he fled into his ship in the sea, and arrested him. The following day the crowd had the deputy publicly humiliated and paraded throughout the city before killing him. The *wali* himself was struck dead in public, his corpse burned, his house pillaged, his women and children robbed of their belongings. An infant son of the *wali* died in his crib, out of fear; another son was taken hostage.[96] The crowd had evidently taken over the city.

Al-Maqrizi, who reports the incidents, was not an eyewitness to these events. He was a contemporary, but being based in Cairo most of his life he was probably not familiar with the names of local figures of a provincial town like Damietta or have as much access to detailed information as he would have for Cairo. Given the information he does provide, several points are interesting. First, al-Maqrizi does not mention any central authorities or Mamluk troops taking part in this *fitna*; indeed, the Mamluk army is conspicuous by its absence, which confirms the idea that such a violent protest could only take place in a provincial town, away from the eyes and hands of the sultan's authorities. Second, the report does not refer to any demands by the crowds or any process of negotiation. The crowd simply wanted the governor's head. They wanted to punish him. Third, no particular mention is made of the elite and notables of the city and what role they might have played in this protest. The only oblique mention of the ulama is that on the day of the assassination the crowd brought some of their qadis and witnesses in order to register a case against the *wali*. This suggests that it was the crowd, rather than the ulama, that had the upper hand and were deciding what would happen. None of the qadis is mentioned by name and none is given a leading role. It also hints at the possibility that some among the crowd might have wanted to conduct a trial of the *wali* and to grant the protest an air of legitimacy.

During the currency fluctuations of 821/1418, it was the people of Mahalla, a town in Egypt, who actively protested a forced purchase of gold coins imposed by the sultan in return for copper coins. Whereas al-Maqrizi reports dissatisfaction, even foot-dragging, by people and traders in Cairo, the people of Mahalla dared to rise against their governor.[97] In fact they also stoned him.[98] Many fled to Cairo to avoid the unjust levy.[99]

In a sense, the populations of provincial Egyptian cities behaved in ways similar to those of Syrian cities. The latter were at a considerable distance from the center of power in Cairo, which meant that the heavy hand of the central government did not reach them as easily as it reached populations closer to the center. The years 1417 and 1418 were momentous. Another wave of the plague passed through, wars were fought, and the Mamluk state under al-Mu'ayyad Shaykh was in the process of reestablishing order. The eruption of violent protest could be one of the indications of this struggle.

In the last years of Qaytbay's rule, Ibn Iyas reports in 898/1493 that news arrived from Damascus that its people had stoned the viceroy, resulting in a great *fitna*, one of the rare occasions in which the term is used for non-military unrest.[100] Later, in 911/1506, early in Qansuh al-Ghawri's reign, Ibn Iyas reports that the people of Damascus rose up against their viceroy, Arkamas min Tarabay, stoned him, and threw him out of the city. The sultan ordered him to return to the capital and appointed another *na'ib* in his place.[101]

Attacks on qadis increased in the Ottoman period as their role and function and that of the courthouse expanded to include more administrative duties.[102] In a sense the Qadi replaced the *muhtasib* as the target of public wrath. The chronicle of Ahmad al-Budayri al-Hallaq includes several references to attacks on qadis and courthouses. In 1156/1743, for example, the people of Damascus stoned the judge to protest a rise in the prices of wheat and bread.[103] When a similar increase in prices and a shortage of bread occurred in 1158/1745, crowds complained to the governor, who ordered them to go to the court and complain to the qadi. The confrontation turned violent and troops attacked the crowd, who in turn pillaged the courthouse. The Qadi was forced to flee the scene by jumping through the rooftops.[104]

Thus, physical attacks on public officials were a likely development during urban riots—a feature that was apparent in both the Mamluk and Ottoman periods. Such attacks were more likely to turn violent in provincial cities that were farther from the control of the central government. More incidents of violent protest are reported to have occurred in Syrian cities. This is especially true when Damascus is compared to Cairo. However, as we have seen, the people of provincial Egyptian cities, such as Damietta, Mahalla, and Qus, did protest in violent ways similar to their Syrian counterparts. This suggests that the reasons behind medieval Cairenes' preference for less direct forms of protest, such as complaints, foot-dragging, and tax evasion, have more to do with the fact that Cairo was the center of political and military power, directly under the heavy hand of the sultans. The bias of many Egyptian historians, who focused in their writings on what was happening in Cairo, prevents us from making detailed comparisons between Cairo and other provincial Egyptian cities. Yet, given the reports that do survive, it appears that medieval Syrian urban dwellers, when faced with an excessively exploitative levy, were more likely to physically attack the official in charge of collecting it or the official perceived to be behind it. In Cairo, on the other hand, in a similar situation, crowds were more likely to appeal to a higher authority, sometimes the sultan himself, to repeal the tax and punish a subordinate official. Tax collectors in the guise of *muhtasib*s were not immune from direct physical attacks. Such attacks, however, seem to have occurred more often at times of extraordinary crisis and mismanagement of the markets than at the imposition of a new levy.

As previously mentioned, protesting against government officials, middle-ranking state employees, or even representatives of the state in provinces distant from the capital was one thing; protesting against ruling sultans was another. In general terms, Islamic political thought is ambiguous with regard to the space it allowed for protesting against rulers. Indeed, even the theoretical discourse on practicing *hisba* against rulers is rather vague. Medieval legal texts include examples of the practice of this duty *against* rulers and men in authority. They are, however, almost exclusively *hisba* of the second order: that is, reprimand and advice. Such anecdotes emphasize the piety of the historical figures who dared to point out to powerful rulers their mistakes and command them to do right, but the reports simultaneously stress the risks that these men were taking by such action. The examples are always narrated as commendable acts, harking back to the golden age of Islam, and are often relayed with a sense of nostalgia bemoaning the authors' own times, which were considered to lack not only pious and daring critics, but the kind of rulers who would tolerate this form of reprimand and advice. They are not clearly examples to be emulated, though they remain exemplary. *Hisba* against rulers was also elevated to a form of jihad in its own right, a tacit admission of the dangers involved and the high price the *muhtasib* might pay for it.[105] In a sense, the pious Muslim approached it as he would going to battle—expecting death and other-worldly rewards. Indeed, by exclusively citing historical anecdotes that referred to the early days of Islam, jurists were simultaneously constructing an ideal while distancing themselves from it. While modern scholars might argue that according to classical political theory the duty of practicing *hisba* against rulers was no longer obligatory and not necessarily even meritorious, especially in public,[106] the texts reveal a more ambivalent attitude that differed from one scholar to another. Thus the motif of the protesting pious man who confronts the caliph is a recurrent one in medieval legal texts, usually within the context of discussions of *hisba*.

Al-Ghazali provides a number of examples of earlier pious men and Companions who rebuked their rulers.[107] Yet, despite his preceding defense of the right of *hisba* against the more rule-oriented ulama, when it came to rulers even al-Ghazali put up more limitations. Taking matters into one's hands to correct a wrong committed by an unjust ruler, acts that would be tantamount to violent political protest (such as seizing property that the ruler has unjustly confiscated, to take a common example, or destroying containers of alcohol in his house), would jeopardize the ruler's awe and prestige in the eyes of his subjects. This might unleash even more evil by disrupting social order, which is also forbidden. Thus, for al-Ghazali, while it is incumbent on the Muslim to inform a sinning ruler of his wrong and to urge him to abstain from it, he should not attempt to use harsh language or violence.[108] In other words, he should safeguard the ruler's authority to some extent. Interestingly, even in such cases al-Ghazali does not advise against *hisba* or suspend the duty; instead, he modifies the method in which it is to be employed.

Other writers, including al-Mawardi, Ibn al-Ukhuwwa, and Ibn Qayyim al-Jawziya, were equally aware of the dangers involved in this manner of practicing *hisba* and sought to restrict it. Yet even the enigmatic Ibn Bassam (fl. 14th–15th centuries), most probably a *muhtasib* himself, includes references to *muhtasib*s reprimanding and advising rulers such as the Abbasid caliph al-Ma'mun and the Turkish sultan of Damascus Taghtin Atabek (d. 522/1128) in his manual *Nihayat al-rutba fi talab al-hisba*.[109] While Ibn Bassam does not dwell on this aspect of *hisba*, he mentions it briefly in both the introduction and the conclusion of his work, where the *muhtasib* is also encouraged to frequent the councils of governors to remind them of their duty to command right and forbid wrong, and preach to them justice and fairness based on the Prophet's sayings, all in a cheerful, encouraging manner to avoid antagonizing them.[110]

A rare historical example of *hisba* against rulers during the late Mamluk period occurred in 822/1419. Sadr al-Din al-'Ajami, the *muhtasib* of Cairo, was rather daring in disagreeing with the consensus of the senior ulama of his time and challenging both their opinion and the sultan's decision to follow it. Sultan al-Mu'ayyad Shaykh had fallen sick and a *faqih* had permitted him to combine his daily prayers into sets of two instead of performing the ritual prayers five times a day. Sadr al-Din al-'Ajami, however, claimed that this was not permissible according to the Hanafi *madhhab* to which both he and the sultan belonged, and he told the sultan as much. Thus it was not a political injustice that Ibn al-'Ajami was seeking to redress, but one related to a religious ritual. However, his act was overtly political, and it was recognized as such. The ulama had him punished on the grounds that in his argument he had defamed one of the Companions of the Prophet. He was imprisoned and deposed. As he was escorted to receive his punishment, crowds accompanied him, shouting their support. Interestingly, he was reappointed to the *hisba* ten days later, much to the delight of the people.[111]

Yet, as Ibn Khaldun cautioned, without having the necessary power to challenge and unseat a ruler—regardless of how unjust or impious he was—the rebelling good Muslim risks unleashing even greater evil.[112] For "rulers and dynasties are strongly entrenched. Their foundations can be undermined and destroyed only through strong efforts backed by the group feeling of tribes and families."[113] Thus Ibn Khaldun does not dispute the religious permissibility of revolt. He does not argue that it is religiously unlawful to rebel against a ruler or that a ruler must always be obeyed, rather that a ruler could be disobeyed if sufficient force can be mustered against him. This raises the stakes of revolt considerably, in a sense legitimizing all-out rebellion but not the everyday type of protest that threatened public order without displacing a regime. Anything less than properly armed and fully supported rebellion would be sheer madness:

With respect to such people, it is necessary to adopt one of the following courses. One may either treat them, if they are insane, or one may punish them either by execution or beatings when they cause trouble, or one may ridicule them and treat them as buffoons.[114]

Interestingly, while a jurist and scholar like Ibn Taymiya, who was renowned for being outspoken with authorities and for going on *hisba* campaigns himself, discusses the duty of the ruler to command right and forbid wrong in his *al-Siyasa al-shar'iya*, he does not refer to rulers being commanded as such.[115] He does, however, refer to the obligation to advise those in power.[116] And while Ibn Taymiya does refer to an example of an injustice by the ruler, namely that of *exceeding* the *hudud* punishments, and states that a governor is to be punished for such a transgression, even he did not detail a course of action if the governor in question is the imam himself rather than one of his subordinates—the implication being that if he were a pious Muslim the imam should in such a case punish himself.[117] As for the pious Muslim, he should stoically and patiently endure the injustices of the ruler, as long as that ruler upholds and leads the Muslim prayers.[118]

Lambton and others have argued that the question of power and the problem of *quis custodiet custodes* did not theoretically arise for Muslim political thinkers, since all power was delegated: from God to the Prophet, to the caliphs and imams, to the governors, qadis, and officials.[119] Ibn Khaldun might have been aware of this lacuna in the theory. In his discussion of injustice and the threat it poses to human civilization, he answers the hypothetical question of why it is that despite its danger, no deterring punishment for injustice is prescribed by the sharia like those listed for other crimes. His explanation stems from the historical realities of his times and does not try to challenge it: contrary to crimes like adultery or murder, "injustice can be committed only by persons who cannot be touched, only by persons who have power and authority. Therefore, injustice has been very much censured, and repeated threats against it have been expressed in the hope that perhaps the persons who are able to commit injustice will find a restraining influence in themselves."[120]

One formula that is explicitly mentioned is that the duty of obeying a ruler ends when he commands a decree that is against the sharia. He is to be obeyed in *everything* and *anything* save that which is in opposition to the sharia. Most Sunni jurists leave the formula at that; they do not mention what exactly constitutes deviating from the sharia or how the imam or ruler is to be disobeyed in this case. Should his command simply not be obeyed? Should he be punished for such a command? Should he be deposed? And who makes these decisions? And who implements them? All these are questions that are conveniently ignored and left unanswered.

Thus, for example, the eleventh-century Maliki jurist al-Baqillani (d. 403/1013) argued that an imam has a right to the obedience of the community as long as his behavior is in accordance with the sharia — regardless of whether he was a descendant of Quraysh or not. If he deviates from the sharia, however, the community should summon him to right behavior; if he committed acts that called for his deposition, he was to be deposed, and allegiance given to another ruler.[121] Though al-Baqillani goes somewhat farther than others in allowing for such possibilities, in true Sunni fashion he ignores the details and does not discuss how such a deposition is to be attempted. Similarly, Abu Mansur 'Abd al-Qahir Tahir al-Baghdadi (d. 429/1037) does not specify how an imam is to be deposed, though he mentions the possibility of an imam deviating from the sharia: "When he deviates from this standard, the Community has to choose between two courses of action in regard to him: either to turn him from his error toward the right, or to turn away from him and give allegiance to another."[122] This idea that the community, presumably with the authority of its *ijma'*, is standing behind the imam to monitor him and act as some sort of check on his authority was not always so explicitly referred to in the theories. For al-Mawardi, for example, the imam could set the qadi right but the imam himself had no one to set him right.[123] But then, by the time of al-Mawardi and later jurists, the conception of the imamate itself had changed considerably. Yet even al-Mawardi allowed for the possibility of the forfeiture of the imamate; the reason would be committing sins or heresy.[124] Indeed, when rival Mamluk factions deposed Sultan al-Nasir Faraj ibn Barquq, they obtained a fatwa from the ulama that the sultan's immoral behavior had made him an apostate and therefore unfit to rule. This also legalized his execution.[125]

Thus the very concept of *hisba* and the circumstances that call for its practice place a limit, at least a theoretical limit, on the duty of obeying the rulers and consequently on their authority. It does open a legitimate—if exceedingly narrow—window for protest.

In the Mamluk period, ulama came to recognize that the sultans were the de facto and de jure rulers and that the prerogatives of the imam/caliph fell to them even though they did not fulfill all the qualifications of the post. The theory of the caliphate as expressed by scholars such as Badr al-Din ibn Jama'a (d. 1333) came to legitimize the sultan's "usurpation" of caliphal authority.[126] Thus many of the attitudes and positions in the literature vis-à-vis the imams were transferred to the Mamluk sultans, making real, meaningful protest against them rather limited. Instead, the sultan was often presented as the judge of last resort and above blame. Some of the juristic writing of the period offers a rationalization that either excuses the injustice of the supreme ruler, the sultan, or else argues it must be borne and tolerated as a way of atoning for other sins. Even in al-Sha'rani's advice to Sufis and officials, in which there is a tension between the idea of *qanun* and sharia, there is the idea that the sultan is appointed by God and therefore, for example, has the right to impose taxes that would be forbidden if imposed by lesser officials.[127] The prerogatives of the sultan are safeguarded even in literature that includes criticism of the way rulers managed the affairs of state. Other state and government officials, however, did not enjoy such sanctity. They were, as we have seen, often the targets of protest and taken as scapegoats. Attacks on government officials were one form of protest that non-elite members of the population occasionally adopted, usually to object to what they perceived as excessive injustices meted out to them by those officials. In previous chapters, we have discussed the transformations that were occurring in Mamluk governance by the fifteenth century. Attacks on officials are one way in which the urban communities showed their objection to some of the policies employed by the changing administration, and how they punished officials who trespassed on the people's rights. In the ideal social order that they imagined, these policies amounted to unjust transgressions.

State-induced Protest

Even though normative discourse discouraged protest against ruling authorities, there were occasions when rulers or ruling factions found the support of popular crowds useful to their struggles for power. The idea of collective voices carried weight and a sense of justice with it, an attitude that rulers tried to turn to their advantage sometimes. Elements within the ruling elite sometimes encouraged and manipulated urban protest. Thus, crowds were encouraged to rebel by various Mamluk factions in their quest for power. When one faction sought to overpower another, they resorted to adding to their numbers from within the urban population. Thus in Tripoli in 802/1399, common people took sides in the fighting that broke out during the interregnum following Sultan Barquq's death.[128] Some of the common people of Aleppo also took sides in the insurgency in 809/1406, during Faraj's reign.[129] The crowds in Damascus supported Faraj later, in 815/1412, during the insurgency of Shaykh and Nawruz.[130] Crowds gave their respective factions additional numbers and some veneer of legitimacy. They could also be urged to attack rivals. During the fighting that erupted between the factions of the *amir* Qansuh Khamsmi'a and the *dawadar* Aqbardi in 901/1496, common people were induced to pillage the houses of the *dawadar* and his allies.[131] While historians often represented the crowds as being easily bought off and ignorantly following the faction that promised them more benefits, the dynamic itself suggests that urban groups sought to maximize the profits they could gain from times of strife among ruling factions by getting each group, if possible, to promise them tax relief and/or other benefits.

In other instances, the state seems to have encouraged crowds to attack senior officials after their fall from favor. This is different from attacking officials in power as a way of protesting their policies. So, for example, when in 1399 the *wali* of Cairo, Shihab al-Din Ahmad ibn al-Zayn, was dismissed from his post, he attempted to flee the inevitable punishment that was expected to follow, but was arrested. As he was being escorted to stand before the new governor, the common people almost killed him out of hatred.[132] The masses probably took their cue from the authorities following Ibn al-Zayn's fall from grace; it was not their protest that cost him his job. A public flogging was part of the humiliation meted out to the man, followed by a fine of 400,000 dirhams.[133] While al-Maqrizi does not explain here what particular offense or injustice the *wali* had committed, it was not unusual for dismissed officials to be heavily fined and/or have their properties confiscated. In fact, by the end of the century when the state faced severe financial crises, this became one of the mechanisms by which the government attempted to retrieve hoarded assets.[134] However, it is obvious that persuading the common people to protest the fallen official added credence to the claims against him, as much as it served to further his public humiliation and confirm state power. It was also meant to induce the official in question to disclose and surrender his assets more quickly in the hope of avoiding further public humiliation. At other times it could also serve the dual function of allowing festering public discontent to vent by offering the public a scapegoat in the form of a fallen official. In 913/1507, on the dismissal of Abul-Khayr al-Nahhas, an official formerly in charge of implementing confiscations of property, the *muhtasib* paraded him through Cairo, where the crowds "almost stoned him."[135]

In 822/1419 the chief Shafi'i qadi al-Harawi was found guilty of embezzling *awqaf* funds after several complaints by people from al-Khalil and Jerusalem, where he had previously served as *awqaf* administrator and teacher.[136] He was briefly held at the Salihiya Madrasa in Cairo, and when he attempted to ride back to his house, the people shouted at him, insulted him, and stoned him.[137] That the man was unpopular is clear from al-Maqrizi's previous reports, which indicate that al-Harawi, a Turk (unusual for the period), was not fluent in Arabic and not familiar with the customs and social norms of Cairo.[138] However, the attacks on him also appear to be part of a pattern of attacks on disgraced officials by crowds of common people. Al-'Ayni, who also reports the incident, interprets it as evidence of the power of various bureaucratic factions and the extent of their rivalries. It was another faction of ulama and senior bureaucrats, headed by the *katib al-sirr* Ibn al-Barizi, who manipulated the common people into denouncing al-Harawi and supporting Jalal al-Din al-Bulqini, al-Harawi's predecessor and eventual replacement. This same faction convinced the sultan that al-Harawi was unpopular with the people.[139]

Such attacks are a further indication of what we may tentatively call "medieval public opinion." While crowds were more likely to gather to express their dissatisfaction and opposition, they also sometimes gathered to express support of a particular policy or the popularity of a certain official. Thus when the downfall and disgrace of the aforementioned qadi al-Harawi was followed by the reappointment of his predecessor al-Bulqini in Rabi' I 822/1419, crowds cheered the sultan's decision. They paraded the new qadi from Bab Zuwayla (outside Sultan al-Mu'ayyad Shaykh's mosque, where the sultan met the qadi and reappointed him) to the Salihiya Madrasa. Incense, candles, and rose water were liberally sprayed and people prayed for Sultan al-Mu'ayyad Shaykh, approving his decision. Al-Maqrizi writes that the popular reaction confirmed the sultan in his decision.[140]

Prayer and Protest

As mentioned previously, prayer was believed to have a real power in the worldview of the late medieval Islamic world. This was part of the strength and appeal of the Sufis and holy men. In reports of protest, medieval narratives often mention prayer as part of the repertoire of behaviors that crowds used. Although historians seldom report the slogans and chants people cried out at riots, it is likely that most riots would have involved slogans that referred to God and appeals to a supreme power to relieve the masses from their misery. Narratives also show that calling out prayer itself could be a form of protest.

In addition to the historiographic topos whereby historians signified growing popular dissatisfaction through the ambiguous phrase "and prayers against the sultan increased," other narratives refer to prayer itself as an act of protest, so that the chanting of "Allahu Akbar" (God is great) is used as a verb *(takbir/kabbar)* to signify a particular type of riot that begins with such chants and rallying cries. They suggest that a certain controlled form of rioting took place within the confines of large urban mosques, using the symbolism of the place and the weight of the sacred discourse as leverages against injustice in addition to the logistical opportunities prayer congregations presented. The very act of uttering prayers to God was itself symbolically charged in a culture that believed in the potential power of words.[141] A poignant example comes from the sixteenth-century chronicle of the Damascene qadi al-Ansari. In one of his entries he reports that soldiers on their way back from Cairo in Rajab 999/April 1591 reported that Cairo's governor, Awis Pasha, had died. They explained, he wrote, that the ulama of Cairo, the *fuqara'*, the pious, and the Sufis had all gathered to "pray against him" and so he instantly suffered a stroke and died the next day, relieving the people of Egypt. God had answered the prayers of his pious believers.[142]

The collective chanting of prayers to God against an injustice was an unmistakable call for action, rallying the believers and the urban dwellers to a cause. Friday congregational prayers, collectively performed by a large number of believers and usually attended by the authorities and dignitaries of the city at its larger mosques, provided potential rebels with a ready crowd. Thus the chanting of "Allahu Akbar" from the tops of minarets was a common call to rioting in medieval cities, especially in Syria. Riots that began in a controlled form within the confines of a mosque could escalate by moving out into the main streets of the city. Similarly, the architectural design of the minaret allowed rebels to use it to transmit their cries within the vicinity of the mosque, attracting crowds from outside it.

We have seen this happen in the 895/1490 riot in Damascus, when crowds chanted "Allahu Akbar" from the Umayyad mosque on Friday following the prayers, and which eventually snowballed into a major riot that had "Damascus upside down," leaving many people killed and others wounded.[143]

Friday afternoon, right after the communal prayers, was in fact the optimal time for rioting in a medieval Muslim city. While historians often do not give us the complete details of the events, sometimes we can piece together circumstantial evidence to arrive at a better picture of the practice of politics. And while the slogans chanted by protesters are not often noted in the sources, formulas that involve prayer and invoke God seem to have been common. Given the strong believe in the power of such prayer, it was a tool that crowds manipulated to their ends.

Satire and Parody

Although Islamic political thought, even in the Mamluk period, remained quite guarded in the spaces it allowed for protest against an established regime, the diffusion of political power allowed for various forms of protest, as we have seen. Not only did people seek to negotiate power and resist particular decrees of the sultans and their subordinates, but urban communities also occasionally made light of power and its trappings. Some ulama might have gone out of their way to legitimize and accommodate the rule of the Mamluk sultans, but their legitimacy remained questionable in the eyes of some members of the public, and many of them did not enjoy the same aura as the earlier, classical Muslim rulers.

It is not hard to imagine that many of the people of Egypt and Syria made fun of their rulers and used mockery and jokes to express their political opinions. This pulse of the streets, however, rarely makes it onto the pages of histories. Some historians have recorded some of the slogans and verses of poetry that were recited in protest of government decisions. For example, the *wali* of Cairo in 823/1420, Nasir al-Din Muhammad, was given the nickname "Bikilmish" because of a slip of the tongue he once uttered. Al-Maqrizi explains that the man paid a heavy bribe to obtain the post of *wali* and made it up by extorting money from the people. He became seriously indebted in the process, which led the common people to lose respect for him and to refer to him by his nickname, a sign of disrespect. Al-Maqrizi also comments that the man dressed more like a woman.[144]

When grain prices increased in Cairo in 874/1470, it was rumored that the cause was a monopoly imposed by the *dawadar* Yashbak min Mahdi on Upper Egyptian grain. A poet responded by composing two lines of poetry that apparently became popular. The verses do not name the unjust man who was the cause of the price increases, but they ask God to punish him severely in the afterlife:

> An unjust [ruler], who (brought us) higher prices,
> On Judgment Day, God will treat him harshly.
> So pray for the man and ask God to wipe
> Out his fortunes and make him suffer in his heart![145]

During a period of general hardship in 892/1486–87, when prices were high and currencies were unstable, the sultan imposed extra levies to fight the Ottomans; the Bedouin were rebellious, wheat disappeared from the markets, and bakers baked corn bread instead. The common people, Ibn Iyas writes, responded by composing a song and dance to make light of their situation: "My husband is a cause for mockery/He feeds me corn bread!"[146]

Later, in 904/1498, the *dawadar* punished a certain singer, 'Ali ibn Rihab, and had him beaten and publicly insulted for siding with one Mamluk faction against another and insulting and satirizing the *amir*s.[147] In fact, popular verses of poetry seem to have been common as a light-hearted form of protest.[148] In 911/1506–1507 the poet Jamal al-Din al-Salmuni satirized the agent of the treasury, Mu'in al-Din Ibn Shams, in verse. The Hanafi qadi, 'Abd al-Birr ibn al-Shihna, had him imprisoned. Upon his release, al-Salmuni duly composed verses satirizing Ibn al-Shihna as well! So popular was al-Salmuni and his verses that when he was brought before the qadis once more at the Salihiya Madrasa, they were dissuaded from issuing a severe punishment by the presence of a large group of commoners with rocks hidden in their sleeves, ready to throw them at Ibn al-Shihna. Indeed, we are told, the qadis ordered him to be merely imprisoned and did not have him pilloried.[149] The fact that singers and poets would be taken to court for composing satirical lines is evidence of their popularity among the community. That rulers and qadis did not ignore them confirms that they were thought to have some influence on the streets and the urban population, as the reference to his supporters attending the hearing would indicate.

These different groups of *'amma* are difficult to identify through the sources. Who were the supporters of 'Ali the singer? Did they form a coherent group? Were there associations of people working in the entertainment field? Were they a "medieval fan club"? Other, equally elusive, groups in the sources include the *harafish*.[150] In an interesting entry in Muharram 895/December 1489, Ibn Tulun described a procession of the *harafish* that took place in Damascus.[151] The procession itself does not indicate outright protest, though it does suggest potentially subversive behavior. The *harafish* had their own "sultan," Ibn Sha'ban, who traveled from Egypt to Damascus, which he entered surrounded by supporters beating drums and carrying yellow banners. They accompanied him to his residence and then went back to join the procession of his wife, also welcomed with drums. Around two hundred women accompanied her, with yellow bandannas wrapped around their head scarves.[152] This procession is an obvious parody of official royal processions, down to the reference to the title of 'sultan' for the leader of the *harafish*. While the sources do not provide sufficient detail, knowing the lowly nature of the *harafish* we can imagine that such a procession was performed with a sense of coarse folk humor, perhaps a form of carnival where members of these groups acted out the roles of sultans, where roles were reversed and the medieval social order turned upside down. As Mikhail Bakhtin commented with respect to medieval European carnivals, the procession of the *harafish* seems to have been held outside the purview of any official or religious establishment; in this it was distinct from popular festivals and processions such as Coptic Nile festivals or the procession of the *mahmal*.[153] The coarse humor and carnivalesque mood and behavior are themselves subversive and not devoid of power. And as with Rabelais's works, on which Bakhtin's study was based, the *harafish* celebration came at a time of flux, transformation, and breakdown of borders. Did the *harafish*'s challenge to state authority, here described in a somewhat carnivalesque fashion, extend to outright protest on other days? The very public and ceremonial nature of the procession suggests a subversive performance, even if it was not directly connected to an act of protest. By granting a member of the lowly classes the title of sultan, the *harafish* were parodying the pomp and glory of the Mamluk sultans.

Similarly carnivalesque behavior is reported for slaves. In the spring of 849/1445, a large group of slaves gathered in Giza and appointed one of their number as their sultan. The parody of the Mamluk sultan extended to the paraphernalia: a royal tent and a throne were set up. Some slaves were appointed to mock positions of state, such as governor of Aleppo or Damascus. Slaves belonging to a rival faction were "executed." Al-'Ayni's report borders on the fantastical: a slave belonging to a Mamluk officer fled and joined the slave "colony" in Giza. When the Mamluk officer went to look for him, he was brought before the Sultan of the Slaves. When the Mamluk had explained his demand, the runaway slave was brought forward, in chains. The Sultan of the Slaves asked the Mamluk:

"Is this your slave?" He said: "Yes," so he said: "Execute him," and so immediately he was cut in half. The Mamluk's fear increased, he asked permission to depart. So he [the Sultan of the Slaves] said: "For how much had you bought that slave?" He said: "For 25 ashrafis." So he lifted the corner of his cushion and beneath it was a pile of gold. He counted 25 ashrafis and said: "Take this and buy another slave instead of yours."[154]

After returning to Cairo, the Mamluk went up to the sultan to inform him of what had happened to him, but the sultan merely inquired whether the slaves were attacking the populace. When he received a negative answer he said, "So let them kill each other off."[155] To what extent the report is factually accurate is difficult to ascertain. If it is true, the behavior of the slaves would also conform with some aspects of carnival, where "carnival is not a spectacle seen by the people; they live in it" and where the distinction between life and spectacle is lost.[156] This allows the Sultan of the Slaves to go so far as to execute a slave.

The reports of this incident imply that the slaves were out in Giza accompanying horses to pasture. Aside from the murder of the Mamluk's slave, their behavior sounds remarkably similar to practices associated with the festival of Nawruz, as does the procession of the *harafish*.[157] Despite the fact that the Mamluk state increasingly restricted the celebration of Coptic Nile festivals such as Nawruz,[158] the social practices associated with such festivals, primarily the appointment of mock leaders and the inversion of social roles and categories, probably continued in various forms. They were occasions for people to mock the authorities and vent some of their frustrations. Such rituals included a protest against the established order while simultaneously working to preserve it and even strengthen it.[159]

Protest and the Mamluk Underworld

Also living on the margins of society, similar to the *harafish* but distinct from them, the *zu'ar* were referred to in the texts as sources of unrest and perpetrators of crime more often than the *harafish*, especially for Damascus.[160] The *zu'ar* formed organized bands or gangs, known as *ahzab*, *'asharat*, and *'usab*, which often resided near the gates of towns, and who would march behind their banners to the sound of their drums and fifes.[161] Apparently armed, at times these bands were directly fought by regular troops, while at other times they might be gradually institutionalized into urban militias.[162] The expression is often used to refer to rowdy and ill-behaved young men and has connotations of 'rascal' and 'scoundrel,' though the *zu'ar* were also frequently connected to the Sufi *tariqas*.[163] Some of the *zu'ar* were also artisans or shopkeepers. Lapidus connects their increased activity from 1485 onward with economic decline and political disintegration.[164] He argues that economic distress led to a swelling in the number of marginals in society. This along with the weakening ability of Mamluk rulers to control the population, allowed such groups as the *zu'ar* to play roles in resisting the established order in society. They played crucial roles particularly in resisting taxation.[165] In 902/1497, the *zu'ar* of Damascus rose up against the *naqibs*. Tumurbugha, the *hajib al-hujjab*, suppressed them by force, killing some and cutting off the hands of others.[166] In Jumada I 907/November 1501, the *zu'ar* reportedly played an important role in the riot that broke out against the *na'ib* of Damascus. The *zu'ar*, presumably of those neighborhoods, fought alongside the people of Harat Maydan al-Hasa and Harat al-Shaghur. However, about three weeks after that riot, on 4 Jumada II 907/15 December 1501, the *na'ib* of Damascus reportedly sent for the chief of the *zu'ar*, a man known by the name Ibn al-Tabbakh (literally, 'the cook's son') to placate him and reprimand him, presumably for the events of Jumada I. Ibn al-Tabbakh was also granted a robe of honor. The *na'ib* promised not to impose the blood money owed for a murder on people who were not responsible for it.[167] This suggests that the *zu'ar* had been fined a sum of money as a collective punishment for a murder, which could have been the cause of their riot. The references to Ibn al-Tabbakh as a chief, and to a fine of *rimaya* imposed on them collectively, suggest that the *zu'ar* were indeed loosely organized, much as a craft group would have been, and that they were at times recognized by state authorities as a group.

They also seem to have represented the interests of particular neighborhoods; at times defending the neighborhoods against authorities, even though at other times they were abusing them.[168] Some *zu'ar* groups not only evaded taxes but also forced merchants to pay them protection money.[169] Despite this criminal activity, Mamluk factions and authorities also resorted to the *zu'ar*, occasionally using them as auxiliary troops in their factional fights and battles.[170] Lapidus is dismissive of the revolutionary potential of the *zu'ar* or the ability of such groups to present a political challenge to the Mamluk regime, since the Mamluks managed to co-opt them and channel their resistance to criminal activities.[171] However, the very rise of such groups, with their organized structures, and their collective behavior, which compelled Mamluk authorities to deal and negotiate with them, especially on matters relating to taxation, is indicative of the changes taking place in the late Mamluk period. Keeping in mind that some of them were artisans or traders, gives an idea of the changing political landscape and the opening of new room for political participation, notwithstanding its limitations.

Ironically, for a regime that was based on a slave system, non-military slaves appear only occasionally in the histories of late medieval Egypt and Syria. The marginalization of domestic and laboring slaves no doubt echoes the biases of the social order to which the historians belonged. However, the instances in which slaves do appear on the scene usually relate either to crime or else, rarely, to protest. These all-too-brief references allow us only minimal views of slaves in society.

One of the rare references to slaves in revolt was of a riot in Muharram 848/April 1444. When the *muhtasib* went out to Bulaq to arrest slaves who worked at the oil presses, a group of slaves rioted and stoned him so that he almost died.[172] It is not clear why the *muhtasib* wanted to arrest the slaves. Al-Sakhawi presents it in the context of pious deeds meant to ward off the plague, which had spread to Cairo at the time. In this narrative, the *muhtasib* went out to Bulaq to arrest two male slaves and two female slaves in a campaign meant to "weaken corruption".[173] It is interesting that the slogans and insults the rioters hurled at Yar 'Ali, the *muhtasib*, accused him of being a secret Shi'i.[174] Had these four slaves fled from their masters, perhaps? Was this the grave threat to social order that the *muhtasib* sought to redress? Were the oil presses at Bulaq a refuge for slaves on the run? Did slaves fleeing from their masters seek regular employment in the city? While the surviving reports do not allow us answers to these questions, such references, as well as reports of the slave colony mentioned earlier, give us an indication of the types of organizations that existed on the fringes of medieval Mamluk society, and the limitations of Mamluk rule.

Protesting Peasants

The surviving literary texts and histories of the late Mamluk period tell us much more about the main urban centers than they do about the countryside. More environmental history, archaeology, and documentary analysis would probably yield a better understanding of the transformations occurring in the countryside during the same time period. However, there are some echoes in the sources used here of the reactions and protest in the rural areas to the changes imposed by ruling authorities in the capital, at least for Egypt. We have discussed in previous chapters the effects that the plagues and the Mamluk administration of agricultural lands in the late fourteenth and fifteenth centuries had on agrarian production. These left peasants suffering from additional burdens, which in effect meant higher rents as well as corvée labor.[175] Although reports are few and far between, some uprisings are reported. On some occasions the trouble was a confrontation between peasants and Bedouin because of increasing Bedouin encroachment into agricultural areas.[176]

Difficult to gauge, but also appearing in the sources, is peasant flight to the cities, which in some cases can be regarded as a form of protest. Peasants would rarely flee from one village to another, since conditions in different areas of the countryside were equally unpredictable, especially when *iqta*'s were rotated periodically.[177] Besides, more opportunities were to be found in Cairo. Since grain was a form of wealth, and crops were stored by the *amir*s as part of their *iqta*' benefits, the major grain stores were in Cairo; in times of dearth it was the logical destination.[178] Dols has pointed out that in the panic that plague outbreaks created, cities were a destination because of the access to religious services, medical treatment, and food reserves that they offered.[179] Occasionally we read in the sources that peasants were arrested in cities and sent back to their villages. For example, al-Maqrizi writes that on 29 Dhu al-Qa'da 827/23 October 1424 a decree was issued ordering peasants to leave Cairo and Fustat and return to their villages. However, it was not implemented, according to al-Maqrizi.[180] In fact, one of the consequences of the plagues that ravished Egypt and Syria in the fourteenth and fifteenth centuries was the depopulation of the countryside, as large numbers of peasants succumbed to the plague and others fled to the cities in search of medicine, food, and support. The effects were compounded, as previously discussed, by mismanagement on the part of the Mamluk regime, which failed to restructure quickly enough to allow for adequate maintenance of waterworks. Their deterioration led to a decrease in arable land and consequently in agrarian production. As a result, the regime gradually lost control over Bedouin tribes in the provinces, allowing some of them to overrun formerly agrarian provinces. All these transformations created added burdens on peasants, which they protested, partially by fleeing their villages for the cities and leaving agriculture behind.

Conclusion

The various political, economic, and social transformations that were occurring in Egypt and Syria in the late Mamluk period allowed room for political participation and for protest. This sometimes resulted in renegotiations of power and allowed for revision of some Mamluk policies and decisions, such as the decrease or abolition of certain levies. Sometimes the protests sought to re-establish or maintain traditional rights in the face of perceived threats. At other times the protests took the forms of passive resistance or subversive behavior. Sometimes they involved attacks on officials by crowds seeking retribution. In all these examples one can discern how medieval populations imagined an ideal social order and sought to create it in reality. In so doing, people navigated very narrow straits, for despite the perceived limitations in normative discourse on the roles of the subject populations, their potential collective power was also acknowledged; it allowed some communities and groups political space at times, and also gave rulers opportunities to manipulate them. In a time of deep transformation and social flux, these interactions between rulers and ruled helped to push history forward.

7
CONCLUSION

This book reads the history of late Mamluk Egypt and Syria "from below," bringing into the narrative the historical experiences of the common people of Egypt and Syria, not only in discussing the social history of the time but also in analyzing its political history. That is, it makes the argument that common people are of interest not only in discussing the premodern history of popular culture or the history of family and private life, but also in discussing political history. It has also argued that a broad transformation occurred in the late fourteenth and fifteenth centuries, one that affected the very institutions of rule through which the Mamluks governed, their economic structure, the societies they ruled, the culture the people produced, and—ultimately—the relations between rulers and ruled. As societies were transformed, members of the non-elite, including the common people, came to express their political opinions often, to negotiate with those in authority, and to protest against injustices more frequently.

As we have seen, various factors combined to make Mamluk power more diffused in the late fourteenth and fifteenth centuries. Even though this development was not one of linear regression and decline, and despite the revival that is evident during the long reign of Sultan Qaytbay, the institutions had certainly altered when compared to the classical Mamluk forms of the thirteenth century or their heyday under al-Nasir Muhammad ibn Qalawun. The economic crises that the Mamluk regime faced, partly induced by the recurrent plagues and their detrimental effects on the population; the drop in the agrarian income of Egypt; the changing balance of regional and world power that saw the rise of regional regimes such as the Ottoman and the Safavids; the threats posed by the Turco-man regimes as well as the growing encroachment of European powers such as the Portuguese into former Mamluk areas of influence; the cash crisis and the shortage of gold— these crises, and others, led to changes in the way the Mamluk institutions worked. The *iqta'* system by which the Mamluk ruling caste was maintained came to be a costly burden on a regime short of cash, and it reached a point of breakdown. The changing recruitment patterns that led to rapid recruitment of older Mamluk sol-diers and their deployment before being fully integrated into the system encouraged factionalization within the Mamluk armies and tense rival-ries between veteran Mamluks and recruits. The shortage of cash made rulers resort to numerous money-levying mechanisms and techniques, which had far-reaching effects in the end. Monopolizing the Red Sea trade brought in cash as the sultans acquired exclusive rights to tax all the spice trade passing through, but they also encouraged the search for an alternative route that ultimately caused the Red Sea route to decline in importance. The trade monopolies also dealt a blow to free trade and the network of Karimi merchants. Bribery and the sale of offices brought in cash to officials but further diffused the power of the top-ranking Mamluk authorities and sometimes brought individuals with substandard qualifications into the state apparatus. Land sales might have appeased Mamluk officers or even brought in cash to the sultans, but they also had the potential of allowing the rise of a new landowning class and thereby changing the landholding system altogether.

These changes in the Mamluk institutions went hand in hand with social transformations that the people of Egypt and Syria were experi-encing. Partly as a result of the political and economic transformations, partly as a result of natural calamities such as the plague, the popula-tions were facing new challenges and new opportunities. The diffusion of power opened up new social and cultural space. More people of common background had access to education and managed to climb up in soci-ety. No longer did a ruling elite monopolize the cultural scene. Instead, new cultural and literary forms were developing. New forms of patronage were possible as members of the middling classes also enjoyed and supported literary and cultural production. People expressed themselves in new genres: the popular poetry, the epic, and even the historiography of the period carry the echoes of the concerns and tastes of a wider group in society. Some degree of social mobility was possible, as individuals from commoner backgrounds moved from one social milieu to another, sometimes moving up in society. In particular, several important government officials of the fifteenth century came from commoner and craft backgrounds. For the same reasons, the culture of the Mamluk courts also came to include elements of popular and vernacular culture.

The cultural production of the period also reflects a sense of civic engagement, and a sense that what happened on the streets of the cities was important and worthy of being historicized. This is particularly clear in the historiography of the period; writers included elements of the everyday life of their cities and their communities as part of their historical narrative. Many of them also took critical stances in their writing vis-à-vis the ruling establishment, and directly or indirectly criticized Mamluk policies.

This form of engagement hints at the beginnings of a certain understanding of public space, and of a commonality in understanding and dealing with the concerns of this space as individuals, perhaps the precursors of public opinion. We have seen how some issues of social concern were debated publicly at the main courthouse or in the open prayer space of the mosque. We have also seen how contemporary writers came to express an awareness of their roles in their societies. These are generations whose male offspring would soon be sitting together at coffee houses, consuming a drink in public, enjoying various forms of entertainment, and discussing matters of public concern.

These generations who were living in a society in flux were also anxious, and their social anxiety is visible in what they wrote. Their anxiety and their communal and civic awareness are also reflected in the ways in which they participated in politics.

The main focus of this book has been urban protest. As a theme, protest is meant to serve a variety of functions and highlight a number of historiographical issues. First, it shows the cracks in the Mamluk system of rule. It shows points of stress when the relationship between rulers and ruled was compromised, and which then opened up new spaces for action. In looking at these cracks we can imagine what the relationship was like and how it was changing. Protest reveals the challenges that these societies, both rulers and ruled, faced and the ways in which they responded to them. Protest also shows us a way in which large numbers of the non-elites made their opinions heard and affected the outcomes of different types of rule, influencing and sometimes manipulating the decisions of rulers. As protest often resulted in negotiation and compromise, it allows us to see how the non-elite negotiated their position vis-à-vis their rulers—in essence, how they participated in politics. It thus brings a larger percentage of the population into the political narrative. Political history should not be assumed to be only the prerogative of Mamluk sultans and *amirs*. Protest allows us to see the ways in which, though un-institutionalized, popular participation in politics was happening in medieval Egypt and Syria. Protest is not alien to the political culture of the Middle East, and it predates the modern period.

Focusing on those transformations in late Mamluk society, and seeing them within the context of interrelated socioeconomic changes and developments rather than simply the decline and fall of a regime, might also open the way to a different understanding of early Ottoman rule in the Arab provinces. The diffusion of political power, the rise of middling classes, the bourgeois trend, and communal awareness in many ways continue under Ottoman rule and take new forms by the eighteenth century. Rather than interpreting them as signs of decline, this time of the Ottoman Empire, future research might link these developments of the late Mamluk period and the early modern period and ask whether there were continuing trends that societies were developing, despite the changes in the ruling regime. Indeed, future research could consider whether the change in the ruling regime, and the new trading maps and routes that came with it, pushed some of these trends to the fore.

This book has read between the lines in order to retrace and imagine the contribution of the urban non-elites. It remains a shortcoming of the historical records that people living outside the main urban centers, and especially in rural areas, are scarcely represented. As readers of history and students of the deep transformations taking place in Egyptian and Syrian societies in the fifteenth century, we need to bear in mind that the majority of the population continued to live outside the cities. This includes the rural as well as the Bedouin populations. Some aspects of Bedouin history can be discerned in the literary material. However, rural history remains elusive. Ongoing investigation, using the tools of archaeology, environmental history, and archival research, might be able to bring more aspects of the social history of the countryside into view.

At the time of writing, protest is very much alive on the streets of various Arab cities, including those of Egypt and Syria. While current societies are quite different from their late Mamluk counterparts, there are recognizable similarities between the two historical junctures. Ours too is a time of deep transformation. There are worldwide changes in the international balance of power, a spread of a new world economic order in the form of neoliberalism, an international economic crisis, deep local economic crises, environmental changes on a grand scale with detrimental effects on the agrarian production of the countries including real threats of drought, changing demographics especially with the majority-young populations of the region, and new forms of expression and mobilization. There are also entrenched ruling apparatuses that are trying to extend their lifespan but failing to deal with those challenges. In the process, they resort to traditional methods to extract wealth: levies, bribes, land sales, intimidation, and coercion. Finally, there are societies unwilling to put up with injustice and which are in continual protest. These similarities might not make the present more intelligible nor the future any more predictable, but they might provide the reader with perspective, if not hope. As they live through "interesting times," perhaps contemporary societies can learn from history, as our Mamluk predecessors would have us do, and try to realize the full potential of our changing times. They might seize the opportunities being opened up by a society in flux.

NOTES

Chapter 1

1 For an overview of the Mamluk institution and Mamluk history see: Linda S. Northrup, "The Bahri Mamluk Sultanate, 1250–1390," in *The Cambridge History of Egypt*, vol. 1, *Islamic Egypt, 640–1517*, ed. Carl F. Petry (Cambridge: Cambridge University Press, 1998), 242–89; Jean-Claude Garcin, "The Regime of the Circassian Mamluks," in *The Cambridge History of Egypt*, vol. 1, *Islamic Egypt, 640–1517*, 290–317; Qasim 'Abduh Qasim, *'Asr salatin al-mamalik: al-tarikh al-siyasi wa-l-ijtima'i* (Cairo: Ein, 1998); P.M. Holt, "Mamluks," in *Encyclopaedia of Islam*, 2nd ed., ed. P. Bearman, Th. Bianquis, C.E. Bosworth, E. van Donzel, and W.P. Heinrichs (Brill Online, 2014), http://referenceworks.brillonline.com/entries/encyclopaedia-of-islam-2/mamluks-COM_0658; D. Ayalon, "Mamluk," in *Encyclopaedia of Islam*, http://referenceworks.brillonline.com/entries/encyclopaedia-of-islam-2/mamluk-COM_0657

2 al-Maqrizi, *Mamluk Economics: A Study and Translation of al-Maqrizi's Ighathah*, trans. Adel Allouche (Salt Lake City: University of Utah Press, 1994), 73.

3 John L. Meloy, "The Privatization of Protection: Extortion and the State in the Circassian Mamluk Period," *Journal of the Economic and Social History of the Orient* 47, no. 2 (2004): 199–200.

4 E. Ashtor, "Levantine Sugar Industry in the Late Middle Ages: A Case of Technological Decline," in *The Islamic Middle East, 700–1900: Studies in Economic and Social History*, ed. A.L. Udovitch (Princeton, NJ: The Darwin Press, 1981), 120; Janet Abu-Lughod, *Before European Hegemony: The World System 1250–1350* (New York and Oxford: Oxford University Press, 1989), 233.

5 Ashtor, "Levantine Sugar Industry," 104–105, 112.

6   Ashtor, "Levantine Sugar Industry," 106.
7   Ashtor, "Levantine Sugar Industry," 119.
8   Tsugitaka Sato, "Sugar in the Economic Life of Mamluk Egypt," *Mamluk Studies Review* 8 (2004): 107. Sato refers to al-Maqrizi's reference to the use of waterwheels *(dulab)* in irrigating sugar cane plantations as evidence of technological innovation. However, this does not relate to the technique of sugar cane pressing, which remained quite labor intensive, depending on laborers cutting up the cane and then the use of mill stones rotated by oxen. Sato, "Sugar in Mamluk Egypt," 94, citing Shihab al-Din Ahmad ibn 'Abd al-Wahab al-Nuwayri, *Nihayat al-'arab fi funun al-adab*, (Cairo: al-Mu'assassa al-Misriya al-'Amma lil-Ta'lif wa al-Tarjama wa al-Nashr, 1964–), 8: 267–71, 272; Hassanein Rabie, "Some Technical Aspects of Agriculture in Medieval Egypt," in *The Islamic Middle East, 700–1900: Studies in Economic and Social History*, ed. A.L. Udovitch (Princeton, NJ: The Darwin Press, 1981), 70–71; Tsugitaka Sato, *State and Rural Society in Medieval Islam: Sultans, Muqta's, and Fallahun* (Leiden and New York: E.J. Brill, 1997), 134n2.
9   Carl F. Petry, *Protectors or Praetorians? The Last Mamluk Sultans and Egypt's Waning as a Great Power* (New York: State University of New York Press, 1994); Petry, *Twilight of Majesty: The Reigns of the Mamluk Sultans al-Ashraf Qaytbay and Qansuh al-Ghawri in Egypt* (Seattle and London: University of Washington Press, 1993).
10   Petry, *Protectors or Praetorians?*, 19–20.
11   Petry, *Protectors or Praetorians?*, 20–21.
12   Petry, *Protectors or Praetorians?*, 23.
13   Petry, *Protectors or Praetorians?*, 74–75.
14   Petry, *Protectors or Praetorians?*, 209.
15   Petry, *Protectors or Praetorians?*, 103.
16   Immanuel Wallerstein, *The Modern World System: Capitalist Agriculture and the Origins of the European World Economy in the Sixteenth Century* (New York: Academic Press, 1976), 325.
17   J.H. Galloway, "The Mediterranean Sugar Industry," *The Geographical Review* 67 (April 1977): 194.
18   Abu-Lughod, *Before European Hegemony*, 235–36.
19   Igarashi Daisuke, "The Establishment and Development of al-Diwan al-Mufrad: Its Background and Implications," *Mamluk Studies Review* 10 (2006): 117–40.
20   Toru Miura, "Administrative Networks in the Mamluk Period: Taxation, Legal Execution and Bribery," in *Islamic Urbanism in Human History: Political Power and Social Networks*, ed. Tsugitaka Sato (London and New York: Kegan Paul International, 1997), 39–76; Meloy, "Privatization of Protection," 208.
21   Meloy, "Privatization of Protection," 209.

22   Jamal al-Din Abu al-Mahasin Yusuf ibn Taghribirdi, *al-Nujum al-zahira fi muluk Misr wa-l-Qahira* (Cairo: al-Mu'assasa al-Misriya al-'Amma li-l-Ta'lif wa-l-Tarjama wa-l-Tiba'a wa-l-Nashr, 1963–71), xv, 375ff.; Shams al-Din Muhammad ibn Abd al-Rahman al-Sakhawi, *al-Daw' al-lami' li ahl al-qarn al-tasi'* (Cairo: Maktabat al-Quds, 1353 [1934–36]), 7:63–66; Richard T. Mortel, "The Decline of Mamluk Civil Bureaucracy in the Fifteenth Century: The Career of Abul Khayr al-Nahhas," *Journal of Islamic Studies* 6, no. 2 (1995): 173–88.

23   Ahmad ibn 'Ali al-Maqrizi, *Kitab al-suluk li ma'rifat duwal al-muluk*, ed. Muhammad Mustafa Ziyada (Cairo: Dar al-Kutub al-Misriya, 1936), 4:543.

24   In classical Marxist thought referring to the Western European historical experience, the culture of the bourgeoisie began with the Renaissance and reached its apogee in the second half of the nineteenth century. By using these terms I am not arguing for a contemporary development of this kind in the eastern Mediterranean, only that there were similarities and that there were changes that indicate the possibilities of deep and radical transformations—a 'trend.'

Chapter 2

1   'Imad Badr al-Din Abu Ghazi, *al-Juzur al-tarikhiya li azmat al-nahda fi Misr* (Cairo: Merit, 2000), 12.

2   Michael Dols, *The Black Death in the Middle East* (Princeton, NJ: Princeton University Press, 1977), 79–80.

3   Petry, *Protectors or Praetorians?*, 83; Muhammad ibn Ahmad ibn Iyas, *Bada'i' al-zuhur fi waqa'i' al-duhur*, ed. Paul Kahle and Muhammad Mustafa (Istanbul: Staatsdruckerei, 1931–45), 3:325.

4   André Raymond, *Cairo*, trans. Willard Wood (Cambridge, MA and London: Harvard University Press, 2000), 140; David Ayalon, "The Plague and Its Effects upon the Mamluk Army," *Journal of the Royal Asiatic Society*, issue 1 (1946): 70.

5   P.M. Holt, *The Age of the Crusades: The Near East from the Eleventh Century to 1517* (London and New York: Longman, 1986), 194.

6   Holt, *Age of the Crusades*, 194; Michael Dols, "The General Mortality of the Black Death in the Mamluk Empire," in *The Islamic Middle East, 700–1900: Studies in Economic and Social History*, ed. A.L. Udovitch (Princeton, NJ: The Darwin Press, 1981), 406; Ayalon, "The Plague and Its Effects," 68, 70–71. Ayalon discusses the reduction in numbers due to the plague epidemics as only one of several causes for what he considers the slow but steady decline of the Mamluk army. For him, the exhaustion of Egypt's resources by the predatory economic system of the Mamluks and the deterioration of discipline within the army because of its officers' preoccupation with internecine political rivalries are also to blame. Ayalon, "The Plague and Its Effects," 67.

7   André Raymond, "Cairo's Area and Population in the Early Fifteenth Century," *Muqarnas* 2 (1984): 22; Dols, "General Mortality of the Black Death," 403.

8   Raymond, "Cairo's Area and Population," 30.

9   Dols, "General Mortality of the Black Death," 403.

10   Dols, "General Mortality of the Black Death," 404.

11   Dols, "General Mortality of the Black Death," 404.

12   Dols, "General Mortality of the Black Death," 415.

13   Raymond, *Cairo*, 136–37, 140; Dols, "General Mortality of the Black Death," 413.

14   Janet Abu-Lughod, *Before European Hegemony: The World System 1250–1350* (New York and Oxford: Oxford University Press, 1989), 237–38.

15   Raymond, *Cairo*, 140.

16   Holt, *Age of the Crusades*, 194.

17   Peasants were possibly fleeing the high taxation and seeking better wages in the cities. Furthermore, in cities they had access to medical and religious services and, more importantly, food reserves. Dols, "General Mortality of the Black Death," 397ff. Grain merchants, including the sultans themselves and senior Mamluk *amir*s, typically stored their grain in storehouses in the cities. Despite such flight, however, the number of peasants arriving in the cities was still not high enough to make up for the loss of total urban population, which further confirms the severe loss of population overall.

18   Jean-Claude Garcin, "The Regime of the Circassian Mamluks," in *The Cambridge History of Egypt*, vol. 1, *Islamic Egypt, 640–1517*, ed. Carl F. Petry (Cambridge: Cambridge University Press, 1998), 293.

19   Carl F. Petry, *Protectors or Praetorians? The Last Mamluk Sultans and Egypt's Waning as a Great Power* (New York: State University of New York Press, 1994), 104.

20   Yahya ibn al-Muqirr ibn al-Ji'an, *Kitab al-tuhfa al-saniya bi asma' al-bilad al-misriya*, ed. Bernhard Moritz (Cairo: Maktabat al-Kulliyat al-Azhariya, 1974).

21   Jean-Claude Garcin, "Note sur les rapports entre bédouins et fellahs à l'époque mamluke," *Annales Islamologiques/ Hawliyyat Islamiyyah* 14 (1978), 155–56.

22   Muhammad Fathi al-Zamil, *al-Tahawwulat al-iqtisadiya fi Misr awakhir al-'usur al-wusta: AH 857–923/1453–1517 CE* (Cairo: al-Majlis al-A'la li-l-Thaqafa, 2008), 50–52, 55.

23   Stuart J. Borsch, *The Black Death in Egypt and England: A Comparative Study* (Cairo: American University in Cairo Press, 2005), 44; Petry, *Protectors or Praetorians?*, 114–15.

24   Petry, *Protectors or Praetorians?*, 115.

25   Raymond, *Cairo*, 141, 160, 168–69.

26 Borsch, *Black Death*, 47.

27 For example: Shams al-Din Muhammad ibn Tulun, *Mufakahat al-khillan fi hawadith al-zaman*, ed. Muhammad Mustafa (Cairo: al-Mu'assasah al-Misriyah al-'Ammah, 1962, 1964), 1:29–30; Ibn Iyas, *Bada'i' al-zuhur*, 4:20, 29; 5:58, 210, 351, 439.

28 Ibn Iyas, *Bada'i' al-zuhur*, 3:184.

29 Ibn Iyas, *Bada'i' al-zuhur*, 4:20, 29.

30 Ibn Iyas, *Bada'i' al-zuhur*, 5:50, 58.

31 Garcin, "Regime of the Circassian Mamluks," 294.

32 John L. Meloy, "Imperial Strategy and Political Exigency: The Red Sea Spice Trade and the Mamluk Sultanate in the Fifteenth Century," *Journal of the American Oriental Society* 123, no. 1 (Jan.–Mar. 2003): 2; Ahmad Darrag, *L'Égypte sous le règne de Barsbay* (Damascus: Institut Français, 1961), 7.

33 Meloy, "Imperial Strategy," 2.

34 Meloy, "Imperial Strategy," 3.

35 Garcin, "Regime of Circassian Mamluks," 294.

36 al-Zamil, *al-Tahawwulat al-iqtisadiya*, 145.

37 al-Zamil, *al-Tahawwulat al-iqtisadiya*, 145.

38 al-Zamil, *al-Tahawwulat al-iqtisadiya*, 146.

39 Ibn Iyas, *Bada'i' al-zuhur*, 3:237.

40 Ibn Iyas, *Bada'i' al-zuhur*, 3:64.

41 Miura, "Administrative Networks in the Mamluk Period," 39–76; John L. Meloy, "The Privatization of Protection: Extortion and the State in the Circassian Mamluk Period," *Journal of the Economic and Social History of the Orient* 47, no. 2 (2004): 208.

42 Meloy, "Privatization of Protection," 203.

43 'Ali ibn Dawud al-Jawhari ibn al-Sayrafi, *Inba' al-hasr bi abna' al-'asr: Annals of Egypt and Syria*, ed. Hasan Habashi (Cairo: Dar al-Fikr al-'Arabi, 1970), 261–62, 361–62.

44 Carl F. Petry, *The Civilian Elite of Cairo in the Late Middle Ages* (Princeton, NJ: Princeton University Press, 1981), 19–25.

45 The sale of the office of *muhtasib* almost became the norm during that period. Ahmad 'Abd ar-Raziq "La *hisba* et le *muhtasib* en Egypte au temps des Mamluks," *Annales Islamologiques/Hawliyyat Islamiyah* 13 (1977): 128.

46 Kirsten Stilt, *Islamic Law in Action: Authority, Discretion, and Everyday Experiences in Mamluk Egypt* (Oxford: Oxford University Press, 2011), 63, citing al-Maqrizi, *al-Suluk*, 3:566 and Ibn Hajar al-'Asqalani, *Inba' al-ghumr bi anba' al-'umar*, ed. Hasan Habashi (Cairo: al-Majlis al-A'la lil-Shu'un al-Islamiya, 1969), 1:337.

47 Petry, *Protectors or Praetorians?*, 167–68; Ibn Iyas, *Bada'i' al-zuhur*, 3:40, 120, 243, 257.

48 Ahmad ibn 'Ali al-Maqrizi, *Kitab al-suluk li ma'rifat duwal al-muluk*, ed. Muhammad Mustafa Ziyada (Cairo: Dar al-Kutub al-Misriya, 1936), 4:534.

49   Igarashi Daisuke, "The Establishment and Development of al-Diwan al-Mufrad: Its Background and Implications," *Mamluk Studies Review* 10 (2006): 117–40.

50   Petry, *Protectors or Praetorians?*, 168.

51   Petry, *Protectors or Praetorians?*, 209.

52   al-Zamil, *al-Tahawwulat al-iqtisadiya*, 27.

53   al-Zamil, *al-Tahawwulat al-iqtisadiya*, 31–35.

54   al-Zamil, *al-Tahawwulat al-iqtisadiya*, 27.

55   The *halqa* regiment typically included non-Mamluk auxiliary military troops, sometimes including sons of Mamluks. Al-Maqrizi, *al-Suluk*, 2:218; Amalia Levanoni, "The *Halqah* in the Mamluk Army: Why Was It Not Dissolved When It Reached Its Nadir?" *Mamluk Studies Review* 15 (2011): 37–65.

56   Jonathan P. Berkey, "The *Muhtasib*s of Cairo under the Mamluks: Toward an Understanding of an Islamic Institution," in *The Mamluks in Egyptian and Syrian Politics and Society*, ed. Michael Winter and Amalia Levanoni (Leiden and Boston: Brill, 2004), 267–68.

57   Stilt, *Islamic Law in Action*, 71.

58   'Abd ar-Raziq, "La *hisba* et le *muhtasib* en Egypte," 125.

59   Adam Sabra, "Introduction," in 'Abd al-Wahhab al-Sha'rani, *The Guidebook for Gullible Jurists and Mendicants to the Conditions for Befriending Emirs and The Abbreviated Guidebook for Gullible Jurists and Mendicants to the Conditions for Befriending Emirs*, ed. Adam Sabra (Cairo: IFAO, 2013), 15.

60   Robert Irwin, "The Privatization of 'Justice' Under the Circassian Mamluks," *Mamluk Studies Review* 6 (2002): 65.

61   Ibn Iyas, *Bada'i' al-zuhur*, 3:42.

62   Irwin, "Privatization of Justice," 68; Jamal al-Din Abu al-Mahasin Yusuf ibn Taghribirdi, *al-Nujum al-zahira fi muluk Misr wa-l-Qahira* (Cairo: al-Mu'assasa al-Misriya al-'Amma li-l-Ta'lif wa-l-Tarjama wa-l-Tiba'a wa-l-Nashr, 1963–71), 7:516f; Ibn Taghribirdi, *History of Egypt, 1382–1469 A.D., translated from the Arabic annals of Abu l-Mahasin ibn Taghrî Birdî by William Popper* (Berkeley: University of California Press, 1954–1963), 6:84–85.

63   Garcin, "Regime of the Circassian Mamluks," 314.

64   Garcin, "Regime of the Circassian Mamluks," 299–300.

65   Garcin, "Regime of the Circassian Mamluks," 300.

66   Garcin, "Regime of the Circassian Mamluks," 302.

Chapter 3

1   Adam Sabra, *Poverty and Charity in Medieval Islam: Mamluk Egypt, 1250–1517* (Cambridge: Cambridge University Press, 2000), 121–129.

2   E. Ashtor, "The Diet of the Salaried Classes in the Medieval Near East," *Journal of Asian History* 4, no.1 (1970): 10–13.

3   For example, Ahmad ibn 'Ali al-Maqrizi, *Kitab al-suluk li ma'rifat duwal al-muluk*, ed. Muhammad Mustafa Ziyada (Cairo: Dar al-Kutub al-Misriya, 1936), 4:636, 638.

4   Michael Winter, *Egyptian Society under Ottoman Rule, 1517–1798* (London: Routledge, 1992), 93.

5   Ulrich Haarmann, "The Sons of Mamluks as Fief-holders in Late Medieval Egypt," in *Land Tenure and Social Transformation in the Middle East*, ed. Tarif Khalidi (Beirut: American University of Beirut, 1984), 142.

6   Haarmann, "Sons of Mamluks," 142n9; Yahya ibn al-Muqirr ibn al-Ji'an, *Kitab al-tuhfa al-saniya bi asma' al-bilad al-misriya*, ed. Bernhard Moritz (Cairo: Maktabat al-Kulliyat al-Azhariya, 1974); A.N. Poliak, *Feudalism in Egypt, Syria, Palestine and the Lebanon, 1250–1900* (London: The Royal Asiatic Society, 1939), 27.

7   Jean-Claude Garcin, "The Regime of the Circassian Mamluks," in *The Cambridge History of Egypt*, vol. 1, *Islamic Egypt, 640–1517*, ed. Carl F. Petry (Cambridge: Cambridge University Press, 1998), 290–317.

8   Stuart J. Borsch, *The Black Death in Egypt and England: A Comparative Study* (Cairo: American University in Cairo Press, 2005), 53.

9   Jean-Claude Garcin, *Un centre musulman de la Haute-Egypte médiévale, Qus* (Cairo: Institut français d'archéologie orientale du Caire, 1976), 468–507; Borsch, *Black Death*, 51.

10   Borsch, *Black Death*, 51; al-Maqrizi, *al-Suluk*, 2:832–33; Carl F. Petry, *Protectors or Praetorians? The Last Mamluk Sultans and Egypt's Waning as a Great Power* (New York: State University of New York Press, 1994), 124–25; Richard Cooper, "Land Classification Terminology and the Assessment of the *Kharaj* Tax in Medieval Egypt," *Journal of the Economic and Social History of the Orient* 17 (1974): 96, 100.

11   Borsch, *Black Death*, 52.

12   Borsch, *Black Death*, 53; Garcin, *Qus*, 468–507.

13   al-Maqrizi, *al-Suluk*, 4:352.

14   al-Maqrizi, *al-Suluk*, 4:443–44.

15   al-Maqrizi, *al-Suluk*, 4:450.

16   al-Maqrizi, *al-Suluk*, 4:495–96.

17   Shams al-Din Muhammad ibn Tulun, *Mufakahat al-khillan fi hawadith al-zaman*, ed. Muhammad Mustafa (Cairo: al-Mu'assasah al-Misriyah al-'Ammah, 1962, 1964), 1:104.

18   Muhammad ibn Ahmad ibn Iyas, *Bada'i' al-zuhur fi waqa'i' al-duhur*, ed. Paul Kahle and Muhammad Mustafa (Istanbul: Staatsdruckerei, 1931–45), 3:416.

19   Ibn Tulun, *Mufakahat*, 1:161.

20   Ibn Tulun, *Mufakahat*, 1:197–98.

21   Ibn Tulun, *Mufakahat*, 1:218.

22   Ibn Tulun, *Mufakahat*, 1:233.

23 Ibn Tulun, *Mufakahat*, 1:314.

24 Shams al-Din Muhammad ibn Tulun, *Hawadith Dimashq al-yamiya ghudat al-ghazw al-'Uthmani li-l-Sham, 926–951: Safahat mafquda tunshar li awal marra min kitab Mufakahat al-khillan fi hawadith al-zaman li Ibn Tulun al-Salihi al-Dimashqi*, ed. Ahmad Ibesch (Damascus: al-Awa'il, 2002), 176.

25 Ahmad al-Budayri al-Hallaq, *Hawadith Dimashq al-Yawmiya 1154–1175/1741–1762*, ed. Ahmad 'Izzat 'Abd al-Karim (Cairo: al-Jam'iya al-Misriya li-l-Dirasat al-Tarikhiya, 1959), 206–208.

26 Ibn Tulun, *Mufakahat*, 1:125.

27 al-Maqrizi, *al-Suluk*, 4:603.

28 al-Maqrizi, *al-Suluk*, 4:610. The rebellion continued throughout the summer: al-Maqrizi, *al-Suluk*, 4:615.

29 Muhammad ibn Ahmad Ibn Iyas, *Bada'i' al-zuhur fi waq'ai' al-duhur*, eds. Paul Kahle and Muhammad Mustafa (Istanbul: Staatsadruckerei, 1931–1945), 4:104.

30 Ibn Iyas, *Bada'i' al-zuhur*, 3:360.

31 Ibn Iyas, *Bada'i' al-zuhur*, 3:67–69.

32 Ibn Tulun, *Mufakahat*, 1:71.

33 Ibn Tulun, *Mufakahat*, 1:87.

34 Borsch, *Black Death*, 49; al-Maqrizi, *al-Suluk*, 2:843, 861, 899–900, 908, 909–10.

35 Carl F. Petry, "From Slaves to Benefactors: The *Habashi*s of Mamluk Cairo," *Sudanic Africa* 5 (1994): 58–62.

36 Petry, "From Slaves to Benefactors," 64.

37 Tamer El-Leithy, "Coptic Culture and Conversion in Medieval Cairo, 1293–1524" (PhD diss., Princeton University, 2005).

38 Bernard Lewis, *Islam: From the Prophet Muhammad to the Capture of Constantinople*, vol. 2, *Religion and Society* (Oxford: Oxford University Press, 1987), 229–32; al-Maqrizi, *al-Suluk*, 1:909-913. This shock at the behavior of non-Muslims in Egypt is also recorded in the manual of the Moroccan Maliki *'alim*, Ibn al-Hajj (d. 1336): *al-Madkhal* (Cairo: al-Matba'a al-Misriya bi al-Azhar, 1929).

39 G. Wiet, "Barsbay," in *Encyclopaedia of Islam*, 2nd ed., ed. P. Bearman, Th. Bianquis, C.E. Bosworth, E. van Donzel, and W.P. Heinrichs (Brill Online, 2014), http://referenceworks.brillonline.com/entries/encyclopaedia-of-islam-2/barsbay-SIM_1243

40 Irmeli Perho, "Climbing the Ladder: Social Mobility in the Mamluk Period," *Mamluk Studies Review* 15 (2011): 35. Perho's study focuses on the fourteenth century by relying on Ibn Hajar's famous biographical dictionary. It also excludes a number of possible entries where the background of the individuals is not certain. The study also gives more importance to individuals having reached senior positions in the administration or the religious establishment than to commoners occupying middling positions.

41   Perho, "Climbing the Ladder," 25.
42   Perho, "Climbing the Ladder," 29.
43   Perho, "Climbing the Ladder," p.34. The study and transmission of Hadith seems to have been one of the more open sub-fields in religious studies, even to women. There are various reasons for this, including the nature of the qualifications needed, as well as the pressure to ensure short chains of transmission of Hadith.
44   Garcin, "Regime of the Circassian Mamluks," 307.
45   Perho, "Climbing the Ladder," 31.
46   Perho, "Climbing the Ladder," 31–32.
47   This is also connected to the development of the genre of bureaucratic manuals and encyclopedias, which were in part meant to safeguard against the loss of this kind of knowledge, as discussed elsewhere in this book.
48   Richard T. Mortel, "The Decline of Mamluk Civil Bureaucracy in the Fifteenth Century: The Career of Abul-Khayr al-Nahhas," *Journal of Islamic Studies* 6, no. 2 (1995): 173–88.
49   Mortel, "Decline of Mamluk Civil Bureaucracy," 177–79.
50   Mortel, "Decline of Mamluk Civil Bureaucracy," 182–83; Jamal al-Din Abu al-Mahasin Yusuf ibn Taghribirdi, *al-Nujum al-zahira fi muluk Misr wa-l-Qahira* (Cairo: al-Mu'assasa al-Misriya al-'Amma li-l-Ta'lif wa-l-Tarjama wa-l-Tiba'a wa-l-Nashr, 1963–71), 15:410–11; Shams al-Din Muhammad ibn Abd al-Rahman al-Sakhawi, *Kitab al-tibr al-masbuk fi dhayl al-suluk* (Cairo: Maktabat al-Kulliyat al-Azhariya, n.d.), 313–14.
51   Mortel, "Decline of Mamluk Civil Bureaucracy," 187.
52   Adam Sabra, "Introduction," in 'Abd al-Wahhab al-Sha'rani, *The Guidebook for Gullible Jurists and Mendicants to the Conditions for Befriending Emirs and The Abbreviated Guidebook for Gullible Jurists and Mendicants to the Conditions for Befriending Emirs*, ed. Adam Sabra (Cairo: IFAO, 2013), 3.
53   Adam Sabra, "Illiterate Sufis and Learned Artisans: The Circle of 'Abd al-Wahhab al-Sha'rani," in *The Development of Sufism in Mamluk Egypt*, ed. Richard McGregor and Adam Sabra, Cahier des Annales islamologiques 27 (Cairo: IFAO, 2006), 153–68.
54   Ibn Iyas, *Bada'i' al-zuhur*, 4:136; 173–5.
55   John L. Meloy, "The Privatization of Protection: Extortion and the State in the Circassian Mamluk Period," *Journal of the Economic and Social History of the Orient* 47, no. 2 (2004): 209, citing Kosei Morimoto, "What Ibn Khaldun Saw: The Judiciary of Mamluk Egypt," *Mamluk Studies Review* 6 (2002): 131.
56   Meloy, "Privatization of Protection," 209.
57   al-Maqrizi, *al-Suluk*, 4:1038–1040; Abul-Mahasin Ibn Tahgribirdi, *History of Egypt, 1382–1469A.D.*, trans. William Popper (Berkeley and Los Angeles: University of California Press, 1958), vol. 4, 149–50; Michael Dols, *The Black Death in the Middle East* (Princeton, NJ: Princeton University Press, 1977), 243–45.

58 Shihab al-Din Ahmad ibn Tawq, *al-Taʿliq: Yawmiyat Shihab al-Din Ahmad ibn Tawq 834–915H/1430–1509M: Mudhakkarat kutibat bi Dimashq fi awakhir al-ʿahd al-mamluki 885–908H/1480–1502M*, ed. Jaʿfar al-Muhajir (Damascus: Institut français d'études arabes, 2000–), 2:611, 612, 624, 641.

59 Ibn Tawq, *al-Taʿliq*, 2:628.

60 Ibn Tawq, *al-Taʿliq*, 2:629.

61 Ibn Tawq, *al-Taʿliq*, 2:631.

62 Ibn Tawq, *al-Taʿliq*, 2:631.

63 Torsten Wollina, "Ibn Tawq's *Taʾliq*: An Ego-Document for Mamluk Studies," in *Ubi Sumus? Quo Vademus? Mamluk Studies: State of the Art*, ed. Stephan Conermann (Göttingen: Vandenhoeck and Ruprecht, 2013), 356, quoting Ibn Tawq, *al-Taʾliq* 3:1107, 1224; the shaykh avoiding the people, 1:546, 2:669; 4:1780.

64 Bernadette Martel-Thoumian, "La mort volontaire: Le traitement du suicide et du suicidé dans les chroniques mameloukes tardives," *Annales Islamologiques* 38 (2004): 414.

65 Steven Stack, "Suicide: A 15-year Review of the Sociological Literature, Part I: Cultural and Economic Factors," *Suicide and Life-threatening Behavior* 30 (Summer 2000): 145–62.

66 Martel-Thoumian, "La mort volontaire," 414.

67 Martel-Thoumian, "La mort volontaire," 415, 435; Ibn Iyas, *Badaʾiʿ al-zuhur*, 4:29.

68 Martel-Thoumian, "La mort volontaire," 416; Ibn al-Himsi, *Hawadith*, 2:44.

69 Martel-Thoumian, "La mort volontaire," 425; Zayn al-Din ʿAbd al-Basit ibn Khalil ibn Shahin al-Zahiri al-Hanafi al-Malati, *Nayl al-amal fi dhayl al-duwal*, ed. ʿUmar ʿAbd al-Salām Tadmuri (Beirut and Sidon: al-Maktaba al-ʿAsriya, 2002), 7:411.

70 Carl F. Petry, "Class Solidarity versus Gender Gain: Women as Custodians of Property in Later Medieval Egypt," in *Women in Middle Eastern History: Shifting Boundaries in Sex and Gender*, ed. Nikki R. Keddie and Beth Baron (New Haven and London: Yale University Press, 1991), 122–42.

Chapter 4

1 Sheila S. Blair and Jonathan M. Bloom, *The Art and Architecture of Islam, 1250–1800* (New Haven and London: Yale University Press, 1994), 105.

2 Blair and Bloom, *Art and Architecture of Islam*, 108.

3 Blair and Bloom, *Art and Architecture of Islam*, 100.

4 Blair and Bloom, *Art and Architecture of Islam*, 108; Janet Abu-Lughod, *Before European Hegemony: The World System 1250–1350* (New York and Oxford: Oxford University Press, 1989), 233.

5 Blair and Bloom, *Art and Architecture of Islam*, 113; Jon Thompson, "Late Mamluk Carpets: Some New Observations," in *The Arts of the Mamluks in*

Egypt and Syria: Evolution and Impact, ed. Doris Behrens-Abouseif (Bonn: V&R Unipress, 2012), 115–40.

6   Thomas Bauer, "Mamluk Literature: Misunderstandings and New Approaches," *Mamluk Studies Review* 9 (2005): 109–10; Thomas Bauer, "Mamluk Literature as a Means of Communication," in *Ubi Sumus? Quo Vademus? Mamluk Studies: State of the Art*, ed. Stephan Conermann (Göttingen:Vandenhoeck and Ruprecht Unipress, 2013), 23.

7   Bauer, "Mamluk Literature: Misunderstandings," 110–11; Bauer, "Mamluk Literature as a Means of Communication," 23; Robert Irwin, "Mamluk Literature," *Mamluk Studies Review* 7 (2003): 1–29.

8   Dwight F. Reynolds, "Popular Prose in the Post-Classical Period," in *The Cambridge History of Arabic Literature: Arabic Literature in the Post-Classical Period*, eds. Roger Allen and D.S. Richards (Cambridge: Cambridge University Press, 2006), 247.

9   Reynolds, "Popular Prose," 254.

10   Bauer, "Mamluk Literature as a Means of Communication," 23.

11   Nelly Hanna, "Culture in Ottoman Egypt," in *The Cambridge History of Egypt*, vol. 2, *Modern Egypt from 1517 to the End of the Twentieth Century*, ed. M.W. Daly (Cambridge: Cambridge University Press, 1998), 87.

12   Ulrich Haarmann argues that the Mamluks' contribution to culture in general was not greatly appreciated by contemporary ulama: "By insidiously declaring the full command and correct pronunciation of Arabic as the first criterion of culture, they barred most Mamluks from their own holy precinct, because these Mamluks continued to use Turkish as the language of the army and must have experienced great difficulty in shaking off completely their alien accent when they spoke Arabic." Ulrich Haarmann, "Arabic in Speech, Turkish in Lineage: Mamluks and Their Sons in the Intellectual Life of Fourteenth-Century Egypt and Syria," *Journal of Semitic Studies* 33, no. 1 (1988): 82–84.

13   Haarmann, "Arabic in Speech," 91.

14   Barbara Flemming, "Literary Activities in Mamluk Halls and Barracks," in *Studies in Memory of Gaston Wiet*, ed. Myriam Rosen-Ayalon (Jerusalem: Institute of Asian and African Studies, 1977), 251–52.

15   Muhammad Zaghlul Sallam, *al-Adab fi-l-'asr al-mamluki* (Cairo: Dar al-Ma'arif, 1971), 2:105.

16   Margaret Larkin, "Popular Poetry in the Post-Classical Period, 1150–1850," in *Arabic Literature in the Post-Classical Period*, ed. Roger Allen and D.S. Richards (Cambridge: Cambridge University Press, 2006), 221.

17   Sallam, *al-Adab fi-l-'asr al-mamluki*, 2:105.

18   Larkin, "Popular Poetry in the Post-Classical Period," 194–95.

19   'Imad Abu Ghazi, *Tattawur al-hiyaza al-zira'iya zaman al-mamalik al-jarakisa: dirasa fi bay' amlak bayt al-mal* (Cairo: 'Ein for Human and Social Studies, 2000), 125; Ulrich Haarmann, "The Sons of Mamluks as Fief-holders in

Late Medieval Egypt," in *Land Tenure and Social Transformation in the Middle East*, ed. Tarif Khalidi (Beirut: American University of Beirut, 1984), 141–68.

20 Haarmann, "Arabic in Speech," 85–86.

21 Larkin, "Popular Poetry in the Post-Classical Period," 220.

22 Sallam, *al-Adab fi-l-'asr al-mamluki*, 1:121; Taj al-Din 'Abd al-Wahhab al-Subki, *Mu'id al-ni'am wa-mubid al-niqam*, ed. Muhammad 'Ali al-Najjar, Abu Zayd Shalabi, and Muhammad Abu al-'Uyun (Cairo: Maktabat al-Khanji, 1948), 186.

23 Adam Sabra, "Illiterate Sufis and Learned Artisans: The Circle of 'Abd al-Wahhab al-Sha'rani," in *The Development of Sufism in Mamluk Egypt*, ed. Richard McGregor and Adam Sabra, Cahier des Annales islamologiques 27 (Cairo: IFAO, 2006), 153.

24 al-Sha'rani, *al-Akhlaq al-Matbuliya* 1:445, quoted in Sabra, "Illiterate Sufis and Learned Artisans," 158.

25 Sabra, "Illiterate Sufis and Learned Artisans," 168.

26 Leonor Fernandes, "The Foundation of Baybars al-Jashankir: Its *Waqf*, History, and Architecture," *Muqarnas* 4 (1987): 21; Leonor Fernandes, *The Evolution of a Sufi Institution in Mamluk Egypt: The Khanqah* (Berlin: Klaus Schwarz Verlag, 1988).

27 Fernandes, *Evolution*, 98.

28 George Makdisi, *The Rise of Colleges: Institutions of Learning in Islam and the West* (Edinburgh: Edinburgh University Press, 1981), 167–8; 179.

29 Haarmann, "Arabic in Speech," 89.

30 Carl F. Petry, "Scholastic Stasis in Medieval Islam Reconsidered: Mamluk Patronage in Cairo," *Poetics Today* 14, no. 2, "Cultural Processes in Muslim and Arab Societies: Medieval and Early Modern Periods" (Summer 1993): 328; Muhammad ibn Ahmad ibn Iyas, *Bada'i' al-zuhur fi waqa'i' al-duhur*, ed. Paul Kahle and Muhammad Mustafa (Istanbul: Staatsdruckerei, 1931–45), 3:47, 101, 169; 'Ali ibn Dawud al-Jawhari ibn al-Sayrafi, *Inba' al-hasr bi abna' al-'asr: Annals of Egypt and Syria*, ed. Hasan Habashi (Cairo: Dar al-Fikr al-'Arabi, 1970), 186, 256–57.

31 Haarmann, "Arabic in Speech," 105–6.

32 Adam Sabra, "Introduction," to *The Guidebook for Gullible Jurists and Mendicants to the Conditions for Befriending Emirs and The Abbreviated Guidebook for Gullible Jurists and Mendicants to the Conditions for Befriending Emirs*, by 'Abd al-Wahhab al-Sha'rani and ed. Adam Sabra (Cairo: IFAO, 2013), 13, 15.

33 Sabra, "Introduction," *Guidebook for Gullible Jurists and Mendicants*, 24.

34 Tarif Khalidi, *Arabic Historical Thought in the Classical Period*, Cambridge Studies in Islamic Civilization (Cambridge: Cambridge University Press, 1994), 211.

35 Khalidi, *Arabic Historical Thought*, 211.

36 Sabra, "Introduction," *Guidebook for Gullible Jurists and Mendicants*, 25.

37 Khalidi, *Arabic Historical Thought*, 192.

38 Sabra, "Illiterate Sufis and Learned Artisans," 153.
39 Arnoud Vrolijk, *Bringing a Laugh to a Scowling Face: A Study and Critical Edition of the "Nuzhat al-nufus wa mudhik al-'abus" by 'Ali ibn Sudun al-Bashbaghawi (Cairo 810/1407–Damascus 868/1464)* (Leiden: Research School CNWS, 1998), 41, 115–7, 141.
40 Sallam, *al-Adab fi-l-'asr al-mamluki*, 2:123.
41 Larkin, "Popular Poetry in the Post-Classical Period," 202–203.
42 Sallam, *al-Adab fi-l-'asr al-mamluki*, 2:243.
43 W.P. Heinrichs, "Safi al-Din 'Abd al-'Aziz b. Saraya al-Hilli," in *Encyclopaedia of Islam*, 2nd ed., ed. P. Bearman, Th. Bianquis, C.E. Bosworth, E. van Donzel, and W.P. Heinrichs (Brill Online, 2014), http://referenceworks.brillonline.com/entries/encyclopaedia-of-islam-2/safi-al-din-abd-al-aziz-b-saraya-al-hilli-COM_0966
44 Larkin, "Popular Poetry in the Post-Classical Period," 203–204.
45 Sallam, *al-Adab fi-l-'asr al-mamluki*, 2:123–25.
46 Sallam, *al-Adab fi-l-'asr al-mamluki*, 2:123.
47 Robert Irwin, "Mamluk History and Historians," in *Arabic Literature in the Post-Classical Period*, ed. Roger Allen and D.S. Richards (Cambridge: Cambridge University Press, 2006), 164.
48 Irwin, "Mamluk History and Historians," 165.
49 Irwin, "Mamluk History and Historians," 165.
50 Benjamin Lellouche, "Le téléphone arabe au Caire au lendemain de la conquête ottomane: On-dits et rumeurs dans Ibn Iyas," *Revue du monde musulman et de la Méditerranée* 75–76 (1995): 117–30.
51 Ulrich Haarmann, "Review of *Weltgeschichte und Weltbeschreibung im mittelalterlichen Islam* by Bernd Radtke," *Journal of the American Oriental Society* 115 (1995): 134–35.
52 For an example of the criticism of Mamluk—and Ottoman—literature as being of lower quality and bad grammar, and mixing the colloquial with the classical, see Bakri Shaykh Amin, *Mutala'at fi-l-shi'r al-mamluki wa-l-'uthmani* (Cairo: Dar al-Shuruq, 1972), 316–24.
53 The procedure of placing women's biographies in a separate section at the end of a biographical dictionary was not uncommon, but it is not clear whether this placement allowed the loss of many such sections from manuscripts of dictionaries other than al-Sakhawi's or whether some of them never included such a section in the first place. Mostly, however, such sections included entries on women Companions of the Prophet and women Hadith transmitters rather than contemporary women per se. See, for example, Huda Lutfi, "Al-Sakhawi's *Kitab al-Nisa'* as a Source for the Social and Economic History of Muslim Women during the Fifteenth Century A.D.," *The Muslim World* 71, no. 2 (April 1981): 106, fn.8; Ruth Roded, *Women in Islamic Biographical Collections: From Ibn Sa'd to Who's Who* (Boulder and London: Lynne Rienner Publishers, 1994), 8–9.

54   Asma Sayeed, "Women and Hadith Transmission: Two Case Studies from Mamluk Damascus," *Studia Islamica* 95 (2002): 71–94.

55   Asma Sayeed, *Women and the Transmission of Religious Knowledge in Islam* (Cambridge: Cambridge University Press, 2013), 185.

56   Roded, *Women in Islamic Biographical Collections*, 72.

57   Sayeed, *Women and Transmission*, 184.

58   Lutfi, "al-Sakhawi's *Kitab al-Nisa*'," 108–109; Roded, *Women in Islamic Biographical Collections*, 72.

59   Nelly Hanna, "Literacy and the Great Divide in the Islamic World, 1300–1800," *Journal of Global History* 2, no. 2, (2007): 184.

60   Adam Sabra, *Poverty and Charity in Medieval Islam: Mamluk Egypt, 1250–1517* (Cambridge: Cambridge University Press, 2000), 80–83.

61   Dana Sajdi, *The Barber of Damascus: Nouveau Literacy in the Eighteenth-century Ottoman Levant* (Palo Alto: Stanford University Press, 2013).

62   On popular eighteenth-century histories see Dana Sajdi, "A Room of His Own: The 'History' of the Barber of Damascus (fl. 1762)," *The MIT Electronic Journal of Middle East Studies. Crossing Boundaries: New Perspectives on the Middle East* 3 (Fall 2003): 21, http://web.mit.edu/cis/www/mitejmes/

63   Amin, *Mutala'at fi-l-shi'r al-mamluki wa-l-'uthmani*, 313; Sallam, *al-Adab fi-l-'asr al-mamluki*, 2:108.

64   Irmeli Perho, "Climbing the Ladder: Social Mobility in the Mamluk Period," *Mamluk Studies Review* 15 (2011): 20; Shihab al-Din Ahmad ibn 'Ali ibn Muhammad Ibn Hajar al-'Asqalani, *al-Durar al-kamina fi a'yan al-mi'a al-thamina*, ed. al-Shaykh 'Abd al-Warith Muhammad 'Ali (Beirut: Dar al-Kutub al-'Ilmiya, 1997), 1:35, 4:285; Sallam, *al-Adab fi-l-'asr al-mamluki*, 2:166.

65   Vrolijk, *Bringing a Laugh*, 12–13.

66   Larkin, "Popular Poetry in the Post-Classical Period," 201.

67   Larkin, "Popular Poetry in the Post-Classical Period," 201; Sallam, *al-Adab fi-l-'asr al-mamluki*, 1:301.

68   Larkin, "Popular Poetry in the Post-Classical Period," 219.

69   Larkin, "Popular Poetry in the Post-Classical Period," 219.

70   Boaz Shoshan, "High Culture and Popular Culture in Medieval Islam," *Studia Islamica* 73 (1991): 78–79.

71   Nelly Hanna, *In Praise of Books: A Cultural History of Cairo's Middle Class, Sixteenth to the Eighteenth Century* (Cairo: American University in Cairo Press, 2004), 172–73.

72   Sallam, *al-Adab fi-l-'asr al-mamluki*, 1:302.

73   Reynolds, "Popular Prose," 259–60.

74   Mia I. Gerhardt, *The Art of Story-telling: A Literary Study of the Thousand and One Nights* (Leiden: Brill, 1963), 190.

75   Dwight F. Reynolds, "A Thousand and One Nights: A History of the Text and its Reception," in *Arabic Literature in the Post-Classical Period*, ed. Roger Allen and D.S. Richards (Cambridge: Cambridge University Press, 2006), 273, 275.

76 Bauer, "Mamluk Literature as a Means of Communication," 23; Sallam, *al-Adab fi-l-'asr al-mamluki*, 2:108.

77 Shoshan, "High Culture and Popular Culture in Medieval Islam," 103–105; Bauer, "Mamluk Literature: Misunderstandings," 110–11.

78 Larkin, "Popular Poetry in the Post-Classical Period," 212.

79 Larkin, "Popular Poetry in the Post-Classical Period," 212–13.

80 Larkin refers to a circa sixteenth-century manuscript studied by Rida Muhsin al-Qurayshi and Kamil Mustafa al-Shaybi which includes poems attributed to one "Fatima al-Jamaliya, shaykhat al-firqa al-misriya al-ni-sawiya li ihya' al-munasabat al-ijtima'iya wa-l-diniya." The MS is Shi'r Taymur, no. 608, Dar al-Kutub al-Misriya. Larkin, "Popular Poetry in the Post-Classical Period," 213.

81 Vrolijk, *Bringing a Laugh*, 22.

82 Larkin, "Popular Poetry in the Post-Classical Period," 219.

83 Larkin, "Popular Poetry in the Post-Classical Period," 220; Joseph Sadan, "al-Bilbaysi," in *Encyclopaedia of Islam, Three*, ed. Gudrun Krämer, Denis Matringe, John Nawas, and Everett Rowson (Brill Online, 2014), http://referenceworks.brillonline.com/entries/encyclopaedia-of-islam-3/al-bil-baysi-COM_23478; Joseph Sadan, "Kings and Craftsmen, a Pattern of Contrasts: On the History of a Medieval Arabic Humoristic Form (Part I)" *Studia Islamica* 56 (1982): 30–32.

84 Khalidi, *Arabic Historical Thought*, 182.

85 Khalidi, *Arabic Historical Thought*, 183.

86 Khalidi, *Arabic Historical Thought*, 184.

87 Donald P. Little, *An Introduction to Mamluk Historiography: An Analysis of Arabic Annalistic and Biographical Sources for the Reign of al-Malik an-Nasir Muhammad ibn Qalawun* (Wiesbaden: F. Steiner, 1970); Li Guo, "Mamluk Historiographic Studies: The State of the Art," *Mamluk Studies Review* 1 (1997): 15–43.

88 There is a lag of around seventy years between it and the next extant chronicle, although some scholars have surmised that some works might have been lost. It is, however, still a noticeable gap; had a work of the same stature been authored it would have been copied frequently, giving it higher chances of survival. There are mentions within other works of titles of some still undiscovered texts. P.M. Holt, "Ottoman Egypt (1517–1798): An Account of Arabic Historical Sources," in *Political and Social Change in Modern Egypt: Historical Studies from the Ottoman Conquest to the United Arab Republic*, ed. P.M. Holt (London: Oxford University Press, 1968), 3; Joseph H. Escovitz, "A Lost Arabic Source for the History of Early Ottoman Egypt," *Journal of the American Oriental Society* 97, no. 4 (Oct.–Dec. 1977): 513.

89 On his dates and works see: Abdul-Karim Rafeq, "Ibn Abi'l-Surur and His Works," *Bulletin of the School of Oriental and African Studies, University of London* 38, no. 1 (1975): 24–31.

90   P.M. Holt, "al-Damurdashi," in *Encyclopaedia of Islam*, 2nd ed., ed. P.
     Bearman, Th. Bianquis, C.E. Bosworth, E. van Donzel, and W.P. Hein-
     richs (Brill Online, 2014), http://referenceworks.brillonline.com/entries/
     encyclopaedia-of-islam-2/al-damurdashi-SIM_1688
91   D. Ayalon, "al-Djabarti," in *Encyclopaedia of Islam*, 2nd ed., ed. P. Bear-
     man, Th. Bianquis, C.E. Bosworth, E. van Donzel, and W.P. Heinrichs
     (Brill Online, 2014), http://referenceworks.brillonline.com/entries/
     encyclopaedia-of-islam-2/al-djabarti-SIM_1894
92   Otfried Weintritt, "Concepts of History as Reflected in Arabic Histo-
     riographical Writing in Ottoman Syria and Egypt (1517–1700)," in *The
     Mamluks in Egyptian Politics and Society*, ed. Thomas Philipp and Ulrich
     Haarman (Cambridge: Cambridge University Press, 1998), 188, 195.
93   Khalidi, *Arabic Historical Thought*, 216.
94   Khalidi, *Arabic Historical Thought*, 183–84.
95   Bernadette Martel-Thoumian, "Les élites urbaines sous les Mamlouks cir-
     cassiens: Quelques éléments de réflexion," in *Egypt and Syria in the Fatimid,
     Ayyubid and Mamluk Eras*, ed. U. Vermeulen and J. Van Steenbergen, vol. 3,
     Proceedings of the 6th, 7th, and 8th International Colloquiums organized
     at the Katholieke Universiteit Leuven in May 1997, 1998, and 1999, Ori-
     entalia Lovaniensia Analecta 102 (Leuven: Uitgeverij Peeters, 2001), 280.
96   Li Guo, "Al-Biqa'i's Chronicle: A fifteenth Century Learned Man's
     Reflection on His Time and World," in *The Historiography of Islamic Egypt*,
     (c.950-1800), ed. Hugh Kennedy (Leiden, Boston and Koln: Brill, 2001), 127.
97   Wadad al-Qadi, "Biographical Dictionaries as the Scholars' Alternative
     History of the Muslim Community," in *Organizing Knowledge: Encyclopedic
     Activities in the Pre-Eighteenth Century Islamic World*, ed. Gerhard Endres
     (Boston: Brill Academic Publishers, 2006), 41.
98   Khalidi, *Arabic Historical Thought*, 184, 204–10; Roded, *Women in Islamic
     Biographical Collections*, 4–5.
99   al-Qadi, "Biographical Dictionaries," 23–75.
100 Khalidi, *Arabic Historical Thought*, 205.
101 Khalidi, *Arabic Historical Thought*, p.210.
102 Michael Chamberlain, *Knowledge and Social Practice in Medieval Damascus,
     1190-135.* (Cambridge: Cambridge University Press, 1994), 156–59.
103 Radiyy al-Din Muhammad ibn Ibrahim ibn Yusuf al-Halabi ibn al-Han-
     bali, *Durr al-habab fi tarikh a'yan Halab, 908–971*, ed. Mahmud Hamad
     al-Fakhuri and Yahya Zakariya 'Abbara (Damascus: Manshurat Wazarat
     al-Thaqafa, 1972).
104 The remark comes in al-Ghazzi's introduction to his *al-Kawakib al-sa'ira*,
     where he names the sources he used in compiling his biographical dic-
     tionary and otherwise compliments Ibn al-Hanbali's work, upon which
     he relied in part of his compilations. Najm al-Din al-Ghazzi, *al-Kawakib
     al-sa'ira bi a'yan al-mi'a al-'ashira*, ed. Jibra'il Sulayman Jabbur (Beirut:

American University of Beirut, 1945), 1:6; Najm al-Din Muhammad
ibn Muhammad al-Ghazzi, *al-Kawakib al-sa'ira bi a'yan al-mi'a al-'ashira*,
ed. Khalil al-Mansur (Beirut: Dar al-Kutub al-'Ilmiya, 1997), 3:38–39;
Muhammad Raghib ibn Mahmud ibn Hisham al-Tabbakh, *I'lam al-nubala' bi tarikh Halab al-shahba'* (Aleppo: Dar al-Qalam, 1923), 6: 67–8;
Abu al-Falah 'Abd al-Hayy ibn al-'Imad al-Hanbali, *Shadharat al-dhahab fi
akhbar min dhahab* (Cairo: Maktabat al-Qudsi, 1931), 8:365.

105 Khalidi, *Arabic Historical Thought*, 209–10.

106 Khalidi, *Arabic Historical Thought*, 183–84.

107 Elias Ibrahim Muhanna, "Encyclopaedism in the Mamluk Period: The
Composition of Shihab al-Din al-Nuwayri's (d. 1333) *Nihayat al-'arab fi
funun al-adab*" (PhD diss., Harvard University, 2012), http://dash.harvard.
edu/handle/1/9366551

108 Muhanna, "Encyclopaedism," 42; Amina Muhammad Jamal al-Din, *al-Nuwayri wa kitabuhu nihayat al-'arab fi funun al-adab: Masadirahu al-adabiya wa
'ara'uhu al-naqdiya* (Cairo: Dar Thabit, 1984), 98–101; Mustafa al-Shak'a,
Manahij al-ta'lif 'ind al-'ulama' al-'arab: Qism al-adab (Beirut: Dar al-'Ilm
Lil-Malayyin, 1974); 'Abd al-Latif Hamza, *al-Haraka al-fikriya fi Misr
fi-l-'asrayn al-ayyubi wa-l-mamluki al-awwal* (Cairo: Dar al-Fikr al-Arabi,
1947), 315; Shawqi Dayf, *al-Fann wa-madhahibuhu fi-l-nathr al-'arabi*
(Cairo: Dar al-Maarif, 1960), 379; Ch. Pellat, Vesel, Ž. and Donzel, E. van,
"Mawsū'a," in *Encyclopaedia of Islam*, eds. P. Bearman, Th. Bianquis, C.E.
Bosworth, E. van Donzel, W.P. Heinrichs. 2nd ed. (Brill Online, 2015);
Josef van Ess, "Encyclopaedic Activities in the Islamic World: A Few Ques-
tions, and No Answers," in *Organizing Knowledge: Encyclopaedic Activities
in the Pre-Eighteenth Century Islamic World*, ed. Gerhard Endress (Leiden:
Brill, 2006), 22.

109 Ibn Khaldun, *The Muqaddimah: An Introduction to History*, trans. Franz
Rosenthal (London: Routledge and Kegan Paul, 1958), 1:64–65. I am
grateful to Professor Basim Musallam for pointing out this section.

110 In addition to Michael Dols's seminal work, *The Black Death in the Middle
East* (Princeton, NJ: Princeton University Press, 1977), see: Lawrence I.
Conrad, "Arabic Plague Chronologies and Treatises: Social and Historical
Factors in the Formation of a Literary Genre," *Studia Islamica* 54 (1981):
51–93.

111 Avner Gil'adi, "'The Child Was Small . . . Not So the Grief for Him:
Sources, Structure, and Content of al-Sakhawi's Consolation Treatise for
Bereaved Parents," *Poetics Today* 14, no. 2 (Summer 1993): 367–86; Avner
Gil'adi, "Concepts of Childhood and Attitudes towards Children in Medi-
eval Islam: A Preliminary Study with Special Reference to Reaction to
Infant and Child Mortality," *Journal of the Economic and Social History of the
Orient* 32, no. 2 (June 1989): 121–52.

112 Conrad, "Arabic Plague Chronologies," 86–89.

113 B.F. Musallam, "Birth Control and Middle Eastern History: Evidence and Hypotheses," in *The Islamic Middle East, 700–1900: Studies in Economic and Social History*, ed. A.L. Udovitch (Princeton, NJ: The Darwin Press, 1981), 437, 446, 447–50.

114 Petry, "Scholastic Stasis in Medieval Islam Reconsidered," 323–48.

115 Ahmad ibn 'Ali al-Maqrizi, *Ighathat al-umma bi kashf al-ghumma*, ed. Muhammad Mustafa Ziyada and Jamal al-Din al-Shayyal (Cairo: Lajnat al-Ta'lif wa-l-Tarjama wa-l-Nashr, 1940).

116 By individuation I mean "the emergence of a person's differentiated identity in relation to the larger group of individuals with whom he or she is situated." Brent C. Sleasman, "Individuation," in *Encyclopedia of Identity*, ed. R. Jackson II (Thousand Oaks, CA: Sage Publications, 2010). In the thought of Habermas the concept of individuation is firmly placed within the public sphere.

117 Stephan Conermann and Tilman Seidensticker, "Some Remarks on Ibn Tawq's (d. 915/1509) Journal *al-Taliq*, Vol. 1 (885/1480 to 890/1485)," *Mamluk Studies Review* 11, no. 2 (2007): 122–23; Irwin, "Mamluk History and Historians," 160.

118 Yossef Rapoport, "Women and Gender in Mamluk Society: An Overview," Mamluk Studies Review 11, no. 2, (2007): 3–4.

119 Torsten Wollina, "Ibn Tawq's *Ta'liq*: An Ego-Document for Mamluk Studies," in *Ubi Sumus? Quo Vademus? Mamluk Studies: State of the Art*, ed. Stephan Conermann (Göttingen: Vandenhoeck and Ruprecht, 2013), 350.

120 Wollina, "Ibn Tawq's *Ta'liq*," 339.

121 Wollina, "Ibn Tawq's *Ta'liq*," 341.

122 Conermann and Seidensticker, "Some Remarks," 123.

123 Dwight Reynolds, ed., *Interpreting the Self: Autobiography in the Arabic Literary Tradition* (Berkeley: University of California Press, 2001), 5. For a study of al-Suyuti's autobiographical text see Elizabeth Sartain, Jalal al-Din al-Suyuti, 2 vols. (Cambridge: Cambridge University Press, 1975.

124 Li Guo, "Tales of a Medieval Cairene Harem: Domestic Life in al-Biqa'i's Autobiographical Chronicle," *Mamluk Studies Review* 9, no. 1 (2005): 101–21.

125 Guo, "Tales of a Medieval Cairene Harem," 102; Li Guo, "Al-Biqa'i"'s Chronicle: A fifteenth Century Learned Man's Reflection on His Time and World," in *The Historiography of Islamic Egypt, (c.950–1800)*, ed. Hugh Kennedy (Leiden, Boston and Koln: Brill, 2001), 131.

126 Guo, "Tales of a Medieval Cairene Harem," 104–105.

127 Shihab al-Din Ahmad ibn Tawq, *al-Ta'liq: Yawmiyat Shihab al-Din Ahmad ibn Tawq 834–915H/1430–1509M: Mudhakkarat kutibat bi Dimashq fi awakhir al-'ahd al-mamluki 885–908H/1480–1502M*, ed. Ja'far al-Muhajir (Damascus: Institut français d'études arabes, 2000–), 1:35.

128 Ibn Tawq, *al-Ta'liq*, 1:29.

129 Ibn Tawq, *al-Taʻliq*, 2:629–31.

130 There are numerous instances when he mentions anecdotes related to himself and his family, for example: Ibn Tawq, *al-Taʻliq* 1:27, 28, 29, 32, 35, 42, 44, 45, 46, 52, 69, 74, 75, 78, 84, 85, 86, 90, 91, 92, 94, 98, 99, 101, 103, 105, 106, 107, 107-8, 108, 110, 112, 113, 115, 117, 118, 120, 121, 124, 125, 128, 129, 130, 131, 132, 134, 137, 138, 139, 140, 141, 142, 144, 146, 147, 148, 149, 150, 151, 152, 153 (fight with wife), 155, 156, 157, 158, 160, 163, 165, 166, 167, 168, 169, 170, 171, 177, 188, 189, 195, 196, 197, 199, 200, 203, 204, 206, 207, 208, 209, 210, 211, 214, 216, 218, 219, 220, 220-221, 222, 226, 227, 228, 232, 233, 237, 240, 241, 242, 244, 249, 250, 251, 253, 259, 260, 261-2, 267, 287, 288, 289, 290, 291, 300, 302, 306, 334, 335, 346, 349, 362, 367, 375, 401, 403, 410 (his full name), 411, 412, 414, 418-9, 422, 427, 428, 437, 442 (debt), 442, 444, 449, 456, 472, 480, 482-3, 486, 490, 492, 496.

131 Bauer, "Mamluk Literature: Misunderstandings," 109–10; Sallam, *al-Adab fi-l-ʻasr al-mamluki*, 2:125.

132 Wollina, "Ibn Tawq's Taʻliq," 345; Irwin, "Mamluk History and Historians," 160.

133 Muhammad Mustafa Ziyada, for example, comments that with the exception of history the late Mamluk period was one of compilation, abridgement, exegesis, and marginalia rather than any original scholarship. Muhammad Mustafa Ziyada, *al-Muʼarikhkhun fi Misr fi-l-qarn al-khamis ʻashr al-miladi* (Cairo: Lajnat al-Taʼlif wa-l-Tarjama wa-l-Nashr, 1949), 61.

134 For example: George Saliba, "Arabic Astronomy during the Age of Discovery," in *Columbus and the New World*, ed. J.C. Schnaubelt and F. Van Fletern (New York: Lang, 1998), 44, 50–51; George Saliba, "A Redeployment of Mathematics in a Sixteenth-century Arabic Critique of Ptolemaic Astronomy," in *Perspectives arabes et médiévales sur la tradition scientifique et philosophique grecque*, ed. Ahmad Hasnawi et al. (Leuven: Peeters, 1997), 121–22; Khaled El-Rouayheb, "Opening the Gate of Verification: The Forgotten Arab–Islamic Florescence of the Seventeenth Century," *International Journal of Middle East Studies* 38 (2006): 263–81; Wael B. Hallaq, "Was the Gate of *Ijtihad* Closed?" *International Journal of Middle East Studies* 16 (1984): 2–41; Wael B. Hallaq, "On the Origins of the Controversy about the Existence of *Mujtahid*s and the Gate of *Ijtihad*," *Studia Islamica* 63 (1986): 129–41.

135 Irwin, "Mamluk History and Historians," 159.

136 Nelly Hanna, "The Chronicles of Ottoman Egypt," in *The Historiography of Islamic Egypt (c. 950–1800)*, ed. Hugh Kennedy (Leiden, Boston, and Cologne: Brill, 2001), 241–42. It is important to remember that the probate records, naturally, refer to individuals who had something to bequeath and who were therefore somewhat privileged and literate people.

137 Hanna, "Chronicles," 199–200.

138 W.M. Brinner, "Ibn Iyās," in *Encyclopaedia of Islam*, eds. P. Bearman, Th. Bianquis, C.E. Bosworth, E. van Donzel, W.P. Heinrichs. 2nd ed. Brill Online, 2015; Hanna, "Chronicles," 242, 245–46.
139 Irwin, "Mamluk History and Historians," 165.
140 Irwin, "Mamluk History and Historians," 165.
141 Ralph S. Hattox, *Coffee and Coffee Houses: The Origins of a Social Beverage in the Medieval Near East* (Seattle and London: University of Washington Press, 1985), 73, 77.
142 Hanna, *In Praise of Books*, 65–69, 96.
143 Ziyada, *al-Mu'arikhkhun*, 75.
144 Edward William Lane, *An Account of the Manners and Customs of the Modern Egyptians* (London: East-West Publications, 1989), 386, 395, 408.
145 Abu al-Faraj 'Abd al-Rahman ibn 'Ali ibn al-Jawzi, *Kitab al-qussas wa-l-mudhakkirin*, ed. Qasim al-Sammarra'i (Riyadh: Dar Umayyah li-l-Nashr wa-l-Tawzi', 1983); Charles Pellat, "Ḳāṣṣ in *Encyclopaedia of Islam*, eds. P. Bearman, Th. Bianquis, C.E. Bosworth, E. van Donzel, W.P. Heinrichs. 2nd ed. Brill Online, 2015; Jonathan Berkey, *Popular Preaching and Religious Authority in the Medieval Islamic Near East* (Seattle and London: University of Washington Press, 2001), 40–44.
146 W. Marçais, "al-A'yni," in *Encyclopaedia of Islam*, eds. P. Bearman, Th. Bianquis, C.E. Bosworth, E. van Donzel, W.P. Heinrichs. 2nd ed. (Brill Online, 2015).
147 Irwin, "Mamluk History and Historians," 168.
148 Ahmad ibn 'Ali al-Maqrizi, *Kitab al-suluk li ma'rifat duwal al-muluk*, ed. Muhammad Mustafa Ziyada (Cairo: Dar al-Kutub al-Misriya, 1936), 4:698; Jamal al-Din Abu al-Mahasin Yusuf ibn Taghribirdi, *al-Nujum al-zahira fi muluk Misr wa-l-Qahira* (Cairo: al-Mu'assasa al-Misriya al-'Amma li-l-Ta'lif wa-l-Tarjama wa-l-Tiba'a wa-l-Nashr, 1963–71), 15:110.
149 Irmeli Perho, "Al-Maqrizi and Ibn Taghri Birdi as Historians of Contemporary Events," in *The Historiography of Islamic Egypt (c. 950–1800): The Medieval Mediterranean People, Economies and Cultures, 400–1453*, ed. Hugh Kennedy (Leiden, Boston, and Cologne: Brill, 2001), 107.
150 Irwin, "Mamluk History and Historians," 168.
151 F. Rosenthal, "al-Makrizi," in *Encyclopaedia of Islam*, eds. P. Bearman, Th. Bianquis, C.E. Bosworth, E. van Donzel, W.P. Heinrichs. 2nd ed. (Brill Online, 2015); Amalia Levanoni, "Al-Maqrizi's Account of the Transition from Turkish to Circassian Mamluk Sultanate: History in the Service of Faith," in *The Historiography of Islamic Egypt (c. 950–1800): The Medieval Mediterranean People, Economies and Cultures, 400–1453*, ed. Hugh Kennedy (Leiden, Boston, and Cologne: Brill, 2001), 103; Nasser Rabbat, "Who Was al-Maqrizi? A Biographical Sketch," *Mamluk Studies Review* 7 (2003): 6–10.
152 al-Maqrizi, *al-Suluk*, 4:388–94.

153 Irwin, "Mamluk History and Historians," 167.
154 E. Geoffroy, "al-Suyuti," in *Encyclopaedia of Islam*, eds. P. Bearman, Th.
     Bianquis, C.E. Bosworth, E. van Donzel, W.P. Heinrichs. 2nd ed. (Brill
     Online, 2015). Some scholars have argued that al-Suyuti was eccentric and
     prone to fights and disagreements with people. Al-Suyuti himself attributed
     his opposition to Qaytbay, and the impetus behind his writing of *Ma
     rawahu al-asatin fi 'adam al-maji' ila al-salatin*, to a disagreement that ensued
     after he broke a code of protocol by ascending to the Citadel wearing his
     taylasan in the sultan's presence. His subsequent refusal to answer the sul-
     tan's summons to the Citadel was interpreted as unacceptable disobedience.
     E.M. Sartain, *Jalal al-Din al-Suyuti* (Cambridge: Cambridge University
     Press, 1975), 1:86–91; Ziyada, *al-Mu'arikhkhun*, 66.
155 Al-Suyuti had occupied various positions, including shaykh of the Sufis
     at al-Baybarsiya, shaykh at Barquq's tomb, and professor of Hadith at
     al-Shaykhuniya, and even sought to create for himself the position of
     qadi-in-chief. Thus, despite his daring attitude toward both Qaytbay and
     Qansuh al-Ghawri and his composition of *Ma rawahu al-asatin*, he was not
     totally above dealing with temporal rulers. However, he was not his mas-
     ter's voice either. Sartain, *Jalal al-Din al-Suyuti*, 1:81, 91–92, 103–104.
156 Irwin, "Mamluk History and Historians," 169.
157 Ziyada, *al-Mu'arikhkhun*, 48.
158 Shams al-Din Muhammad ibn Abd al-Rahman al-Sakhawi, *al-Daw' al-lami'
     li ahl al-qarn al-tasi'* (Cairo: Maktabat al-Quds, 1353 [1934–36]), 5:738; Ibn
     al-Sayrafi, *Inba' al-hasr*, 10.
159 al-Sakhawi, *al-Daw'*, 5:217–19; Ibn Iyas, *Bada'i' al-zuhur*, 3:309.
160 Shams al-Din Muhammad ibn Tulun, *Hawadith Dimashq al-yamiya ghudat
     al-ghazw al-'Uthmani li-l-Sham, 926–951: Safahat mafquda tunshar li awal
     marra min kitab Mufakahat al-khillan fi hawadith al-zaman li Ibn Tulun al-Sa-
     lihi al-Dimashqi*, ed. Ahmad Ibesch (Damascus: al-Awa'il, 2002), 63.
161 Shams al-Din Muhammad ibn Tulun, *Mufakahat al-khillan fi hawadith
     al-zaman*, ed. Muhammad Mustafa (Cairo: al-Mu'assasah al-Misriyah
     al-'Ammah, 1962, 1964), 2:14; Ibn Tulun, *Hawadith*, 332, 364–65.
162 Ibn Tulun, *Mufakahat*, 10–11, 14.
163 Ibn Tulun, *Mufakahat*, 12.
164 Petry, "Scholastic Stasis in Medieval Islam Reconsidered," 323–48.
165 Konrad Hirschler, *Medieval Arabic Historiography: Authors as Actors* (London
     and New York: Routledge, 2006), 122.
166 Hirschler, *Medieval Arabic Historiography*, 122.
167 Amina A. Elbendary, "The Sultan, the Tyrant, and the Hero: Changing
     Medieval Perceptions of al-Zahir Baybars," *Mamluk Studies Review* 5
     (2001): 156.
168 F. Rosenthal, *A History of Muslim Historiography* (Leiden: Brill, 1968),
     61–62; Hirschler, *Medieval Arabic Historiography*, 122.

169 This is what Quentin Skinner and others term the 'illocutionary force of the linguistic action.' For example: James Tully, "The Pen Is a Mighty Sword: Quentin Skinner's Analysis of Politics," in *Meaning and Context: Quentin Skinner and His Critics*, ed. James Tully (Cambridge, UK: Polity Press, 1988), 8–9.

170 Badr al-Din Mahmud ibn Ahmad al-'Ayni, *al-Rawd al-zahir fi sirat al-Malik al-Zahir Tatar*, ed. Hans Ernst (Cairo: al-Halabi, 1962); Badr al-Din Mahmud ibn Ahmad al-'Ayni, *al-Sayf al-muhannad fi Sirat al-Malik al-Mu'ayyad Shaykh al-Mahmudi*, ed. Fahim Muhammad Shaltut (Cairo: Dar al-Katib al-'Arabi li-l-Tiba'ah wa-l-Nashr, 1967).

171 *Inter alia* Nasser Rabbat, "Representing the Mamluks in Mamluk Historical Writing," in *The Historiography of Islamic Egypt (c. 950–1800): The Medieval Mediterranean People, Economies and Cultures, 400–1453*, ed. Hugh Kennedy (Leiden, Boston, and Cologne: Brill, 2001), 59–75; Perho, "Al-Maqrizi and Ibn Taghri Birdi," 107–20; Levanoni, "al-Maqrizi's Account," 102.

172 al-Subki, *Mu'id al ni'am*, 69; Sallam, *al-Adab fi-l-'asr al-mamluki*, 1:174–75.

173 al-Maqrizi, *al-Suluk*, 1:7.

174 al-Maqrizi, *al-Suluk*, 1:8.

175 Abu Hamid al-Qudsi al-Shafi'i, *Kitab duwal al-Islam al-sharifa al-bahiya wa dhikr mazahar li min hikam Allah al-khafiya fi jalb ta'ifat al-atrak ila al-diyar al-misriya*, ed. Subhi Labib and Ulrich Haarmann (Beirut: Orient-Institut; Berlin: Das Arabische Buch, 1997).

176 al-Qudsi, *Duwal al-Islam*, 128–31.

177 al-Maqrizi, *Ighathat al-umma*, 4.

178 Medieval scholars have often stressed al-Maqrizi's Fatimid genealogy. It might partly explain his fascination with the Fatimid regime. Al-Sakhawi, *al-Daw'*, 2:21–25; Rabbat, "Who Was al-Maqrizi?," 6–10.

179 al-Maqrizi, *al-Suluk*, 4:429.

180 al-Maqrizi, *al-Suluk*, 4:453–54.

181 al-Maqrizi, *al-Suluk*, 4:274–75.

182 al-Maqrizi, *al-Suluk*, 4:502.

183 al-Maqrizi, *al-Suluk*, 4:388–94.

184 al-Maqrizi, *al-Suluk*, 4:543.

185 Badr al-Din Mahmud al-'Ayni, *'Iqd al-juman fi tarikh ahl al-zaman li Badr al-Din Mahmud al-'Ayni al-mutawwafi sanat AH 855/AD 1451 al-Hawadith wa-l-tarajim min sanat AH 815–824*, ed. 'Abd al-Raziq al-Tantawi al-Qarmut (Cairo: Matba'at 'Ala', 1985), 1:347.

186 al-'Ayni, *'Iqd al-juman*, 1:384.

187 For example: al-'Ayni, *'Iqd al-juman*, 2:422–23, 437, 651, 659–60.

188 Ibn al-Sayrafi, *Inba' al-hasr*, 189.

189 Irwin, "Mamluk History and Historians," 170.

190 Irwin, "Mamluk History and Historians," 168.

Chapter 5

1   Igarashi Daisuke, "The Establishment and Development of al-Diwan al-Mufrad: Its Background and Implications, *Mamluk Studies Review* 10 (2006): 117–40.

2   For example, see Kirsten Stilt, *Islamic Law in Action: Authority, Discretion, and Everyday Experiences in Mamluk Egypt* (Oxford: Oxford University Press, 2011).

3   Ira M. Lapidus, *Muslim Cities in the Later Middle Ages* (Cambridge, MA: Harvard University Press, 1967).

4   Lapidus, *Muslim Cities*, 144.

5   Lapidus, *Muslim Cities*, 183.

6   Lapidus, *Muslim Cities*, 184.

7   A.N. Poliak, "Les révoltes populaires en Égypte à l'époque des Mamelouks et leurs causes économiques," *Revue des Études Islamiques* 8 (1934): 251–73.

8   E.P. Thompson, "The moral economy of the English crowd in the eighteenth century," *Past and Present* 50 (1971): 76–136.

9   'Abd al-Wahhab al-Sha'rani, *The Guidebook for Gullible Jurists and Mendicants to the Conditions for Befriending Emirs and The Abbreviated Guidebook for Gullible Jurists and Mendicants to the Conditions for Befriending Emirs*, ed. Adam Sabra (Cairo: IFAO, 2013), 13, 15.

10   It is the unjust ruler that al-Ghazali was discussing, but there was also an assumption that after the classical period most rulers were unjust rulers who had to be tolerated for the welfare of the community. Abu Hamid Muhammad ibn Muhammad ibn Muhammad al-Ghazali, *Ihya' 'ulum al-din* (Cairo: al-Halabi, 1929), 2:106, 112.

11   Wadad al-Qadi, "Biographical Dictionaries as the Scholars' Alternative History of the Muslim Community," in *Organizing Knowledge: Encyclopedic Activities in the Pre-Eighteenth Century Islamic World*, ed. Gerhard Endres (Boston: Brill Academic Publishers, 2006), 48; Ira M. Lapidus, "The Separation of State and Religion in the Development of Early Islamic Society," *International Journal of Middle East Studies* 6, no. 4 (October 1975): 364.

12   al-Sha'rani, *Guidebook for Gullible Jurists and Mendicants*, 17.

13   Shams al-Din Muhammad ibn Tulun, *Mufakahat al-khillan fi hawadith al-zaman*, ed. Muhammad Mustafa (Cairo: al-Mu'assasah al-Misriyah al-'Ammah, 1962, 1964), 1:48; Shihab al-Din Ahmad ibn Tawq, *al-Ta'liq: Yawmiyat Shihab al-Din Ahmad ibn Tawq 834–915H/1430–1509M: Mudhakkarat kutibat bi Dimashq fi awakhir al-'ahd al-mamluki 885–908H/1480–1502M*, ed. Ja'far al-Muhajir (Damascus: Institut français d'études arabes, 2000–), 1:62–64, 66, 70–75, 80.

14   Ibn Tulun, *Mufakahat*, 1:250–51.

15   Rather than assassinate the *na'ib*, the crowd eventually killed a man (identified as a *ballas*, possibly a person who was famous for bribery) and burned his corpse on their way back from *musalla al-'idayn* (the open

space where feast prayers were performed), even after the agreement with the delegation had been reached.

16 Radiyy al-Din Muhammad ibn Ibrahim ibn Yusuf al-Halabi ibn al-Hanbali, *Durr al-habab fi tarikh a'yan Halab, 908–971*, ed. Mahmud Hamad al-Fakhuri and Yahya Zakariya 'Abbara (Damascus: Manshurat Wazarat al-Thaqafa, 1972), 1:23; Najm al-Din Muhammad ibn Muhammad al-Ghazzi, *al-Kawakib al-sa'ira bi a'yan al-mi'a al-'ashira*, ed. Khalil al-Mansur (Beirut: Dar al-Kutub al-'Ilmiya, 1997), 2:21; Abu al-Falah 'Abd al-Hayy ibn al-'Imad al-Hanbali, *Shadharat al-dhahab fi akhbar min dhahab* (Cairo: Maktabat al-Qudsi, 1931), 8:208. For biographies of (Taqi al-Din) Abu Bakr ibn 'Abdallah ibn Qadi 'Ajlun (d. 928/1522): Shams al-Din Muhammad ibn Abd al-Rahman al-Sakhawi, *al-Daw' al-lami' li ahl al-qarn al-tasi'* (Cairo: Maktabat al-Quds, 1353 [1934–36]), 11:38–39; al-Ghazzi, *al-Kawakib* (1997), 1:115–19; Ibn al-'Imad al-Hanbali, *Shadharat al-dhahab*, 8:157; Ibn Tulun, *Hawadith*, 145.

17 Thompson, "Moral economy."

18 Ibn Tulun, *Mufakahat* 1:124–25; 127; 132.

19 Ibn Tawq, *al-Ta'liq*, 2:951.

20 Ibn Tawq does mention Yusuf al-Bahlul, but apparently in relation to another event: also on Friday, Yusuf al-Bahlul of Maydan al-Hasa complained of the merchant Ibn Qandil before the qadi's hall and the man was arrested. Ibn Tawq, *al-Ta'liq*, 2:951. The epithet 'Bahlul' suggests that the man might have been a holy fool, or *majdhub*, possibly with some Sufi connection.

21 Ibn Tawq, *al-Ta'liq*, 2:951.

22 Ibn Tawq also writes that the people of Maydan al-Hasa convinced Burhan al-Din [Ibrahim] al-Naji to lead them in the Saturday demonstration. He comments that it was not accurate that al-Naji went to the *khassaki*'s residence, but that in fact he went to the Umayyad Mosque and sat at al-Kamiliya madrasa. While the "rabble of commoners" gathered outside, the *hajib* went in to al-Kamiliya and met with him in private. Ibn Tawq, *al-Ta'liq*, 2:951–52. Al-Naji is one of the personalities who make several appearances in Ibn Tawq's narrative. In 890 he was one of the ulama who brokered a truce between the disputing neighborhoods of al-Qubaybat and Maydan al-Hasa. Ibn Tawq, *al-Ta'liq*, 1:488.

23 It is worth noting that in other reports from the city these two neighborhoods are portrayed as rivals rather than allies; fighting often erupted between them. For example: Ibn Tulun, *Mufakahat*, 1:27, 182.

24 Ibn Tulun, *Mufakahat*, 1:124–27, 132. *Fitna* is a term laden with meanings in Islamic discourse. Semantically it is a test that reveals the true nature or mettle of something; historically it is used to refer to the First Civil War in Islam (656–661), which started with the murder of the Caliph 'Uthman ibn 'Affan and dominated the Caliphate of 'Ali ibn Abi Talib and which developed into a test of faith for the nascent Muslim community. The First Fitna involved various Companions of the Prophet and one of its consequences was the rise of

the split between Ahl al-Sunna wa-l-Jama'a and the Shi'a 'Ali. The use of the term in medieval histories for particular instances of fighting reveals how they were perceived as grave occasions. For more on the meaning of *fitna* see: L. Gardet, "Fitna," in *Encyclopaedia of Islam*, eds. P. Bearman, Th. Bianquis, C.E. Bosworth, E. van Donzel, W.P. Heinrichs. 2nd ed. (Brill Online, 2015).

25 The source does not indicate whether the merchants' complaint took the form of a written petition submitted to the *mazalim* or whether a delegation of the aggrieved merchants was allowed to address the sultan and voice their complaint orally. Muhammad ibn Ahmad ibn Iyas, *Bada'i' al-zuhur fi waqa'i' al-duhur*, ed. Paul Kahle and Muhammad Mustafa (Istanbul: Staatsdruckerei, 1931–45), 4:177–79.

26 Ibn Iyas, *Bada'i' al-zuhur* 3:237.

27 Ibn Iyas, *Bada'i' al-zuhur* 3:262.

28 'Ali ibn Dawud al-Jawhari ibn al-Sayrafi, *Inba' al-hasr bi abna' al-'asr: Annals of Egypt and Syria*, ed. Hasan Habashi (Cairo: Dar al-Fikr al-'Arabi, 1970), 261–62, 361–62.

29 Ibn al-Sayrafi refers to them once in this report as coming from Bayn al-Qasrayn and another time as coming from Bayn al-Surayn. It is more likely that he meant Bayn al-Qasrayn, since this was a commercial district and a bustling market, while Bayn al-Surayn seems to have been more residential. Ahmad ibn 'Ali al-Maqrizi, *al-Mawa'iz wa-l-i'tibar fi dhikr al-khitat wa-l-athar*, ed. Ayman Fu'ad Sayyid (London: al-Furqan Islamic Heritage Foundation, 2002), 3:71, 81.

30 Ibn al-Sayrafi, *Inba' al-hasr*, 261–62.

31 Ibn al-Sayrafi, *Inba' al-hasr*, 361–62.

32 Carl F. Petry, "Class Solidarity versus Gender Gain: Women as Custodians of Property in Later Medieval Egypt," in *Women in Middle Eastern History: Shifting Boundaries in Sex and Gender*, ed. Nikki R. Keddie and Beth Baron (New Haven and London: Yale University Press, 1991), 123.

33 Petry, "Class Solidarity," 125–26.

34 Petry notices that Qaytbay generally respected patrimonies entrusted to female relatives of deceased Mamluk competitors. Qansuh al-Ghawri, on the other hand, undermined this tacit agreement, even arresting Qaytbay's own concubine and mother of his heir. Carl F. Petry, *Protectors or Praetorians? The Last Mamluk Sultans and Egypt's Waning as a Great Power* (New York: State University of New York Press, 1994), 171.

35 For example, Ibn al-Sayrafi, *Inba' al-hasr*, 286.

36 For example, Ibn al-Sayrafi, *Inba' al-hasr*, 336.

37 Ibn al-Sayrafi, *Inba' al-hasr*, 388.

38 Ibn al-Sayrafi, *Inba' al-hasr*, 388.

39 Ibn Iyas does not explain the nature of the dispute, but it probably involved a *waqf* under the qadi's supervision and of which the woman was a beneficiary. Ibn Iyas, *Bada'i' al-zuhur*, 3:267.

40 Adrian Randall and Andrew Charlesworth, "The Moral Economy: Riot, Markets and Social Conflict," in *Moral Economy and Popular Protest: Crowd, Conflict and Authority*, ed. Adrian Randall and Andrew Charlesworth (London and New York: Macmillan and St. Martin's, 2000), 4.

41 Thompson, "Moral Economy," 78.

42 For example: Michael Mullett, *Popular Culture and Popular Protest in Late Medieval and Early Modern Europe* (London, New York, and Sydney: Croom Helm, 1987), 1–3.

43 For example: Ibn Tulun, *Mufakahat*, 1:29–30; Ibn Iyas, *Bada'i' al-zuhur*, 4:20, 29, 5:58, 210, 351, 439.

44 Ibn Iyas, *Bada'i' al-zuhur*, 3:184.

45 Ahmad ibn 'Ali al-Maqrizi, *Kitab al-suluk li ma'rifat duwal al-muluk*, ed. Muhammad Mustafa Ziyada (Cairo: Dar al-Kutub al-Misriya), 4:133–34.

46 al-Maqrizi, *al-Suluk*, 4:195.

47 al-Maqrizi, *al-Suluk*, 4:196.

48 Ibn Tulun, *Mufakahat*, 1:29–30.

49 Ibn Iyas, *Bada'i' al-zuhur*, 4:20, 29.

50 Ibn Iyas, *Bada'i' al-zuhur*, 5:50, 58.

51 Since this was the holy month of Ramadan, the impalement was rumored to be scheduled to take place after the end of the Lesser Feast. Ibn Iyas, *Bada'i' al-zuhur*, 5:210.

52 Lapidus, *Muslim Cities*, 148.

53 We have seen how the people of Damascus rose up against the sultan's agent, Ibn al-Nabulsi, in 880/1475: Ibn Iyas, *Bada'i' al-zuhur*, 3:107. The *khassaki* Qarqamas who arrived in Damascus to confiscate properties was the target of the famous riot of 895/1490; another *khassaki* who went to tax the silk weavers in 897/1491 met with a similar reception: Ibn Tulun, *Mufakahat*, 1:124–27, 146. A *khassaki* who arrived in 902/1497 to tax the *awqaf* was denounced from the minarets of the Umayyad Mosque: Ibn Tulun, *Mufakahat*, 1:178.

54 Ibn Tulun, *Mufakahat*, 1:24.

55 Ibn Tulun, *Mufakahat*, 1:95.

56 James C. Scott, *Weapons of the Weak: Everyday Forms of Peasant Resistance* (New Haven: Yale University Press, 1985), 29–36. Quoted in Stephen Duncombe, ed., *Cultural Resistance Reader* (London and New York: Verso, 2002), 93.

57 Stilt, *Islamic Law in Action*, 204.

58 Michael Dols, "Historical Perspective: Insanity in Islamic Law," *Journal of Muslim Mental Health* 2 (2007), 91–3.

59 Ibn Taghribirdi, *History of Egypt*, 4:146.

60 Ibn Taghribirdi, *History of Egypt*, 4: 149.

61 Ibn al-Sayrafi, *Inba al-hasr*, 125.

62 For a general discussion of *mukus* see W. Björkman, "Maks," in *Encyclopaedia of Islam*, 2d ed., ed. P. Bearman, Th. Bianquis, C.E. Bosworth, E. van

Donzel, and W.P. Heinrichs (Brill Online, 2014), http://referenceworks. brillonline.com/entries/encyclopaedia-of-islam-2/maks-SIM_4839

63   Jalal al-Din al-Suyuti, *Ma rawahu al-asatin fi 'adam al-maji' ila al-salatin: dhammu al-qada' wa taqallud al-ahkam: dhammu al-muks*, ed. Majdi Fathi al-Sayyid (Tanta: Dar al-Sahabah li-l-Turath, 1991).

64   al-Maqrizi, *Kitab al-mawa'iz wa-l-'itibar fi dhikr al-khitat wa-l-athar* (Cairo: Dar al-Tiba'a al-Misriya, 1853–54), 1:111.

65   Ibn Iyas, *Bada'i' al-zuhur*, 3:64.

66   Scott, *Weapons of the Weak*, 29–36.

67   Jamal al-Din Abu al-Mahasin Yusuf ibn Taghribirdi, *al-Nujum al-zahira fi muluk Misr wa-l-Qahira* (Cairo: al-Mu'assasa al-Misriya al-'Amma li-l-Ta'lif wa-l-Tarjama wa-l-Tiba'a wa-l-Nashr, 1963–71), 14:282.

68   al-Maqrizi, *al-Suluk*, 4:698.

69   Ibn Iyas, *Bada'i' al-zuhur*, 3:257.

70   Sharaf al-Din Musa ibn Yusuf al-Ansari, *Nuzhat al-khatir wa bahjat al-nazir* (Damascus: Ministry of Culture, 1991), 1:205–206.

71   Ibn al-Sayrafi, *Inba' al-hasr*, 476–77.

72   The *khassakiya* were the bodyguard and entourage of the ruling sultan, chosen from among the Royal Mamluks. Ibn Tulun, *Mufakahat*, 1:24–25.

73   Ibn Tulun, *Mufakahat*, 1:178.

74   al-Maqrizi, *al-Suluk*, 4:1181–83; Ibn Iyas, *Bada'i' al-zuhur*, 2:222; Zayn al-Din 'Abd al-Basit ibn Khalil ibn Shahin al-Zahiri al-Hanafi al-Malati, *Nayl al-amal fi dhayl al-duwal*, ed. 'Umar 'Abd al-Salam Tadmuri (Beirut and Sidon: al-Maktaba al-'Asriya, 2002), vol. 2, pt. 5, 110–11; Badr al-Din Mahmud al-'Ayni, *'Iqd al-juman fi tarikh ahl al-zaman li Badr al-Din Mahmud al-'Ayni al-mutawwafi sanat AH 855/AD 1451 al-Hawadith wa-l-tarajim min sanat AH 815–824*, ed. 'Abd al-Raziq al-Tantawi al-Qarmut (Cairo: Matba'at 'Ala', 1985), 2:551.

75   Lapidus, *Muslim Cities*, 146.

76   Lapidus, *Muslim Cities*, 146.

77   Ibn Iyas, *Bada'i' al-zuhur*, 3:107.

78   Thus in Jumada II 823/July 1420, when the Nile stopped rising, grain prices increased. Sultan al-Mu'ayyad Shaykh immediately joined the people in collective prayers for rain, emphasizing his piety and humility. This increased his popularity and, instead of attacking him, the crowds prayed for him. Ibn Taghribirdi, *al-Nujum al-zahira*, 14:97–98.

79   Boaz Shoshan, "Grain Riots and the 'Moral Economy': Cairo, 1350–1517," *Journal of Interdisciplinary History* 10 (1980): 467.

80   Shoshan, "Grain Riots," 462.

81   Lapidus, *Muslim Cities*, 51; Lapidus, "The Grain Economy of Mamluk Egypt," *Journal of the Economic and Social History of the Orient* 12 (1969): 5; Shoshan, "Grain Riots," 463.

82   Ibn Tulun, *Mufakahat*, 1:84.

83   George Rudé, *The Crowd in History: A Study of Popular Disturbances in France and England, 1730–1848,* (London: Serif, 1995), 218.

84   Rudé, *Crowd in History,* 219.

85   Shoshan, "Grain Riots," 475–77.

86   Jean-Claude Garcin, "The Regime of the Circassian Mamluks," in *The Cambridge History of Egypt,* vol. 1, *Islamic Egypt, 640–1517,* ed. Carl F. Petry (Cambridge: Cambridge University Press, 1998), 301–302; Petry, *Protectors or Praetorians?,* 81.

87   Garcin, "Regime of the Circassian Mamluks," 296.

88   Ibn Iyas, *Bada'i' al-zuhur,* 3:228.

89   Garcin, "Regime of the Circassian Mamluks," 296.

90   Petry, *Protectors or Praetorians?,* 171–72.

91   Garcin, "Regime of the Circassian Mamluks," 298.

92   Ibn Iyas, *Bada'i' al-zuhur,* 4:177.

93   Ibn Iyas, *Bada'i' al-zuhur,* 4:170.

94   It is interesting to note that Mu'allim 'Ali was punished once more that year. In Shawwal 916/January 1511, that is, after the end of the fasting month of Ramadan and the Lesser Feast, the sultan ordered Mu'allim 'Ali to pay an unspecified sum of money that was apparently beyond his means. Unable to pay, Mu'allim 'Ali fled and disappeared. Another man was appointed in his place but a meat shortage occurred. Ibn Iyas, *Bada'i' al-zuhur,* 4:200.

95   It was highly unusual, for example, when Qaytbay ignored this custom in 873/1469 on the pretext that he was out of Cairo during the feast (Ibn al-Sayrafi, *Inba' al-hasr,* 74). Much earlier, in 827/1424, when Sultan Barsbay paid his troops a dinar each instead of giving them meat rations on the feast, they rioted. The Mamluks threw rocks at the *amir*s from their *tibaq*s as the customary sacrificial animals were being slaughtered and tore at the carcasses. al-Maqrizi, *al-Suluk,* 4:678.

96   Ibn Iyas, *Bada'i' al-zuhur,* 4:170.

97   Ibn Iyas, *Bada'i' al-zuhur,* 4:179.

98   Ibn Iyas, *Bada'i' al-zuhur,* 4:483–86.

99   Ibn Iyas, *Bada'i' al-zuhur,* 5:5–6.

100 We are not told, however, whether the state did anything to relieve the bread shortage, but al-'Ayni was replaced a month later. Al-Maqrizi, *al-Suluk,* 4:698, 706; Ibn Taghribirdi, *al-Nujum al-zahira,* 14:281–82.

101 This is a rare reference to a collective grievance voiced through the *mazalim.* Even though Ibn al-Sayrafi himself was an eyewitness to such sessions in his capacity as deputy Hanafi judge, there are few such references in his text. Ibn al-Sayraf, *Inba' al-hasr,* 367.

102 Ibn Iyas, *Bada'i' al-zuhur,* 4:328–29. This was a.year of plague. Watermelon was used in plague remedies—as were other fruit juices— possibly for its thirst-quenching properties, which might explain its importance on the

market and the state's decision to tax it separately. The same taxes were abolished once more in 922/1516. Ibn Iyas, *Bada'i' al-zuhur*, 5:16–18.

103 Ibn Shahin al-Zahiri, *Nayl al-amal*, vol. 2, pt. 5, 110–11.

104 Ibn Tulun, *Mufakahat*, 1:83–84.

105 Ibn Tulun, *Mufakahat*, 1:84.

106 Ibn Tulun, *Mufakahat*, 1:146.

107 The camels were taken as booty after the viceroy defeated the Al Mirri Bedouin. Ibn Tulun, *Mufakahat*, 1:904.

108 Ibn Tulun, *Mufakahat*, 1:24.

109 Ibn Tulun, *Mufakahat*, 1:62.

Chapter 6

1 The best study on *hisba* in Islamic law remains Michael Cook's classic *Commanding Right and Forbidding Wrong in Islamic Thought* (Cambridge: Cambridge University Press, 2000).

2 Abu al-Hasan 'Ali ibn Muhammad ibn Habib al-Mawardi, *al-Ahkam al-sultaniya wa-l-wilayat al-diniya* (Cairo: Mustafa al-Halabi, 1966), 240.

3 Muhammad ibn Muhammad ibn Ahmad al-Qurashi ibn al-Ukhuwwa, *Kitab ma'alim al-qirba fi ahkam al-hisba*, ed. R. Levy (Cambridge: Matba'at Dar al-Funun, 1937), 29–30, 197.

4 Ibn al-Ukhuwwa, *Ahkam al-hisba*, 195.

5 Muhammad ibn Abi Bakr ibn Qayyim al-Jawziya, *al-Turuq al-hukmiya fi-l-siyasa al-shar'iya*, ed. Muhammad Jamil Ahmad (Cairo: Matba'at al-Madani, 1961), 257.

6 al-Shaykh al-Imam Taqi al-Din Ahmad ibn Taymiya, *Public Duties in Islam: The Institution of the Hisba* [Risala fi'l hisba], trans. Muhtar Holland (London: The Islamic Foundation, 1982), 77; Ibn Taymiya, *Majmu' fatawa Shaykh al-Islam Ahmad ibn Taymiya*, ed. 'Abd al-Rahman ibn Muhammad ibn Qasim al-'Asimi al-Najdi al-Hanbali (Beirut: Mu'assasat al-Risala, 1997), 28:126.

7 Throughout this discussion I use *muhtasib* to refer to the individual Muslim who practices *hisba* in general, not exclusively the official appointed by the state, the market inspector.

8 Ibn Taymiya, *Majmu' fatawa*, 28:129.

9 Abu Hamid Muhammad ibn Muhammad ibn Muhammad al-Ghazali, *Ihya' 'ulum al-din* (Cairo: al-Halabi, 1928–29), 2:276–27; Basim Musallam, "The Ordering of Muslim Societies," *The Cambridge Illustrated History of the Islamic World*, ed. Francis Robinson (Cambridge: Cambridge University Press, 1996), 176.

10 Muslim, *Sahih Muslim, Being Traditions of the Sayings and Doings of the Prophet Muhammad as Narrated by His Companions and Compiled under the Title al-Jami'-us-Sahih*, trans. 'Abdul Hamid Siddiqi (New Delhi: Kitab Bhavan, 1982), 1:41, 1:33.

11 'Abd al-Rahman ibn Muhammad ibn Khaldun, *Muqadimmat Ibn Khaldun*, ed. 'Ali 'Abd al-Wafi (Cairo: Lajnat al-Bayan al-'Arabi, 1966), 2:639; Ibn Khaldun, *The Muqaddimah: An Introduction to History*, trans. Franz Rosenthal (London: Routledge and Kegan Paul, 1958), 1:323–24.

12 Shams al-Din Muhammad ibn Tulun, *Mufakahat al-khillan fi hawadith al-zaman*, ed. Muhammad Mustafa (Cairo: al-Mu'assasah al-Misriyah al-'Ammah, 1962, 1964), 1:21.

13 Ibn Tulun, *Mufakahat*, 1:32.

14 Ibn Tulun, *Mufakahat*, 1:65.

15 Shihab al-Din Ahmad ibn Tawq, *al-Ta'liq: Yawmiyat Shihab al-Din Ahmad ibn Tawq 834–915H/1430–1509M: Mudhakkarat kutibat bi Dimashq fi awakhir al-'ahd al-mamluki 885–908H/1480–1502M*, ed. Ja'far al-Muhajir (Damascus: Institut français d'études arabes, 2000–), 1:431–32.

16 Ibn Tulun, *Mufakahat*, 1:65.

17 Ibn Tulun, *Mufakahat*, 1:158. Ibn Tawq offers a more detailed account of the confrontations. In his version, the trigger is not the destruction of alcohol, but an unexplained dispute between the Sufi shaykh Mubarak and Arqamas, the sultan's *dawadar*. Ibn Tawq, *al-Ta'liq*, 3:1287–88.

18 Ibn Tulun, *Mufakahat*, 1:62.

19 Ibn Tawq, *al-Ta'liq*, 1:127.

20 The riot only ended with the mediation of the *na'ib al-qal'a*, who announced that the *hajib* would be removed from the position of *na'ib al-ghayba* until an order arrived from Cairo. Ibn Tulun, *Mufakahat*, 1:280.

21 Ibn Tulun, *Mufakahat*, 1:299.

22 Terry G. Wilfong, "The Non-Muslim Communities: Christian Communities," in *The Cambridge History of Egypt*, vol. 1, *Islamic Egypt, 640–1517*, ed. Carl F. Petry (Cambridge: Cambridge University Press, 1998), 197.

23 The history of the Islamization of Syria is by contrast less studied. This is in part a consequence of the historical sources themselves, which offer far less detail on conversion in Syria than in Egypt. It could also be a reflection of the Islamization of Syria itself, which is assumed to have been quicker than that of Egypt: the pre-Islamic presence of Arab tribes in Syria as well as the post-conquest resettlement patterns of Arab tribes probably meant the demographic balance shifted in favor of Muslims much sooner in Syria than in Egypt. While there is reason to assume that discriminatory decrees issued in Cairo (such as those prohibiting the employment of Coptic scribes) were also applied in Syrian cities, the fact that the contemporary historians pay less attention to Syrian Christian communities might suggest that it was the senior Coptic bureaucrats, based in the capital, who were the primary targets of such decrees. The historians' silence is remarkable given the evidence of anti-Christian and anti-Jewish polemics in Syria, especially during and in the aftermath of the Crusades and the Mongol attacks. For example:

Muhammad ibn Abi Bakr ibn Qayyim al-Jawziya, *Hidayat al-hayara fi-l-radd 'ala al-yahud wa-l-nasara*, ed. Sayf al-Din al-Katib (Beirut: Dar Maktabat al-Hayah, 1980).

24 Tamer El-Leithy, "Coptic Culture and Conversion in Medieval Cairo, 1293–1524 AD" (PhD diss., Princeton University, 2005).

25 Wilfong, "Non-Muslim Communities," 184; Donald P. Little, "Coptic Conversions to Islam during the Bahri Mamluk Period," in *Conversion and Continuity: Indigenous Christian Communities in Islamic Lands, Eighth to Eighteenth Centuries*, ed. Michael Gervers and Ramzi Jibran Bikhazi (Toronto: Pontifical Institute of Medieval Studies, 1990), 263–88.

26 The *shurut* reflect the concerns and anxieties of the Arab Muslim conquerors at a time when they were a minority among the populations. Albrecht Noth, "Problems of Differentiations between Muslims and non-Muslims: Re-reading the 'Ordinance of 'Umar' (al-Shurut al-'Umariya)," in *Muslims and Others in Early Islamic Society*, ed. Robert Hoyland (Aldershot: Ashgate Variorium, 2004), 103–24.

27 M. Perlmann, "Notes on Anti-Christian Propaganda in the Mamluk Empire," *Bulletin of the School of Oriental and African Studies* 10, no. 4 (1942): 843–61.

28 Kirsten Stilt, *Islamic Law in Action: Authority, Discretion, and Everyday Experiences in Mamluk Egypt* (Oxford: Oxford University Press, 2011), 118.

29 Stilt, *Islamic Law in Action*, 112.

30 Ahmad ibn 'Ali al-Maqrizi, *Kitab al-suluk li ma'rifat duwal al-muluk*, ed. Muhammad Mustafa Ziyada (Cairo: Dar al-Kutub al-Misriya, 1936), 4:486, 494, 495.

31 al-Maqrizi, *al-Suluk*, 4:416.

32 al-Maqrizi, *al-Suluk*, 4:486.

33 Michael Dols, *The Black Death in the Middle East* (Princeton, NJ: Princeton University Press, 1977), 114.

34 Badr al-Din Mahmud al-'Ayni, *'Iqd al-juman fi tarikh ahl al-zaman li Badr al-Din Mahmud al-'Ayni al-mutawwafi sanat AH 855/AD 1451 al-Hawadith wa-l-tarajim min sanat AH 815–824*, ed. 'Abd al-Raziq al-Tantawi al-Qarmut (Cairo: Matba'at 'Ala', 1985), 1:361. Berkey, in an analysis of the changing functions of the *muhtasib*, interprets these actions as exceptions that prove the rule and refers them to the piety and zeal of Sadr al-Din al-'Ajami, who was unusual among his generation of *muhtasib*s in evoking the post's moral and religious obligations. Jonathan P. Berkey, "The *Muhtasib*s of Cairo under the Mamluks: Toward an Understanding of an Islamic Institution," in *The Mamluks in Egyptian and Syrian Politics and Society*, ed. Michael Winter and Amalia Levanoni (Leiden and Boston: Brill, 2004), 263–64. Yet Ibn al-'Ajami's forceful and pious personality notwithstanding, the general historical climate of the period, and in particular the trauma caused by the plague, cannot be ignored.

35 On 26 Rajab 822/18 August 1419, a crowd carrying arms and rocks destroyed three hundred barrels of alcohol which belonged to Franks (foreigners) living in the city, at a cost of 4,000 dinars. The crowd then moved to attack the houses and stores of the Franks as well as the houses of glassmakers, destroying more alcohol and pillaging their belongings. Presumably the glassmakers were targeted for manufacturing containers for the alcohol. Al-Maqrizi, *al-Suluk*, 4:503.

36 al-Maqrizi, *al-Suluk*, 4:610.

37 Thus also al-Maqrizi, *al-Suluk*, 3:1040 (803/1400), 4:486 (Rabi' I 822/ March 1419), 4:493–94 (Jumada I 822/June 1419); al-'Ayni, *'Iqd al-juman* 1:303 (Sha'ban 820/September 1417), 1:361 (Rabi' I 822/March 1419), 1:361–62 (Jumada I 822/June 1419).

38 Zayn al-Din 'Abd al-Basit ibn Khalil ibn Shahin al-Zahiri, *Nayl al-amal fi dhayl al-duwal*, ed. 'Umar 'Abd al-Salam Tadmuri (Beirut and Sidon: al-Maktaba al-'Asriya, 2002), vol. 2, pt. 5, 100–101.

39 'Ali ibn Dawud al-Jawhari ibn al-Sayrafi, *Inba' al-hasr bi abna' al-'asr: Annals of Egypt and Syria*, ed. Hasan Habashi (Cairo: Dar al-Fikr al-'Arabi, 1970), 424.

40 Qaytbay presided over other murder cases, for example, the murder of a Mamluk by his slaves and concubines: Ibn al-Sayrafi, *Inba' al-hasr*, 425.

41 Ibn al-Sayrafi takes issue with this ruling: the conversion of a *dhimmi*, unless he is a non-Muslim in battle with Muslims, does not absolve him of murder, he argues. Ibn al-Sayrafi, *Inba' al-hasr*, 424.

42 Ibn al-Sayrafi, *Inba' al-hasr*, 424.

43 Ibn al-Sayrafi, *Inba' al-hasr*, 424.

44 al-Maqrizi, *al-Suluk*, 4:486.

45 al-'Ayni, *'Iqd al-juman*, 1:361–62. Al-'Ayni's comment is indicative of a prevailing attitude: even when they tried to acquiesce and converted to Islam, the Coptic converts were still considered suspect and their dedication to Islam questionable.

46 al-Maqrizi, *al-Suluk*, 4:494–95.

47 al-Maqrizi, *al-Suluk*, 4:495.

48 Shams al-Din Muhammad ibn Abd al-Rahman al-Sakhawi, *Kitab al-tibr al-masbuk fi dhayl al-suluk* (Cairo: Maktabat al-Kulliyat al-Azhariya, n.d.), 36–40. Ibn Shahin al-Zahiri offers a short account: *Nayl al-amal*, vol. 2, pt. 5, 157.

49 By the fifteenth century this was no longer an option for many converts, especially those from elite bureaucratic families, as their Mamluk patrons often insisted that the whole family and household convert together. El-Leithy, "Coptic Culture and Conversion," 67–78.

50 Thus, for example, female converts resorted to the Maliki school, which insisted that children were not to follow their mother's religion, to ensure that their children could remain *dhimmi*. El-Leithy, "Coptic Culture and Conversion," 84, 94–96.

51   El-Leithy, "Coptic Culture and Conversion," 125.

52   al-Maqrizi, *al-Suluk*, 4:511.

53   In the *fiqh* manual *al-Madkhal* by the Maliki jurist Ibn al-Hajj, the author expresses shock at the behavior of men and women in Egypt. Huda Lutfi, "Manners and Customs of Fourteenth-century Cairene Women: Female Anarchy versus Male Shar'i Order in Muslim Prescriptive Treatises," in *Women in Middle Eastern History*, ed. Nikki Keddie and Beth Baron (New Haven: Yale University Press, 1991), 99–121.

54   al-Maqrizi, *al-Suluk*, 4:594.

55   Christopher S. Taylor, *In the Vicinity of the Righteous: Ziyara and the Veneration of Muslim Saints in Late Medieval Egypt* (Leiden: Brill, 1999), 57–60.

56   al-Maqrizi, *al-Suluk*, 4:619.

57   al-Maqrizi, *al-Suluk*, 4:614.

58   Ibn Shahin al-Zahiri, *Nayl al-amal*, vol. 2, pt. 5, 24–25; al-Maqrizi, *al-Suluk*, 4:1031, 1033; Jamal al-Din Abu al-Mahasin Yusuf ibn Taghribirdi, *al-Nujum al-zahira fi muluk Misr wa-l-Qahira* (Cairo: al-Mu'assasa al-Misriya al-'Amma li-l-Ta'lif wa-l-Tarjama wa-l-Tiba'a wa-l-Nashr, 1963–71), 15:93–94; Muhammad ibn Ahmad ibn Iyas, *Bada'i' al-zuhur fi waqa'i' al-duhur*, ed. Paul Kahle and Muhammad Mustafa (Istanbul: Staatsdruckerei, 1931–45), 2:182.

59   Ibn Shahin al-Zahiri, *Nayl al-amal*, vol. 2, pt. 5, 28–29; al-Maqrizi, *al-Suluk*, 4:1038; Ibn Taghribirdi, *al-Nujum al-zahira*, 15:93–95.

60   al-Maqrizi, *al-Suluk*, 4:1209; Ibn Iyas, *Bada'i' al-zuhur*, 2:225; Ibn Shahin al-Zahiri, *Nayl al-amal*, vol. 2, pt. 5, 123; Ibn Taghribirdi, *History of Egypt*, 4:149.

61   This was another attempt to introduce an indirect tax. Ibn Iyas, *Bada'i' al-zuhar*, 3:64.

62   Ibn al-Sayrafi, *Inba' al-hasr*, 226–29.

63   The reference to exactly three suitors, only one of whom is identified, is rather suspicious. It is quite reminiscent of folk tales and the *Alf layla* tradition. The choice of suitors could very well have been a fictitious formula included in such documents.

64   The text is not clear. News had reached the *dawadar* that "he had coerced the girl, him and his master, and they used to do to her what was not permissible to do, so she fled from them. Her aunt was angered and he unlawfully wrote a complaint against her." Ibn al-Sayrafi, *Inba' al-hasr*, 228.

65   They appropriated commodities that belonged to the people of the neighborhood, essentially forcing an illegal tax on them: a fraction of straw, clover, fodder, chickens, and anything that went through the *hara*. When they "bought" something from the market they paid only a quarter of its value. Al-Maqrizi describes Harat Qaraqush as lying inside Bab al-Futuh in his days. Taqi al-Din Ahmad ibn 'Ali ibn 'Abd al-Qadir al-Maqrizi, *al-Mawa'iz wa-l-i'tibar fi dhikr al-khitat wa-l-athar*, ed. Ayman Fu'ad Sayyid (London: al-Furqan Islamic Heritage Foundation, 2002), 3:3–4.

66 Petry stresses the status of the girl as a member of the Mamluk class. This is based on the reference to the petition she supposedly presented to the Hanafi chief qadi asking him to find her a suitable match. The text that Ibn al-Sayrafi quotes reads, after the *basmalla*, "the *mamluka*, the relative of so-and-so [female], the adolescent virgin . . . ." This is the only reference in Ibn al-Sayrafi's text to Mamluks or Mamluk descent. Her parents are not named, nor is she. The petition states that she is "poor and had tired of begging," which, along with her parents' abandoning her, suggests that she did not come from a privileged background, much less a Mamluk one. Petry seems to consider her a member of the elite by virtue of the *mamluka* reference. However, this seems more in line with the conventional formulaic used in petitions; *mamluka* probably means 'your slave' in a figurative sense. It is used in this manner in petitions included in the Haram collection, such as Haram no. 215. Carl F. Petry, "Conjugal Rights versus Class Prerogatives: A Divorce Case in Mamluk Cairo," in *Women in the Medieval Islamic World: Power, Patronage, and Piety*, ed. Gavin R.G. Hambly (London: Macmillan, 1998), 227–40. Little reproduces and translates Haram no. 215 in Donald P. Little, "A Fourteenth-century Jerusalem Court Record of a Divorce Hearing: A Case Study," in *Mamluks and Ottomans: Studies in Honour of Michael Winter*, ed. David J. Wasserstein and Ami Ayalon (London and New York: Routledge, 2006), 69–71.

67 Petry, "Conjugal Rights," 236–37.

68 Harat Qaraqush was at a distance from Bulaq, so it is unlikely that this particular soldier's evil had spanned both neighborhoods.

69 Ibn Taghribirdi, *al-Nujum al-zahira*, 14:282; al-Maqrizi, *al-Suluk*, 4:698.

70 Stilt, *Islamic Law in Action*, 203.

71 Berkey, "*Muhtasibs*," 267–68.

72 Berkey, "*Muhtasibs*," 254–56. The short tenures can also be appreciated from a reading of the tables combined by 'Abd ar-Raziq: Ahmad 'Abd ar-Raziq, "La *hisba* et le *muhtasib* en Egypte au temps des Mamluks," *Annales Islamologiques/Hawliyyat Islamiyah* 13 (1977): 115–78; 'Abd ar-Raziq, "Les *muhtasibs* de Fostat au temps des Mamluks," *Annales Islamologiques* 14 (1978): 127–46.

73 With brief interruptions, he was *muhtasib* from Sha'ban 910/1505 to Ramadan 914/1509, Dhu al-Qa'da 914/1509 to Rabi' I 922/1516, and Rabi' II 922/1516 to Ramadan 922/1516, and was reappointed under the Ottoman administration in Muharram 923/1517. 'Abd ar-Raziq, "La *hisba* et le *muhtasib* en Egypte," 177–78.

74 'Abd ar-Raziq, "Les *muhtasibs* de Fostat," 143–44.

75 The sale of the office of *muhtasib* almost became the norm during that period. 'Abd ar-Raziq, "La *hisba* et le *muhtasib* en Egypte," 128.

76 al-Maqrizi, *al-Suluk*, 4:534.

77 Adam Sabra, *Poverty and Charity in Medieval Islam: Mamluk Egypt, 1250–1517* (Cambridge: Cambridge University Press, 2000), 136.

78 al-Maqrizi, *al-Suluk*, 4:330.
79 al-Maqrizi, *al-Suluk*, 4:330–31.
80 al-Maqrizi, *al-Suluk*, 4:332.
81 al-'Ayni, *'Iqd al-juman*, 1:255.
82 al-'Ayni himself does not allude to the incident but other contemporary historians report it: al-Maqrizi, *al-Suluk*, 4:698; Ibn Taghribirdi, *al-Nujum al-zahira*, 14:281–82.
83 Ibn Taghribirdi, *al-Nujum al-zahira*, 15:397–401.
84 Ibn Iyas, *Bada'i' al-zuhur*, 3:257.
85 For example, the stoning of 'Abd al-Qadir, the *muhtasib* of Damascus in 892/1487 discussed on page 148. Ibn Tulun, *Mufakahat*, 1:84.
86 We have seen how the people of Damascus rose up against the sultan's agent, Ibn al-Nabulsi, in 880/1475: Ibn Iyas, *Bada'i' al-zuhur*, 3:107. The *khassaki* Qarqamas who arrived in Damascus to confiscate properties was the target of the famous riot of 895/1490, while another official who went to tax the silk weavers was attacked in 897/1491: Ibn Tulun, *Mufakahat*, 1:124–27, 146. A *khassaki* who arrived in 902/1497 to tax the *awqaf* was denounced from the minarets of the Umayyad Mosque: Ibn Tulun, *Mufakahat*, 1:178.
87 Ibn Tulun, *Mufakahat*, 1:95.
88 Ridicule and satire, rather than outright violent attacks, seem to have been the fate of qadis under the Mamluks.
89 Donald P. Little, "A Fourteenth-century Jerusalem Court Record," 68. Little cites Ibn Qadi Shuhba for a biography of the qadi, whose archives survive.
90 Ibn Tulun, *Mufakahat*, 1:24.
91 The position of *wakil al-sultan* was often occupied by men from merchant families. As with other senior state positions, posts often returned to members of the same family. Ibn al-Sawwa's nephew Abu Bakr would later be appointed as *wakil al-sultan*: Shams al-Din Muhammad ibn Abd al-Rahman al-Sakhawi, *al-Daw' al-lami' li ahl al-qarn al-tasi'* (Cairo: Maktabat al-Quds, 1353 [1934–36]), 11:255.
92 Ibn Tulun, *Mufakahat*, 1:95.
93 al-Maqrizi, *al-Suluk*, 3:1053.
94 al-Maqrizi, *al-Suluk*, 3:1056.
95 al-Maqrizi, *al-Suluk*, 4:429–30.
96 al-Maqrizi, *al-Suluk*, 4:429–30.
97 Dissatisfaction reported in Cairo: al-Maqrizi, *al-Suluk*, 4:436–38.
98 al-Maqrizi, *al-Suluk*, 4:439.
99 al-'Ayni, *'Iqd al-juman*, 1:326.
100 Ibn Iyas, *Bada'i' al-zuhur*, 3:289. The events of the year 898 are completely missing from Ibn Tulun's manuscript of *Mufakahat al-khillan*, which would most probably have reported on this incident.

101 Ibn Iyas, *Bada'i' al-zuhur*, 4:88–89. Interestingly, the Damascene historian Ibn Tulun does not include a riot in his report of the viceroy's dismissal from office. It is highly unlikely that he was not aware of such a development, had it taken place. It is more likely that it was Ibn Iyas whose information was less accurate: in reporting on "trouble in Damascus" he assumed it involved a riot, or else embellished his account by including a riot. His report suggests that a riot was not an unlikely occurrence and hints at a perception that Damascenes were likely to riot and stone officials.

102 James P. Grehan, "Street Violence and Social Imagination in Late-Mamluk and Ottoman Damascus (Ca. 1500–1800)," *International Journal of Middle East Studies* 35 (2003): 215–36.

103 Ahmad al-Budayri al-Hallaq, *Hawadith Dimashq al-Yawmiya 1154– 1175/1741–1762*, ed Ahmad 'Izzat 'Abd al-Karim (Cairo: al-Jam'iya al-Misriya li-l-Dirasat al-Tarikhiya, 1959), 52.

104 al-Budayri *Hawadith*, 63-64.

105 Ibn al-Ukhuwwa, *Ahkam al-hisba*, 19–21.

106 Patricia Crone, *Medieval Islamic Political Thought* (Edinburgh: Edinburgh University Press, 2005), 301.

107 Cook, *Commanding Right and Forbidding Wrong*, 75.

108 al-Ghazali, *Ihya' 'ulum al-din*, 2: 300; Cook, *Commanding Right and Forbidding Wrong*, 82.

109 The earliest surviving manuscript of Ibn Bassam's manual dates to 844/1440, suggesting he lived before that date and during the Mamluk period. Muhammad ibn Ahmad ibn Bassam al-Muhtasib, *Nihayat al-rutba fi talab al-hisba*, ed. Husam al-Din al-Samarra'i (Baghdad: Matba'at al-Ma'arif, 1968), 12–14.

110 Ibn Bassam, *Nihayat al-rutba*, 215.

111 al-Maqrizi, *al-Suluk*, 4:498–500.

112 This rationale informs Ibn Khaldun's evaluation of the first two *fitnas*: Ibn Khaldun, *Muqaddimat Ibn Khaldun*, ed. 'Abd al-Wafi, 2:714, 725, 731–33.

113 Ibn Khaldun, *Muqaddimat Ibn Khaldun*, ed. 'Abd al-Wafi, 2:639; Ibn Khaldun, *Muqaddimah*, trans. Rosenthal, 1:324.

114 Ibn Khaldun, *Muqaddimat Ibn Khaldun*, ed. 'Abd al-Wafi, 2:641; Ibn Khaldun, *Muqaddimah*, trans. Rosenthal, 1:326.

115 Ibn Taymiya, *al-Siyasa al-shar'iya fi islah al-ra'i wa-l-ra'iya*, ed. Abu Ya'li al-Quwaysni (Beirut: Dar al-Kutub al-'Ilmiya, 1988), 72–75.

116 Ibn Taymiya, *al-Siyasa al-shar'iya*, 137–39.

117 Ibn Taymiya, *al-Siyasa al-shar'iya*, 130. He quotes a Hadith by 'Umar ibn al-Khattab in which, as caliph, he stresses the injunction that his delegates are not to treat Muslims unjustly or take their money without due cause, and if anyone did he would punish them himself; he also affirmed that he had seen the Prophet exercising *qisas* against himself: *"wa qad ra'aytu rasul Allah salla Allahu 'alayhi wa sallam yaqus min nafsihi."*

118 Ibn Taymiya, *Majmuʿ fatawa*, 28:128.
119 A.K.S. Lambton, "*Quis custodiet custodes?* Some Reflections on the Persian Theory of Government," *Studia Islamica* 5 (1956): 125–26, reprinted in A.K.S. Lambton, *Theory and Practice in Medieval Persian Government* (London: Variorum Reprints, 1980); A.K.S. Lambton, *State and Government in Medieval Islam: An Introduction to the Study of Islamic Political Theory: The Jurists* (Oxford: Oxford University Press, 1981), 94–95; Leonard Binder, "Al-Ghazali's Theory of Islamic Government," *The Muslim World* 14 (1955): 230.
120 Ibn Khaldun, *Muqaddimat Ibn Khaldun*, ed. ʿAbd al-Wafi, 2:852; Ibn Khaldun, *Muqaddimah*, trans. Rosenthal, 2:107–108.
121 Lambton, *State and Government*, 77.
122 Quoted by Lambton, *State and Government*, 80.
123 Lambton, *State and Government*, 85, citing Abu al-Hasan ʿAli ibn Muhammad al-Mawardi, *Adab al-qadi*, ed. Muhiyy Hilal al-Sarhan (Baghdad: al-Jumhuriya al-ʿIraqiya, Diwan al-Awqaf, 1971), 1:644.
124 There were also the possibilities of the curtailment of the imam's liberty or his being taken captive, situations that were very much part of the historical context of late Abbasid Baghdad. They also applied to later times when sultans, especially under the Mamluk regime, were often deposed and imprisoned while rivals seized the throne. Al-Mawardi, *al-Ahkam al-sultaniya*, 17; Lambton, *State and Government*, 92.
125 al-Maqrizi, *al-Suluk*, 4:220, 223.
126 The rise of the Mamluk regime led Ibn Taymiya, by contrast, to develop political thought to transcend the institution of the caliphate. Circumventing any debate about who the legitimate caliph is, or the qualifications of the caliph, Ibn Taymiya focuses instead on the application of the sharia in practice. What is essential for a Muslim society according to this analysis is not that a caliph should rule but that the sharia is upheld; it does not matter who is applying it. Linda S. Northrup, "The Bahri Mamluk Sultanate, 1250–1390," in *The Cambridge History of Egypt*, vol. 1, *Islamic Egypt, 640–1517*, ed. Carl Petry (Cambridge: Cambridge University Press, 1998), 256; E.I.J. Rosenthal, *Political Thought in Medieval Islam* (Cambridge: Cambridge University Press, 1962), 44–45, 52.
127 Abd al-Wahhab al-Shaʿrani, *The Guidebook for Gullible Jurists and Mendicants to the Conditions for Befriending Emirs and The Abbreviated Guidebook for Gullible Jurists and Mendicants to the Conditions for Befriending Emirs*, ed. Adam Sabra (Cairo: IFAO, 2013), 29.
128 al-Maqrizi, *al-Suluk*, 3:990–91.
129 al-Maqrizi, *al-Suluk*, 4:34.
130 al-ʿAyni, *ʿIqd al-juman*, 1:108.
131 Ibn Iyas, *Badaʾiʿ al-zuhur*, 3:314.
132 al-Maqrizi, *al-Suluk*, 3:964.

133 al-Maqrizi, *al-Suluk*, 3:964.

134 Toru Miura, "Administrative Networks in the Mamluk Period: Taxation, Legal Execution, and Bribery," in *Islamic Urbanism in Human History: Political Power and Social Networks*, ed. Tsugitaka Sato (London and New York: Kegan Paul International, 1997), 55.

135 Ibn Iyas, *Bada'i' al-zuhur*, 4:114–15.

136 al-Maqrizi, *al-Suluk*, 4:448, 483.

137 al-Maqrizi, *al-Suluk*, 4:484.

138 al-Maqrizi, *al-Suluk*, 4:447, 453.

139 al-'Ayni, *'Iqd al-juman*, 1: 226–28, 351–53.

140 al-Maqrizi, *al-Suluk*, 4:485–86.

141 Theories of semantics recognize both the denotational and connotational meanings of words. For example: G. Leech, *Semantics* (Harmondsworth: Penguin, 1985), 18. Grehan discusses the symbolic power of words in Damascus culture in the seventeenth and eighteenth centuries, yet it is arguable that the weight of uttering specific formulations, especially in prayer to God, had deeper roots in medieval Arab culture. James P. Grehan, "The Mysterious Power of Words: Language, Law, and Culture in Ottoman Damascus (17th–18th Centuries)," *Journal of Social History* 37, no. 4 (2004): 991–1015.

142 Sharaf al-Din Musa ibn Yusuf al-Ansari, *Nuzhat al-khatir wa bahjat al-nazir* (Damascus: Ministry of Culture, 1991), 2:194.

143 Ibn Tulun, *Mufakahat*, 1:124–25, 127, 132; Ibn Tawq, *al-Ta'liq*, 2:951.

144 al-Maqrizi, *al-Suluk*, 4:536.

145 يلع سمطأ انربر اولوقو هل اوعداف مبر نم رشحلا يف هليو اي الغلا اناتأ منم ملاظو ملاوماً هلبق ىلع ددشاو Ibn Iyas, *Bada'i' al-zuhur*, 3:39. I thank my colleague Adam Talib for helping with this translation.

146 "قردلا زبخ ينمعطي ةركسملا يذ يجوز" Ibn Iyas, *Bada'i' al-zuhur*, 3:231–32.

147 Ibn Iyas, *Bada'i' al-zuhur*, 3:397–98.

148 Such as, for example, the verses Ibn Iyas quotes satirizing the Shafi'i qadi Ibn al-Naqib, who had paid a bribe to obtain the position of chief qadi: Ibn Iyas, *Bada'i' al-zuhur*, 4:91–92.

149 Ibn Iyas, *Bada'i' al-zuhur*, 4:87, 112–14.

150 Some modern sources translate *harafish* as "vagabonds."

151 Modern historians have differed in their definition of the *harafish* of the Middle Ages. The term was sometimes used in the sources to refer to generic common people, the 'rabble.' At other times it was used for specific, apparently organized groups. As Brinner shows, begging seems to have been one of their main occupations. William M. Brinner, "The Significance of the *Harafish* and Their 'Sultan,'" *Journal of the Economic and Social History of the Orient* 6, no. 2 (July 1963): 196. For example: when beggars clamored upon the sultan al-Ashraf Barsbay while he was out on a procession one day, the angered sultan sent for the sultan of the *harafish* and the procession

one day, the angered sultan sent for the sultan of the harafish and the shaykh of the beggars and ordered them to prevent professional beggars from begging on the streets and to obligate them to find employment. Ibn Taghribirdi, *History of Egypt*, 4:148. This, and other references, suggest a link between the harafish and beggars and confirm some form of organization and leadership for both groups.

152 Ibn Tulun, *Mufakahat*, 1:114.

153 Mikhail Bakhtin, *Rabelais and His World*, trans. Hélène Iswolsky (Bloomington: Indiana University Press, 1984), 7.

154 Al-'Ayni, *'Iqd al-juman*, 2:646.

155 Al-'Ayni, *'Iqd al-juman*, 2:646. The incident is also reported in al-Sakhawi, *Kitab al-tibr*, 126–27.

156 Bakhtin, *Rabelais*, 7.

157 Boaz Shoshan, *Popular Culture in Medieval Cairo*, (Cambridge: Cambridge University Press, 1993), 46, 48, 50–51.

158 Huda Lutfi, "Coptic Festivals of the Nile: Aberrations of the Past?" in *The Mamluks in Egyptian Politics and Society*, ed. Thomas Philipp and Ulrich Haarman (Cambridge: Cambridge University Press, 1998), 254–82.

159 Nicholas B. Dirks, "Ritual and Resistance: Subversion as a Social Fact," in *Culture/Power/History: A Reader in Contemporary Social Theory*, ed. Nicholas B. Dirks, Geoff Eley, and Sherry B. Otner (Princeton, NJ: Princeton University Press, 1994), 485; Natalie Zemon Davis, *Society and Culture in Early Modern France: Eight Essays* (Cambridge, UK: Polity, 1987), 130.

160 Ibn Iyas, *Bada'i' al-zuhur*, 3:200, 214, 235, 365; 4:96, 232–33; 5:82.

161 Th. Bianquis, "Zu'ar," in *Encyclopaedia of Islam*, 2nd ed., ed. P. Bearman, Th. Bianquis, C.E. Bosworth, E. van Donzel, and W.P. Heinrichs (Brill Online, 2014), http://referenceworks.brillonline.com/entries/encyclopaedia-of-islam-2/zuar-SIM_8185

162 Bianquis, "Zu'ar"; Cl. Cahen, "Mouvements populaires et autonomisme urbain dans l'Asie musulmane," *Arabica* 5 (1958): 225–50; 6 (1959): 25–56, 233–65.

163 Bianquis, "Zu'ar"; E. Geoffroy, *Le soufisme en Égypte et en Syrie sous les derniers Mamelouks et les premiers Ottomans*, Orientations spirituelles et enjeux culturels (Damascus: Publications de l'Institut français de Damas, 1995), index s.v.

164 Ira M. Lapidus, *Muslim Cities in the Later Middle Ages* (Cambridge, MA: Harvard University Press, 1967), 155.

165 Lapidus, *Muslim Cities*, 156.

166 Ibn Tulun, *Mufakahat*, 1:176.

167 Ibn Tulun, *Mufakahat*, 1:251–52.

168 Lapidus, *Muslim Cities*, 156–58.

169 Lapidus, *Muslim Cities*, 158.

170 Lapidus, *Muslim Cities*, 159–62.

171 Lapidus, *Muslim Cities*, 162.

172 al-Sakhawi, *al-Tibr al-masbuk*, 87; Ibn Shahin al-Zahiri, *Nayl al-amal*, vol. 2, pt. 5, 184; al-'Ayni, *'Iqd al-juman*, 2:620.
173 al-Sakhawi, *al-Tibr al-masbuk*, 87.
174 al-'Ayni, *'Iqd al-juman*, 2:620; al-Sakhawi, *al-Tibr al-masbuk*, 87. For references to Shi'ism in popular Egyptian culture, including the derogatory use of the term *rafadi*, see Devin J. Stewart, "Popular Shiism in Medieval Egypt: Vestiges of Islamic Sectarian Polemics in Egyptian Arabic," *Studia Islamica* 84 (1996): 35–66.
175 Stuart J. Borsch, *The Black Death in Egypt and England: A Comparative Study* (Cairo: American University in Cairo Press, 2005), 48.
176 Borsch, *Black Death*, 49.
177 Borsch, *Black Death*, 49.
178 Ira M. Lapidus, "The Grain Economy of Mamluk Egypt," *Journal of the Economic and Social History of the Orient* 12 (1969): 8, 11–14.
179 Dols, *Black Death*, 163–65.
180 al-Maqrizi, *al-Suluk*, 4:672.

BIBLIOGRAPHY

Primary Sources

al-Ansari, Sharaf al-Din Musa ibn Yusuf. *Nuzhat al-khatir wa bahjat al-nazir*. 2 vols. Damascus: Ministry of Culture, 1991.

al-'Ayni, Badr al-Din Mahmud. *'Iqd al-juman fi tarikh ahl al-zaman li Badr al-Din Mahmud al-'Ayni al-mutawwafi sanat AH 855/AD 1451 al-Hawadith wa-l-tarajim min sanat AH 815–824*, edited by 'Abd al-Raziq al-Tantawi al-Qarmut. 2 vols. Cairo: Matba'at 'Ala', 1985.

———. *al-Rawd al-zahir fi sirat al-Malik al-Zahir Tatar*, edited by Hans Ernst. Cairo: al-Halabi, 1962.

———. *al-Sayf al-Muhannad fi sirat al-Malik al-Mu'ayyad Shaykh al-Mahmudi*, edited by Fahim Muhammad Shaltut. Cairo: Dar al-Katib al-'Arabi li-l-Tiba'a wa-l-Nashr, 1967.

Ben Shemesh, A. *Taxation in Islam*, vol. 3, *Abu Yusuf's Kitab al-Kharaj*, edited and translated by A. Ben Shemesh. Leiden and London: E.J. Brill and Luzac & Co., 1969.

al-Budayri al-Hallaq, Ahmad. *Hawadith Dimashq al-yawmiya 1154–1175/1741–1762*, edited by Ahmad 'Izzat 'Abd al-Karim. Cairo: al-Jam'iya al-Misriya li-l-Dirasat al-Tarikhiya, 1959.

Crecelius, Daniel, and 'Abd al-Wahab Bakr, trans. *al-Damurdashi's Chronicle of Egypt. 1688–1755*. Leiden, New York, Copenhagen, and Cologne: E.J. Brill, 1991.

al-Damurdashi, Ahmad Katkhuda 'Azaban. *Kitab al-durra al-musana fi akhbar al-kinana fi akhbar ma waqa' fi Misr fi dawlat al-mamalik min al-sanajik wa-l-kushshaf w-al-sab'at ujaqat wa-l-dawla wa 'awaydhum wa-l-basha ila akhir sanat thaman wa sittin wa mi'a wa alf*, edited by 'Abd al-Rahim 'Abd al-Rahman 'Abd al-Rahim. Cairo: IFAO, 1989.

"Sahih Muslim." *Encyclopedia of Hadith. Jam' jawami' al-ahadith wa-l-asanid wa-maknaz al-sihah wa-l-sunan wa-l-masanid*. Vaduz, Liechtenstein and Cairo: Thesaurus Islamicus Foundation, 2000.

al-Ghazali, Abu Hamid Muhammad ibn Muhammad ibn Muhammad. *Ihya' 'ulum al-din*. 4 vols. Cairo: al-Halabi, 1969.

———. *Kitab al-iqtisaad fi-l-i'tiqad*. Cairo: al-Khanji, 1909.

———. *al-Tibr al-masbuk fi nasihat al-muluk*. Cairo: Maktabat al-Kulliyat al-Azhariya, 1968.

al-Ghazzi, Najm al-Din. *al-Kawakib al-sa'ira bi a'yan al-mi'a al-'ashira*, edited by Jibra'il Sulayman Jabbur. 3 vols. Beirut: American University of Beirut, 1945–58.

———. *al-Kawakib al-sa'ira bi a'yan al-mi'a al-'ashira*, edited by Khalil al-Mansur. 3 vols. Beirut: Dar al-Kutub al-'Ilmiya, 1997.

Ibn Bassam al-Muhtasib, Muhammad ibn Ahmad *Nihayat al-rutba fi talab al-hisba*, edited by Husam al-Din al-Samarra'i. Baghdad: Matba'at al-Ma'arif, 1968.

Ibn Hajar al-'Asqalani, Shihab al-Din Ahmad ibn 'Ali ibn Muhammad. *al-Durar al-kamina fi a'yan al-mi'a al-thamina*, edited by al-Shaykh 'Abd al-Warith Muhammad 'Ali. 4 vols. Beirut: Dar al-Kutub al-'Ilmiya, 1997.

Ibn Hajar al-'Asqalani, *Inba' al-ghumr bi anba' al-'umar*, edited by Hasan Habashi. 3 vols. Cairo: al-Majlis al-A'la lil-Shu'un al-Islamiya, 1969.

Ibn al-Hajj. *al-Madkhal*. Cairo: al-Matba'a al-Misriya bi al-Azhar, 1929.

Ibn al-Hanbali, Radiyy al-Din Muhammad ibn Ibrahim ibn Yusuf al-Halabi. *Durr al-habab fi tarikh a'yan Halab, 908–971*, edited by Mahmud Hamad al-Fakhuri and Yahya Zakariya 'Abbara. Damascus: Manshurat Wazarat al-Thaqafa, 1972.

Ibn al-Himsi, Shihab al-Din Ahmad ibn Muhammad. *Hawadith al-zaman wa wafayat al-shuyukh wa-l-aqran*, edited by 'Umar 'Abd al-Salam Tadmuri. 3 vols. Sidon and Beirut: al-Maktaba al-'Asriya, 1999

Ibn al-'Imad al-Hanbali, Abu al-Falah 'Abd al-Hayy *Shadharat al-dhahab fi akhbar min dhahab*. 8 vols. Cairo: Maktabat al-Qudsi, 1931.

Ibn Iyas, Muhammad ibn Ahmad. *Bada'i' al-zuhur fi waqa'i' al-duhur*, edited by Paul Kahle and Muhammad Mustafa. 5 vols. Istanbul: Staatsdruckerei, 1931–45.

Ibn al-Jawzi, Abu al-Faraj 'Abd al-Rahman ibn 'Ali. *Kitab al-qusas wa-l-mudhak-kirin*, edited by Qasim al-Sammarra'i. Riyadh: Dar Umayyah li-l-Nashr wa-l-Tawzi', 1983.

Ibn al-Ji'an, Yahya ibn al-Muqirr. *Kitab al-tuhfa al-saniya bi asma' al-bilad al-mis-riya*, edited by Bernhard Moritz. Cairo: Maktabat al-Kulliyat al-Azhariya, 1974.

Ibn Kannan al-Salihi, Muhammad. *Yawmiyat shamiya aw al-hawadith al-yawmiya min tarikh ahad 'ashr wa alf wa mi'a*, edited by Akram Hasan al-'Ulabi. Damascus: Dar al-Tabba', n.d.

Ibn Khaldun, 'Abd al-Rahman ibn Muhammad. *Muqadimmat Ibn Khaldun*, edited by 'Ali 'Abd al-Wafi. 4 vols. Cairo: Lajnat al-Bayan al-'Arabi, 1966.
———. *The Muqaddimah: An Introduction to History*. Translated by Franz Rosenthal. 3 vols. London: Routledge and Kegan Paul, 1958.

Ibn Qayyim al-Jawziya, Muhammad ibn Abi Bakr. *Hidayat al-hayara fi-l-radd 'ala al-yahud wa-l-nasara*, edited by Sayf al-Din al-Katib. Beirut: Dar Maktabat al-Hayah, 1980.
———. *al-Turuq al-hukmiya fi-l-siyasa al-shar'iya*, edited by Muhammad Jamil Ahmad. Cairo: Matba'at al-Madani, 1961.

Ibn al-Sayrafi, 'Ali ibn Dawud al-Jawhari. *Inba' al-hasr bi abna' al-'asr: Annals of Egypt and Syria*, edited by Hasan Habashi. Cairo: Dar al-Fikr al-'Arabi, 1970.

Ibn Shahin al-Zahiri al-Hanafi al-Malati, Zayn al-Din 'Abd al-Basit Ibn Khalil. *Nayl al-amal fi dhayl al-duwal*, edited by 'Umar 'Abd al-Salam Tadmuri. 9 vols. Beirut and Sidon: al-Maktaba al-'Asriya, 2002.

Ibn Taghribirdi, *History of Egypt, 1382–1469 A.D. Translated from the Arabic annals of Abu l-Mahasin ibn Taghri Birdi by William Popper*. Berkeley: University of California Press, 1954–1963.

Ibn Taghribirdi, Jamal al-Din Abu al-Mahasin Yusuf. *al-Nujum al-zahira fi muluk Misr wa-l-Qahira*. 16 vols. Cairo: al-Mu'assasa al-Misriya al-'Amma li-l-Ta'lif wa-l-Tarjama wa-l-Tiba'a wa-l-Nashr, 1963–71.

Ibn Tawq, Shihab al-Din Ahmad. *al-Ta'liq: Yawmiyat Shihab al-Din Ahmad ibn Tawq 834–915H/1430–1509M: Mudhakkarat kutibat bi Dimashq fi awakhir al-'ahd al-mamluki 885–908H/1480–1502M*, edited by Ja'far al-Muhajir. 4 vols. Damascus: Institut français d'études arabes, 2000–2007.

Ibn Taymiya, al-Shaykh al-Imam Taqi al-Din Ahmad. *Public Duties in Islam: The Institution of the Hisba [Risala fi-l-hisba]*. Translated by Muhtar Holland. London: The Islamic Foundation, 1982.
———. *al-Siyasa al-shar'iya fi islah al-ra'i wa-l-ra'iya*, edited by Abu Ya'li al-Quwayasni. Beirut: Dar al-Kutub al-'Ilmiya, 1988.
———. *Majmu' fatawa Shaykh al-Islam Ahmad ibn Taymiya*, edited by 'Abd al-Rahman ibn Muhammad ibn Qasim al-'Asimi al-Najdi al-Hanbali. 37 vols. Beirut: Mu'assasat al-Risala, 1997.

Ibn Tulun, Shams al-Din Muhammad. *Hawadith Dimashq al-yamiya ghudat al-ghazw al-'uthmani li-l-Sham, 926–951: Safahat mafquda tunshar li awwal marra min kitab mufakahat al-khillan fi hawadith al-zaman li Ibn Tulun al-Salihi al-Dimashqi*, edited by Ahmad Ibesch. Damascus: al-Awa'il, 2002.
———. *Mufakahat al-khillan fi hawadith al-zaman*, edited by Muhammad Mustafa. 2 vols. Cairo: al-Mu'assasah al-Misriyah al-'Ammah, 1962, 1964.

Ibn al-Ukhuwwa, Muhammad ibn Muhammad ibn Ahmad al-Qurashi. *Kitab ma'alim al-qirba fi ahkam al-hisba*, edited by R. Levy. Cambridge: Matba'at Dar al-Funun, 1937.

al-Maqrizi, Taqi al-Din Ahmad ibn 'Ali. *Ighathat al-umma bi kashf al-ghumma*, edited by Muhammad Mustafa Ziyada and Jamal al-Din al-Shayyal. Cairo: Lajnat al-Ta'lif wa-l-Tarjama wa-l-Nashr, 1940.

———. *Kitab al-suluk li ma'rifat duwal al-muluk*, , edited by Muhammad Mustafa Ziyada. 4 vols. Cairo: Dar al-Kutub al-Misriya, 1936.

———. *Mamluk Economics: A Study and Translation of al-Maqrizi's* Ighathah. Translated by Adel Allouche. Salt Lake City: University of Utah Press, 1994.

———. *al-Mawa'iz wa-l-i'tibar fi dhikr al-khitat wa-l-athar*, edited by Ayman Fu'ad Sayyid. 4 vols. London: al-Furqan Islamic Heritage Foundation, 2002.

———. *Kitab al-mawa'iz wa-l-i'tibar bi dhikr al-khitat wa-l-athar yakhtassu dhalika bi akhbar iqlim Misr wa-l-Nil wa dhikr al-Qahira wa ma yata'allaq biha wa bi iqlimha*. 2 vols. Cairo: Dar al-Tiba'a al-Misriya, 1853–54.

al-Mawardi, Abu al-Hasan 'Ali ibn Muhammad ibn Habib. *Adab al-qadi*, edited by Muhiyy Hilal Sarhan. 2 vols. Baghdad: al-Jumhuriya al-'Iraqiya, Diwan al-Awqaf, 1971.

———. *al-Ahkam al-sultaniya wa-l-wilayat al-diniya*. Cairo: Mustafa al-Halabi, 1966.

Muslim. *Sahih Muslim, Being Traditions of the Sayings and Doings of the Prophet Muhammad as Narrated by His Companions and Compiled under the Title al-Jami'-us-Sahih.* Translated by 'Abdul Hamid Siddiqi. 4 vols. New Delhi: Kitab Bhavan, 1982.

Nizam al-Mulk. *The Book of Government or Rules for Kings: The Siyar al-Muluk or Siyasat-nama of Nizam al-Mulk.* Translated by Hubert Darke. London, Henley, and Boston: Routledge and Kegan Paul, 1978.

al-Nuwayri, Shihab al-Din Ahmad ibn 'Abd al-Wahab. *Nihayat al-'arab fi funun al-adab*, (Cairo: al-Mu'assassa al-Misriya al-'Amma lil-Ta'lif wa al-Tarjama wa al-Nashr, 1964–).

Pellat, Charles. *Ibn al-Muqaffa' (Mort vers 140/757): "Conseilleur" du Calife.* Paris: G.-P. Maisonneuve et Larose, 1976.

al-Qudsi al-Shafi'i, Abu Hamid. *Kitab duwal al-Islam al-sharifa al-bahiya wa dhikr mazahar li min hikam Allah al-khafiya fi jalb ta'ifat al-atrak ila al-diyar al-misriya*, edited by Subhi Labib and Ulrich Haarmann. Beirut: Orient-Institut; Berlin: Das Arabische Buch, 1997.

al-Sakhawi, Shams al-Din Muhammad ibn Abd al-Rahman. *al-Daw' al-lami' li ahl al-qarn al-tasi'.* 12 vols. Cairo: Maktabat al-Quds, 1353 [1934–36].

———. *Kitab al-tibr al-masbuk fi dhayl al-suluk.* Cairo: Maktabat al-Kulliyat al-Azhariya, n.d.

al-Shak'a, Mustafa. *Manahij al-ta'lif 'ind al-'ulama' al-'arab: Qism al-adab.* Beirut: Dar al-'Ilm Lil-Malayyin, 1974.

al-Sha'rani, Abd al-Wahhab. *The Guidebook for Gullible Jurists and Mendicants to the Conditions for Befriending Emirs and The Abbreviated Guidebook for Gullible Jurists and Mendicants to the Conditions for Befriending Emirs*, edited by Adam Sabra. Cairo: IFAO, 2013.

al-Subki, Taj al-Din 'Abd al-Wahhab. *Mu'id al-ni'am wa mubid al-niqam*, edited by Muhammad 'Ali al-Najjar, Abu Zayd Shalabi, and Muhammad Abu al-'Uyun. Cairo: Maktabat al-Khanji, 1948.

al-Suyuti, Jalal al-Din. *Ma rawahu al-asatin fi 'adam al-maji' ila al-salatin: dhammu al-qada' wa taqallud al-ahkam: dhammu al-muks*, edited by Majdi Fathi al-Sayyid. Tanta: Dar al-Sahabah li-l-Turath, 1991.

al-Tabbakh, Muhammad Raghib ibn Mahmud ibn Hisham. *I'lam al-nubala' bi tarikh Halab al-shahba'*. 8 vols. Aleppo: Dar al-Qalam, 1923.

Secondary Sources

'Abd ar-Raziq, Ahmad. "La *hisba* et le *muhtasib* en Egypte au temps des Mamluks." *Annales Islamologiques/Hawliyyat Islamiyah* 13 (1977): 115–78.

———. "Les *muhtasib*s de Fostat au temps des Mamluks." *Annales Islamologiques* 14 (1978): 127–46.

Abu Ghazi, 'Imad Badr al-Din. *al-Juzur al-tarikhiya li azmat al-nahda fi Misr*. Cairo: Merit, 2000.

Abu Ghazi, 'Imad. *Tatawwur al-hiyaza al-zira'iya zaman al-mamalik al-jarakisa: dirasa fi bay' amlak bayt al-mal*. Cairo: 'Ein for Human and Social Studies, 2000.

Abu-Lughod, Janet. *Before European Hegemony: The World System 1250–1350*. New York and Oxford: Oxford University Press, 1989.

Amin, Bakri Shaykh. *Mutala'at fi-l-shi'r al-mamluki wa-l-'uthmani*. Cairo: Dar al-Shuruq, 1972.

Ashtor, E. "The Diet of the Salaried Classes in the Medieval Neart East." *Journal of Asian History* 4, no.1 (1970): 1–24.

Ashtor, E. "Levantine Sugar Industry in the Late Middle Ages: A Case of Technological Decline." In *The Islamic Middle East, 700–1900: Studies in Economic and Social History*, edited by A.L. Udovitch. Princeton, NJ: The Darwin Press, 1981, 91–132.

Ayalon, D. "Al-Djabarti." In *Encyclopaedia of Islam*, edited by P. Bearman, Th. Bianquis, C.E. Bosworth, E. van Donzel, and W.P. Heinrichs. 2nd ed. Brill Online, 2014. http://referenceworks.brillonline.com/entries/encyclopaedia-of-islam-2/al-djabarti-SIM_1894

Ayalon, D. "Mamluk." In *Encyclopaedia of Islam*, edited by P. Bearman, Th. Bianquis, C.E. Bosworth, E. van Donzel, and W.P. Heinrichs. 2nd ed. Brill Online, 2014. http://referenceworks.brillonline.com/entries/encyclopaedia-of-islam-2/mamluk-COM_0657

———. "The Plague and Its Effects upon the Mamluk Army." *Journal of the Royal Asiatic Society*, issue 1 (1946): 67–73.

Bakhtin, Mikhail. *Rabelais and His World*. Translated by Hélène Iswolsky. Bloomington: Indiana University Press, 1984.

Bauer, Thomas. "Mamluk Literature as a Means of Communication." In *Ubi Sumus? Quo Vademus? Mamluk Studies: State of the Art*, edited by Stephan Conermann, 23–56. Bonn: V&R Unipress, 2013.

————. "Mamluk Literature: Misunderstandings and New Approaches." *Mamluk Studies Review* 9 (2005): 105–132.

Behrens-Abouseif, Doris. "Craftsmen, Upstarts and Sufis in the Late Mamluk Period." *Bulletin of the School of Oriental and African Studies* 74 (2011): 375–95.

Berkey, Jonathan P. "The *Muhtasib*s of Cairo under the Mamluks: Toward an Understanding of an Islamic Institution." In *The Mamluks in Egyptian and Syrian Politics and Society*, edited by Michael Winter and Amalia Levanoni, 245–276. Leiden and Boston: Brill, 2004.

Berkey, Jonathan. *Popular Preaching and Religious Authority in the Medieval Islamic Near East*. Seattle and London: University of Washington Press, 2001.

Bianquis, Th. "Zu'ar." In *Encyclopaedia of Islam*, edited by P. Bearman, Th. Bianquis, C.E. Bosworth, E. van Donzel, and W.P. Heinrichs. 2nd ed. Brill Online, 2014. http://referenceworks.brillonline.com/entries/encyclopaedia-of-islam-2/zuar-SIM_8185

Binder, Leonard. "Al-Ghazali's Theory of Islamic Government." *The Muslim World* 14 (1955): 229–241.

Björkman, W. "Maks." In *Encyclopaedia of Islam*, edited by P. Bearman, Th. Bianquis, C.E. Bosworth, E. van Donzel, and W.P. Heinrichs. 2nd ed. Brill Online, 2014. http://referenceworks.brillonline.com/entries/encyclopaedia-of-islam-2/maks-SIM_4839

Blair, Sheila S., and Jonathan M. Bloom. *The Art and Architecture of Islam, 1250–1800*. New Haven and London: Yale University Press, 1994.

Borsch, Stuart J. *The Black Death in Egypt and England: A Comparative Study*. Cairo: American University in Cairo Press, 2005.

Brinner, W.M. "Ibn Iyās." In *Encyclopaedia of Islam, Second Edition*, edited by: P. Bearman, Th. Bianquis, C.E. Bosworth, E. van Donzel, W.P. Heinrichs. 2nd ed. Brill Online, 2015. Reference. American University in Cairo. 07 July 2015. http://referenceworks.brillonline.com/entries/encyclopaedia-of-islam-2/ibn-iyas-SIM_3225

Brinner, William M. "The Significance of the *Harafish* and Their 'Sultan.'" *Journal of the Economic and Social History of the Orient* 6, no. 2 (July 1963): 190–215.

Cahen, Cl. "Mouvements populaires et autonomisme urbain dans l'Asie musulmane." *Arabica* 5 (1958): 225–50; 6 (1959): 25–56, 233–65.

Chamberlain, Michael. *Knowledge and Social Practice in Medieval Damascus, 1190–135*. Cambridge, Cambridge University Press, 1994.

Conermann, Stephan, and Tilman Seidensticker. "Some Remarks on Ibn Tawq's (d. 915/1509) Journal *al-Taliq*, Vol. 1 (885/1480 to 890/1485)." *Mamluk Studies Review* 11, no. 2 (2007): 121–135.

Conrad, Lawrence I. "Arabic Plague Chronologies and Treatises: Social and Historical Factors in the Formation of a Literary Genre." *Studia Islamica* 54 (1981): 51–93.

Cook, Michael. *Commanding Right and Forbidding Wrong in Islamic Thought.* Cambridge: Cambridge University Press, 2000.

Cooper, Richard. "Land Classification Terminology and the Assessment of the *Kharaj* Tax in Medieval Egypt." *Journal of the Economic and Social History of the Orient* 17 (1974): 91–102.

Crone, Patricia. *Medieval Islamic Political Thought.* Edinburgh: Edinburgh University Press, 2005.

Daisuke, Igarashi. "The Establishment and Development of al-Diwan al-Mufrad: Its Background and Implications." *Mamluk Studies Review* 10 (2006): 117–40.

Darrag, Ahmad. *L'Égypte sous le règne de Barsbay.* Damascus: Institut Français, 1961.

Davis, Natalie Zemon. *Society and Culture in Early Modern France: Eight Essays.* Cambridge, UK: Polity, 1987.

Dayf, Shawqi. *al-Fann wa-madhahibuhu fi-l-nathr al-'arabi.* Cairo: Dar al-Maarif, 1960.

Dirks, Nicholas B. "Ritual and Resistance: Subversion as a Social Fact." In *Culture/Power/History: A Reader in Contemporary Social Theory*, ed. Nicholas B. Dirks, Geoff Eley, and Sherry B. Otner, 483–503. Princeton, NJ: Princeton University Press, 1994.

Dols, Michael. *The Black Death in the Middle East.* Princeton, NJ: Princeton University Press, 1977.

———. "The General Mortality of the Black Death in the Mamluk Empire." In *The Islamic Middle East, 700–1900: Studies in Economic and Social History*, edited by A.L. Udovitch, 397–428. Princeton, NJ: The Darwin Press, 1981.

———. "Historical Perspective: Insanity in Islamic Law." *Journal of Muslim Mental Health* 2 (2007): 81–99.

Duncombe, Stephen, ed. *Cultural Resistance Reader.* London and New York: Verso, 2002.

Elbendary, Amina A. "The Sultan, the Tyrant, and the Hero: Changing Medieval Perceptions of al-Zahir Baybars." *Mamluk Studies Review* 5 (2001): 141–157.

Escovitz, Joseph H. "A Lost Arabic Source for the History of Early Ottoman Egypt." *Journal of the American Oriental Society* 97, no. 4 (Oct.–Dec. 1977): 513–518.

Fernandes, Leonor. *The Evolution of a Sufi Institution in Mamluk Egypt: The Khanqah.* Berlin: Klaus Schwarz Verlag, 1988.

Fernandes, Leonor. "The Foundation of Baybars al-Jashankir: Its *Waqf*, History, and Architecture." *Muqarnas* 4 (1987): 21–42.

Flemming, Barbara. "Literary Activities in Mamluk Halls and Barracks." In *Studies in Memory of Gaston Wiet*, edited by Myriam Rosen-Ayalon, 249–60. Jerusalem: Institute of Asian and African Studies, 1977.

Galloway, J.H. "The Mediterranean Sugar Industry." *The Geographical Review* 67 (April 1977): 177–194.

Garcin, Jean-Claude. "Note sur les rapports entre bédouins et fellahs à l'époque mamluke." *Annales Islamologiques/ Hawliyyat Islamiyyah* 14 (1978): 147–163. Qus
————. *Un centre musulman de la Haute-Egypte médiévale, Qus.* Cairo: Institut français d'archéologie orientale du Caire, 1976.
————. "The Regime of the Circassian Mamluks." In *The Cambridge History of Egypt*, vol. 1, *Islamic Egypt, 640–1517*, edited by Carl F. Petry, 290–317. Cambridge: Cambridge University Press, 1998.
Gardet, L. "Fitna." In *Encyclopaedia of Islam*, edited by: P. Bearman, Th. Bianquis, C.E. Bosworth, E. van Donzel, W.P. Heinrichs. 2nd ed. Brill Online, 2015. Reference. American University in Cairo. 10 July 2015. http://referenceworks.brillonline.com/entries/encyclopaedia-of-islam-2/fitna-SIM_2389
Geoffroy, E. *Le soufisme en Égypte et en Syrie sous les derniers Mamelouks et les premiers Ottomans: Orientations spirituelles et enjeux culturels.* Damascus: Publications de l'Institut français de Damas, 1995.
————. "al-Suyuti." In *Encyclopaedia of Islam*, edited by: P. Bearman, Th. Bianquis, C.E. Bosworth, E. van Donzel, W.P. Heinrichs. 2nd ed. Brill Online, 2015. Reference. American University in Cairo. 07 July 2015. http://referenceworks.brillonline.com/entries/encyclopaedia-of-islam-2/al-suyuti-COM_1130
Gerhardt, Mia I. *The Art of Story-telling: A Literary Study of the Thousand and One Nights.* Leiden: Brill, 1963.
Gil'adi, Avner. "The Child Was Small . . . Not So the Grief for Him: Sources, Structure, and Content of al-Sakhawi's Consolation Treatise for Bereaved Parents." *Poetics Today* 14, no. 2 (Summer 1993): 367–86.
————. "Concepts of Childhood and Attitudes towards Children in Medieval Islam: A Preliminary Study with Special Reference to Reaction to Infant and Child Mortality." *Journal of the Economic and Social History of the Orient* 32, no. 2 (June 1989): 121–52.
Grehan, James P. "The Mysterious Power of Words: Language, Law, and Culture in Ottoman Damascus (17th–18th Centuries)." *Journal of Social History* 37, no. 4 (2004): 991–1015.
————. "Street Violence and Social Imagination in Late-Mamluk and Ottoman Damascus (Ca. 1500-1800)." *International Journal of Middle East Studies* 35 (2003): 215–36.
Guo, Li, "Al-Biqa'i's Chronicle: A fifteenth Century Learned Man's Reflection on His Time and World." In *The Historiography of Islamic Egypt, (c.950-1800)*, edited by Hugh Kennedy, 121–48. Leiden, Boston and Koln: Brill, 2001.
————. "Mamluk Historiographic Studies: The State of the Art." *Mamluk Studies Review* 1 (1997): 15–43.
————. "Tales of a Medieval Cairene Harem: Domestic Life in al-Biqa'i's Autobiographical Chronicle." *Mamluk Studies Review* 9, no. 1 (2005): 101–21.
Haarmann, Ulrich. "Arabic in Speech, Turkish in Lineage: Mamluks and Their Sons in the Intellectual Life of Fourteenth-century Egypt and Syria." *Journal of Semitic Studies* 33, no. 1 (1988): 81–114.

Haarmann, Ulrich. "Review of *Weltgeschichte und Weltbeschreibung im mittelalter-lichen Islam* by Bernd Radtke." *Journal of the American Oriental Society* 115 (1995): 133–135.

———. "The Sons of Mamluks as Fief-holders in Late Medieval Egypt." In *Land Tenure and Social Transformation in the Middle East,* edited by Tarif Khal-idi, 141–168. Beirut: American University of Beirut, 1984.

Hallaq, Wael B. "On the Origins of the Controversy about the Existence of *Mujtahid*s and the Gate of *Ijtihad.*" *Studia Islamica* 63 (1986): 129–41.

———. "Was the Gate of *Ijtihad* Closed?" *International Journal of Middle East Studies* 16 (1984): 3–41.

Hamza, 'Abd al-Latif. *al-Haraka al-fikriya fi Misr fi-l-'asrayn al-ayyubi wa-l-mam-luki al-awwal.* Cairo: Dar al-Fikr al-Arabi, 1947.

Hanna, Nelly. "The Chronicles of Ottoman Egypt." In *The Historiography of Islamic Egypt (c. 950–1800),* edited by Hugh Kennedy, 237–250. Leiden, Boston, and Cologne: Brill, 2001.

———. "Culture in Ottoman Egypt." In *The Cambridge History of Egypt,* vol. 2, *Modern Egypt from 1517 to the End of the Twentieth Century,* edited by M.W. Daly, 87–112. Cambridge: Cambridge University Press, 1998.

———. *In Praise of Books: A Cultural History of Cairo's Middle Class, Sixteenth to the Eighteenth Century.* Cairo: American University in Cairo Press, 2004.

———. "Literacy and the Great Divide in the Islamic World, 1300–1800." *Journal of Global History* 2, no. 2 (2007): 175–193.

Hattox, Ralph S. *Coffee and Coffee Houses: The Origins of a Social Beverage in the Medi-eval Near East.* Seattle and London: University of Washington Press, 1985.

Heinrichs, W.P. "Safi al-Din 'Abd al-'Aziz b. Saraya al-Hilli." In *Ency-clopaedia of Islam,* 2nd ed., edited by P. Bearman, Th. Bianquis, C.E. Bosworth, E. van Donzel, and W.P. Heinrichs. Brill Online, 2014. http://referenceworks.brillonline.com/entries/encyclopaedia-of-islam-2/safi-al-din-abd-al-aziz-b-saraya-al-hilli-COM_0966

Hirschler, Konrad. *The Age of the Crusades: The Near East from the Eleventh Cen-tury to 1517.* London and New York: Longman, 1986.

———. "Mamluks." In *Encyclopaedia of Islam,* 2nd ed., edited by P. Bear-man, Th. Bianquis, C.E. Bosworth, E. van Donzel, and W.P. Heinrichs. Brill Online, 2014. http://referenceworks.brillonline.com/entries/encyclopaedia-of-islam-2/mamluks-COM_0658

———. *Medieval Arabic Historiography: Authors as Actors.* London and New York: Routledge, 2006.

Holt, P. M. *The Age of the Crusades: The Near East from the Eleventh Century to 1517.* London and New York: Longman, 1986.

———. "Al-Damurdashi." In *Encyclopaedia of Islam,* edited by P. Bearman, Th. Bianquis, C.E. Bosworth, E. van Donzel, and W.P. Heinrichs. 2nd ed. Brill Online, 2014. http://referenceworks.brillonline.com/entries/encyclopaedia-of-islam-2/al-damurdashi-SIM_1688

————. "Mamluks." In *Encyclopaedia of Islam*, edited by P. Bearman, Th. Bianquis, C.E. Bosworth, E. van Donzel, and W.P. Heinrichs. 2nd ed. Brill Online, 2014. http://referenceworks.brillonline.com/entries/encyclopaedia-of-islam-2/mamluks-COM_0658

————. "Ottoman Egypt (1517–1798): An Account of Arabic Historical Sources." In *Political and Social Change in Modern Egypt: Historical studies from the Ottoman conquest to the United Arab Republic*, edited by P.M. Holt, 312–** London: Oxford University Press, 1968.

Irwin, Robert. "Mamluk History and Historians." In *Arabic Literature in the Post-Classical Period*, edited by Roger Allen and D.S. Richards, 159–170. Cambridge: Cambridge University Press, 2006.

————. "Mamluk Literature." *Mamluk Studies Review* 7 (2003): 1–29.

————. "The Privatization of 'Justice' Under the Circassian Mamluks." *Mamluk Studies Review* 6 (2002): 63–70.

Jamal al-Din, Amina Muhammad. *al-Nuwayri wa kitabuhu nihayat al-'arab fi funun al-adab: Masadirahu al-adabiya wa 'ara'uhu al-naqdiya* (Cairo: Dar Thabit, 1984).

Khalidi, Tarif. *Arabic Historical Thought in the Classical Period.* Cambridge Studies in Islamic Civilization. Cambridge: Cambridge University Press, 1994.

Lambton, A.K.S. "*Quis custodiet custodes?* Some Reflections on the Persian Theory of Government." *Studia Islamica* 5 (1956): 125–148. Reprinted in A.K.S. Lambton, *Theory and Practice in Medieval Persian Government*, 125–148. London: Variorum Reprints, 1980.

————. *State and Government in Medieval Islam: An Introduction to the Study of Islamic Political Theory: The Jurists.* Oxford: Oxford University Press, 1981.

Lane, Edward William. *An Account of the Manners and Customs of the Modern Egyptians.* London: East-West Publications, 1989.

Lapidus, Ira M. "The Grain Economy of Mamluk Egypt." *Journal of the Economic and Social History of the Orient* 12 (1969): 1–15.

————. *Muslim Cities in the Later Middle Ages.* Cambridge, MA: Harvard University Press, 1967.

————. "The Separation of State and Religion in the Development of Early Islamic Society." *International Journal of Middle East Studies* 6, no. 4 (October 1975): 363–385.

Larkin, Margaret. "Popular Poetry in the Post-Classical Period, 1150–1850." In *Arabic Literature in the Post-Classical Period*, edited by Roger Allen and D.S. Richards, 189–242. Cambridge: Cambridge University Press, 2006.

Leech, G. *Semantics.* Harmondsworth: Penguin, 1985.

El-Leithy, Tamer. "Coptic Culture and Conversion in Medieval Cairo, 1293–1524 AD." PhD diss., Princeton University, 2005.

Lellouche, Benjamin. "Le téléphone arabe au Caire au lendemain de la conquête ottomane: On-dits et rumeurs dans Ibn Iyas." *Revue du monde musulman et de la Méditerranée* 75–76 (1995): 117–130.

Levanoni, Amalia. "The *Halqah* in the Mamluk Army: Why Was It Not Dissolved When It Reached Its Nadir?" *Mamluk Studies Review* 15 (2011): 37–65.

———. "Al-Maqrizi's Account of the Transition from Turkish to Circassian Mamluk Sultanate: History in the Service of Faith." In *The Historiography of Islamic Egypt (c. 950–1800): The Medieval Mediterranean People, Economies and Cultures, 400–1453*, edited by Hugh Kennedy, 93–105. Leiden, Boston, and Cologne: Brill, 2001.

Lewis, Bernard. *Islam: From the Prophet Muhammad to the Capture of Constantinople*, vol. 2, *Religion and Society*. Oxford: Oxford University Press, 1987.

Little, Donald P. "Coptic Conversions to Islam during the Bahri Mamluk Period." In *Conversion and Continuity: Indigenous Christian Communities in Islamic Lands, Eighth to Eighteenth Centuries*, edited by Michael Gervers and Ramzi Jibran Bikhazi, 263–88. Toronto: Pontifical Institute of Medieval Studies, 1990.

———. "A Fourteenth-century Jerusalem Court Record of a Divorce Hearing: A Case Study." In *Mamluks and Ottomans: Studies in Honour of Michael Winter*, ed. David J. Wasserstein and Ami Ayalon, 67–85. London and New York: Routledge, 2006.

———. *An Introduction to Mamluk Historiography: An Analysis of Arabic Annalistic and Biographical Sources for the Reign of al-Malik an-Nasir Muhammad ibn Qalawun*. Wiesbaden: F. Steiner, 1970.

Lutfi, Huda. "Coptic Festivals of the Nile: Aberrations of the Past?" In *The Mamluks in Egyptian Politics and Society*, edited by Thomas Philipp and Ulrich Haarman, 254–82. Cambridge: Cambridge University Press, 1998.

———. "Manners and Customs of Fourteenth-century Cairene Women: Female Anarchy versus Male Shar'i Order in Muslim Prescriptive Treatises." In *Women in Middle Eastern History*, edited by Nikki Keddie and Beth Baron, 99–121. New Haven: Yale University Press, 1991.

———. "Al-Sakhawi's *Kitab al-Nisa'* as a Source for the Social and Economic History of Muslim Women during the Fifteenth Century AD." *The Muslim World* 71, no. 2 (April 1981): 104–124.

Makdisi, George. *The Rise of Colleges: Institutions of Learning in Islam and the West* (Edinburgh: Edinburgh University Press, 1981).

Marçais, W. "al-A'yni." In *Encyclopaedia of Islam*, edited by P. Bearman, Th. Bianquis, C.E. Bosworth, E. van Donzel, W.P. Heinrichs. 2nd ed. Brill Online, 2015. Reference. American University in Cairo. 07 July 2015. http://referenceworks.brillonline.com/entries/encyclopaedia-of-islam-2/al-ayni-SIM_0920

Martel-Thoumian, Bernadette. "Les élites urbaines sous les Mamlouks circassiens: Quelques éléments de réflexion." In *Egypt and Syria in the Fatimid, Ayyubid and Mamluk Eras*, edited by U. Vermeulen and J. Van Steenbergen. Vol. 3, *Proceedings of the 6th, 7th, and 8th International Colloquiums organized at the Katholieke Universiteit Leuven in May 1997, 1998, and 1999*, 271–308. Orientalia Lovaniensia Analecta 102. Leuven: Uitgeverij Peeters, 2001.

————. "La mort volontaire: Le traitement du suicide et du suicidé dans les chroniques mameloukes tardives." *Annales Islamologiques* 38 (2004): 405–435.

Meloy, John L. "Imperial Strategy and Political Exigency: The Red Sea Spice Trade and the Mamluk Sultanate in the Fifteenth Century." *Journal of the American Oriental Society* 123, no. 1 (Jan.–Mar. 2003): 1–19.

————. "The Privatization of Protection: Extortion and the State in the Circassian Mamluk Period." *Journal of the Economic and Social History of the Orient* 47, no. 2 (2004): 195–212.

Miura, Toru. "Administrative Networks in the Mamluk Period: Taxation, Legal Execution, and Bribery." In *Islamic Urbanism in Human History: Political Power and Social Networks*, edited by Tsugitaka Sato, 39–76. London and New York: Kegan Paul International, 1997.

Morimoto, Kosei. "What Ibn Khaldun Saw: The Judiciary of Mamluk Egypt." *Mamluk Studies Review* 6 (2002): 109–131.

Mortel, Richard T. "The Decline of Mamluk Civil Bureaucracy in the Fifteenth Century: The Career of Abul-Khayr al-Nahhas." *Journal of Islamic Studies* 6, no. 2 (1995): 173–88.

Muhanna, Elias Ibrahim. "Encyclopaedism in the Mamluk Period: The Composition of Shihab al-Din al-Nuwayri's (d. 1333) *Nihayat al-'arab fi funun al-adab*." PhD diss., Harvard University, 2012. http://dash.harvard.edu/handle/1/9366551

Mullett, Michael. *Popular Culture and Popular Protest in Late Medieval and Early Modern Europe*. London, New York, and Sydney: Croom Helm, 1987.

Musallam, B.F. "Birth Control and Middle Eastern History: Evidence and Hypotheses." In *The Islamic Middle East, 700–1900: Studies in Economic and Social History*, edited by A.L. Udovitch, 429–469. Princeton, NJ: The Darwin Press, 1981.

Musallam, Basim. "The Ordering of Muslim Societies." In *The Cambridge Illustrated History of the Islamic World*, edited by Francis Robinson, 164–207. Cambridge: Cambridge University Press, 1996.

Northrup, Linda S. "The Bahri Mamluk Sultanate, 1250–1390." In *The Cambridge History of Egypt*. Vol. 1, *Islamic Egypt, 640–1517*, edited by Carl F. Petry, 242–89. Cambridge: Cambridge University Press, 1998.

Noth, Albrecht. "Problems of Differentiations between Muslims and Non-Muslims: Re-reading the 'Ordinance of 'Umar' (al-Shurut al-'Umariya)." In *Muslims and Others in Early Islamic Society*, edited by Robert Hoyland, 103–24. Aldershot: Ashgate Variorium, 2004.

Pellat, Ch. "Ḳāṣṣ." In *Encyclopaedia of Islam*, edited by P. Bearman, Th. Bianquis, C.E. Bosworth, E. van Donzel, W.P. Heinrichs. 2nd ed. Brill Online, 2015. Reference. American University in Cairo. 07 July 2015. http://referenceworks.brillonline.com/entries/encyclopaedia-of-islam-2/kass-SIM_4002

Pellat, Ch.; Vesel, Ž.; Donzel, E. van. "Mawsūʿa." In *Encyclopaedia of Islam*, edited by P. Bearman, Th. Bianquis, C.E. Bosworth, E. van Donzel, W.P.

Heinrichs. 2nd ed. Brill Online, 2015. Reference. American University in Cairo. 06 July 2015. http://referenceworks.brillonline.com/entries/encyclopaedia-of-islam-2/mawsua-COM_0718

Perho, Irmeli. "Climbing the Ladder: Social Mobility in the Mamluk Period." *Mamluk Studies Review* 15 (2011): 19–35.

———. "Al-Maqrizi and Ibn Taghri Birdi as Historians of Contemporary Events." In *The Historiography of Islamic Egypt (c. 950–1800): The Medieval Mediterranean People, Economies and Cultures, 400–1453*, edited by Hugh Kennedy, 107–20. Leiden, Boston, and Cologne: Brill, 2001.

Perlmann, M. "Notes on Anti-Christian Propaganda in the Mamluk Empire." *Bulletin of the School of Oriental and African Studies* 10, no. 4 (1942): 843–61.

Petry, Carl F. *The Civilian Elite of Cairo in the Late Middle Ages*. Princeton, N.J.: Princeton University Press, 1981.

———. "Class Solidarity versus Gender Gain: Women as Custodians of Property in Later Medieval Egypt." In *Women in Middle Eastern History: Shifting Boundaries in Sex and Gender*, edited by Nikki R. Keddie and Beth Baron, 122–42. New Haven and London: Yale University Press, 1991.

———. "Conjugal Rights versus Class Prerogatives: A Divorce Case in Mamluk Cairo." In *Women in the Medieval Islamic World: Power, Patronage, and Piety*, edited by Gavin R.G. Hambly, 227–40. London: Macmillan, 1998.

———. "From Slaves to Benefactors: The *Habashi*s of Mamluk Cairo." *Sudanic Africa* 5 (1994): 57–66.

———. *Protectors or Praetorians? The Last Mamluk Sultans and Egypt's Waning as a Great Power*. New York: State University of New York Press, 1994.

———. "Scholastic Stasis in Medieval Islam Reconsidered: Mamluk Patronage in Cairo." *Poetics Today* 14, no. 2, "Cultural Processes in Muslim and Arab Societies: Medieval and Early Modern Periods" (Summer 1993): 323–348.

———. *Twilight of Majesty: The Reigns of the Mamluk Sultans al-Ashraf Qaytbay and Qansuh al-Ghawri in Egypt*. Seattle and London: University of Washington Press, 1993.

Poliak, A. N., *Feudalism in Egypt, Syria, Palestine and the Lebanon, 1250–1900*. London: The Royal Asiatic Society, 1939.

———. "Les révoltes populaires en Égypte à l'époque des Mamelouks et leurs causes économiques." *Revue des Études Islamiques* 8 (1934): 251–73.

al-Qadi, Wadad. "Biographical Dictionaries as the Scholars' Alternative History of the Muslim Community." In *Organizing Knowledge: Encyclopedic Activities in the Pre-Eighteenth Century Islamic World*, edited by Gerhard Endres, 23–76. Boston: Brill Academic Publishers, 2006.

Qasim, Qasim 'Abduh. *'Asr salatin al-mamalik: al-tarikh al-siyasi wa-l-ijtima'i*. Cairo: Ein, 1998.

Rabbat, Nasser. "Representing the Mamluks in Mamluk Historical Writing." In *The Historiography of Islamic Egypt (c. 950–1800): The Medieval Mediterranean*

People, Economies and Cultures, 400–1453, edited by Hugh Kennedy, 59–75. Leiden, Boston, and Cologne: Brill, 2001.

Rabbat, Nasser. "Who Was al-Maqrizi? A Biographical Sketch." *Mamluk Studies Review* 7 (2003): 1–19.

Rabie, Hassanein, "Some Technical Aspects of Agriculture in Medieval Egypt." In *The Islamic Middle East, 700–1900: Studies in Economic and Social History*, edited by A.L. Udovitch, 59–90. Princeton, NJ: The Darwin Press, 1981.

Rafeq, Abdul-Karim. "Ibn Abi'l-Surur and His Works." *Bulletin of the School of Oriental and African Studies, University of London* 38, no. 1 (1975): 24–31.

Randall, Adrian, and Andrew Charlesworth. "The Moral Economy: Riot, Markets and Social Conflict." In *Moral Economy and Popular Protest: Crowd, Conflict and Authority*, edited by Adrian Randall and Andrew Charlesworth, 1–32. London and New York: Macmillan and St. Martin's, 2000.

Rapoport, Yossef. "Women and Gender in Mamluk Society: An Overview." *Mamluk Studies Review* 11, no. 2, (2007): 1–47.

Raymond, André. *Cairo.* Translated by Willard Wood. Cambridge, MA and London: Harvard University Press, 2000.

———. "Cairo's Area and Population in the Early Fifteenth Century." *Muqarnas* 2 (1984): 21–31.

Reynolds, Dwight F. "*A Thousand and One Nights*: A History of the Text and its Reception." In *The Cambridge History of Arabic Literature: Arabic Literature in the Post-Classical Period*, edited by Roger Allen and D.S. Richards, 270–291. Cambridge: Cambridge University Press, 2006.

Reynolds, Dwight, ed. *Interpreting the Self: Autobiography in the Arabic Literary Tradition.* Berkeley: University of California Press, 2001.

Reynolds, Dwight F. "Popular Prose in the Post-Classical Period." In *The Cambridge History of Arabic Literature: Arabic Literature in the Post-Classical Period*, edited by Roger Allen and D.S. Richards, 245–269. Cambridge: Cambridge University Press, 2006.

Roded, Ruth. *Women in Islamic Biographical Collections: From Ibn Sa'd to Who's Who.* Boulder and London: Lynne Rienner Publishers, 1994.

Rosenthal, E.I.J. *Political Thought in Medieval Islam.* Cambridge: Cambridge University Press, 1962.

Rosenthal, F. *A History of Muslim Historiography.* Leiden: Brill, 1968.

Rosenthal, F. "al-Makrizi." In *Encyclopaedia of Islam*, edited by P. Bearman, Th. Bianquis, C.E. Bosworth, E. van Donzel, W.P. Heinrichs. 2nd ed. Brill Online, 2015. Reference. American University in Cairo. 07 July 2015. http://referenceworks.brillonline.com/entries/encyclopaedia-of-islam-2/al-makrizi-SIM_4838

El-Rouayheb, Khaled. "Opening the Gate of Verification: The Forgotten Arab–Islamic Florescence of the Seventeenth Century." *International Journal of Middle East Studies* 38 (2006): 263–81.

Rudé, George. *The Crowd in History: A Study of Popular Disturbances in France and England, 1730–1848*. London: Serif, 1995.

Sabra, Adam. "Illiterate Sufis and Learned Artisans: The Circle of 'Abd al-Wahhab al-Sha'rani." In *The Development of Sufism in Mamluk Egypt*, edited by Richard McGregor and Adam Sabra, 153–168. Cahier des Annales islamologiques 27. Cairo: IFAO, 2006.

———. *Poverty and Charity in Medieval Islam: Mamluk Egypt, 1250–1517*. Cambridge: Cambridge University Press, 2000.

Sadan, Joseph. "Al-Bilbaysi." In *Encyclopaedia of Islam, Three*, edited by Gudrun Krämer, Denis Matringe, John Nawas, and Everett Rowson. Brill Online, 2014. http://referenceworks.brillonline.com/entries/encyclopaedia-of-islam-3/al-bilbaysi-COM_23478

Sadan, Joseph. "Kings and Craftsmen, a Pattern of Contrasts: On the History of a Medieval Arabic Humoristic Form (Part I)." *Studia Islamica* 56 (1982): 89–120.

Sajdi, Dana. *The Barber of Damascus: Nouveau Literacy in the Eighteenth-century Ottoman Levant*. Palo Alto: Stanford University Press, 2013.

———. "A Room of His Own: The 'History' of the Barber of Damascus (fl. 1762)." *The MIT Electronic Journal of Middle East Studies. Crossing Boundaries: New Perspectives on the Middle East* 3 (Fall 2003): 19–35. http://web.mit.edu/cis/www/mitejmes/

Saliba, George. "Arabic Astronomy during the Age of Discovery." In *Columbus and the New World*, edited by J.C. Schnaubelt and F. Van Fletern, 41–66. New York: Lang, 1998.

Saliba, George. "A Redeployment of Mathematics in a Sixteenth-century Arabic Critique of Ptolemaic Astronomy." In *Perspectives arabes et médiévales sur la tradition scientifique et philosophique grecque*, edited by Ahmad Hasnawi et al., 105–122. Leuven: Peeters, 1997.

Sallam, Muhammad Zaghlul. *al-Adab fi-l-'asr al-mamluki*. 2 vols. Cairo: Dar al-Ma'arif, 1971.

Sartain, E.M. *Jalal al-Din al-Suyuti*. 2 vols. Cambridge: Cambridge University Press, 1975.

Sato, Tsugitaka. *State and Rural Society in Medieval Islam: Sultans, Muqta's, and Fallahun*. Leiden and New York: E.J. Brill, 1997.

Sato, Tsugitaka. "Sugar in the Economic Life of Mamluk Egypt." *Mamluk Studies Review* 8 (2004): 87–107.

Sayeed, Asma. "Women and Hadith Transmission: Two Case Studies from Mamluk Damascus." *Studia Islamica* 95 (2002): 71–94.

Scott, James C. *Weapons of the Weak: Everyday Forms of Peasant Resistance*. New Haven: Yale University Press, 1985.

Shoshan, Boaz. "Grain Riots and the 'Moral Economy': Cairo, 1350–1517." *Journal of Interdisciplinary History* 10 (1980): 459–78.

———. "High Culture and Popular Culture in Medieval Islam." *Studia Islamica* 73 (1991): 67–107.

———. *Popular Culture in Medieval Cairo*. Cambridge: Cambridge University Press, 1993.

Sleasman, Brent C. "Individuation." In *Encyclopedia of Identity*, edited by R. Jackson II. Thousand Oaks, CA: Sage Publications, 2010. http://search.credoreference.com.library.aucegypt.edu:2048/content/entry/sageidentity/individuation/0

Stack, Steven. "Suicide: A 15-year Review of the Sociological Literature, Part I: Cultural and Economic Factors." *Suicide and Life-threatening Behavior* 30 (Summer 2000): 145–62.

Stewart, Devin J. "Popular Shiism in Medieval Egypt: Vestiges of Islamic Sectarian Polemics in Egyptian Arabic." *Studia Islamica* 84 (1996): 35–66.

Stilt, Kirsten. *Islamic Law in Action: Authority, Discretion, and Everyday Experiences in Mamluk Egypt*. Oxford: Oxford University Press, 2011.

Taylor, Christopher S. *In the Vicinity of the Righteous: Ziyara and the Veneration of Muslim Saints in Late Medieval Egypt*. Leiden: Brill, 1999.

Thompson, E.P. "The moral economy of the English crowd in the eighteenth century." *Past and Present* 50 (1971): 76–136.

Thompson, Jon. "Late Mamluk Carpets: Some New Observations." In *The Arts of the Mamluks in Egypt and Syria: Evolution and Impact*, edited by Doris Behrens-Abouseif, 115–40. Bonn: V&R Unipress, 2012.

Tully, James. "The Pen Is a Mighty Sword: Quentin Skinner's Analysis of Politics." In *Meaning and Context: Quentin Skinner and His Critics*, edited by James Tully, 7–28. Cambridge, UK: Polity Press, 1988.

van Ess, Josef. "Encyclopaedic Activities in the Islamic World: A Few Questions, and No Answers." In *Organizing Knowledge: Encyclopaedic Activities in the Pre-Eighteenth Century Islamic World*, edited by Gerhard Endress, 3–19. Leiden: Brill, 2006.

Vrolijk, Arnoud. *Bringing a Laugh to a Scowling Face: A Study and Critical Edition of the "Nuzhat al-nufus wa mudhik al-'abus" by 'Ali ibn Sudun al-Bashbaghawi (Cairo 810/1407–Damascus 868/1464)*. Leiden: Research School CNWS, 1998.

Wallerstein, Immanuel. *The Modern World System: Capitalist Agriculture and the Origins of the European World Economy in the Sixteenth Century*. New York: Academic Press, 1976.

Weintritt, Otfried. "Concepts of History as Reflected in Arabic Historiographical Writing in Ottoman Syria and Egypt (1517–1700)." In *The Mamluks in Egyptian Politics and Society*, edited by Thomas Philipp and Ulrich Haarman, 188–195. Cambridge: Cambridge University Press, 1998.

Wiet, G. "Barsbay." In *Encyclopaedia of Islam*, edited by P. Bearman, Th. Bianquis, C.E. Bosworth, E. van Donzel, and W.P. Heinrichs. 2nd ed. Brill Online, 2014. http://referenceworks.brillonline.com/entries/encyclopaedia-of-islam-2/barsbay-SIM_1243

Wilfong, Terry G. "The Non-Muslim Communities: Christian Communities." In *The Cambridge History of Egypt*, vol. 1, *Islamic Egypt, 640–1517*, edited by Carl F. Petry, 175–97. Cambridge: Cambridge University Press, 1998.

Winter, Michael. *Egyptian Society under Ottoman Rule, 1517–1798*. London: Routledge, 1992.

Wollina, Torsten. "Ibn Tawq's *Ta'liq*: An Ego-Document for Mamluk Studies." In *Ubi Sumus? Quo Vademus? Mamluk Studies: State of the Art*, edited by Stephan Conermann, 337–362. Göttingen: Vandenhoeck and Ruprecht Unipress, 2013,

al-Zamil, Muhammad Fathi. *al-Tahawwulat al-iqtisadiya fi Misr awakhir al-'usur al-wusta: AH 857–923/1453–1517 CE*. Cairo: al-Majlis al-A'la li-l-Thaqafa, 2008.

Ziyada, Muhammad Mustafa. *al-Mu'arikhkhun fi Misr fi-l-qarn al-khamis 'ashr al-miladi*. Cairo: Lajnat al-Ta'lif wa-l-Tarjama wa-l-Nashr, 1949.

INDEX